WHOM THESE PRESENTS DO OR MAY CONCERN
t, Baron of Yeochrie, Commander of the Royal Victorian Order, Writer to Her Majesty's
g: WHEREAS, Jeffery Page Rein Wadsworth, Chancellor, for and on behalf of the ✷ ✷ ✷

SITY OF WATERLOO

on unto Us of date 16 July 1986, Shewn; THAT the said University of Waterloo was incorporated as Waterloo ✷
Act 1953 with classes commencing of date 1 July 1957; THAT by succeeding Acts of the Legislature of the ✷
s changed to University of Waterloo; AND the Petitioner having prayed that there might be granted unto him
h Ensigns Armorial as might be found suitable and according to the Laws of Arms, KNOW-YE-THEREFORE
ssign, Ratify and Confirm unto the Petitioner for and on behalf of the University of Waterloo the following
eof, and matriculated of even date with These Presents upon the 56th page of the 69th Volume of Our ✷ ✷
tland, VIDELICET: Or, on a chevron Sable between
ent. Above the Shield is placed an Helm suitable to an
ined Gules) with a Mantling Sable doubled Or, and on a
en two maple branches in saltire a trillium displayed
the same this Motto "CONCORDIA CUM VERITATE," by
he said University is, amongst all Nobles and in all ✷ ✷
unted and received as an Incorporation Noble in the ✷ ✷
WHEREOF We have Subscribed These Presents and the
rgh this 5th day of August in the 36th Year of the Reign of
he Grace of God, of the United Kingdom of Great Britain
ms and Territories, Queen, Head of the Commonwealth, ✷
Lord One Thousand Nine Hundred and Eighty-seven. ✷

Malcolm R. Innes of Edingight
Lyon.

16th DECember, 1998
Dinner with
Dr James Downey.

Kenneth McLaughlin

WATERLOO

THE UNCONVENTIONAL FOUNDING OF AN
UNCONVENTIONAL UNIVERSITY

University of
Waterloo

Canadian Cataloguing in Publication Data

McLaughlin, Kenneth, 1943-
Waterloo: the unconventional founding of an
unconventional university

Includes bibliographical references
ISBN 0-9682827-0-9

First Published in 1997 by
University of Waterloo
200 University Avenue West
Waterloo, Ontario, Canada N2L 3G1

To reorder additional copies, please call
University of Waterloo Bookstore
Telephone: (519) 888-4567
Fax: (519) 747-2859
email: bookstore@bg1.uwaterloo.ca

Design and Production
Sue Breen & Chris McCorkindale
McCorkindale Advertising & Design

Printed in Canada by
Cober Printing Limited

A note about the photographs. The contemporary
colour photographs are by Chris Hughes; the
historical colour folios are by Marjorie Barber
from the Marjorie Barber Collection in the
University of Waterloo Archives. Photographs
from the Kitchener-Waterloo Record
Photographic Negative Collection, Dana Porter
Library, University of Waterloo are identified as
KWR; those from the University of Waterloo
Archives are cited as UWA; those from the
Wilfrid Laurier University Archives are WLU;
those from the St. Jeromes College Archives
are SJC; Bochsler Photographics & Imaging
are identified as Bochsler; Shore Tilbe Irwin &
Partners as Shore Tilbe; individual photographers
are identified separately.

Photographic Credits

Cover: UWA/M. Barber
Back: (Top) UWA/M. Barber
        (Middle) UWA/M. Barber
        (Bottom) Chris Hughes
End Papers: Pirak Studios Limited
Pages 1-5: UWA/M. Barber
Page 8: UWA/M. Barber
Pages 14-15: Waterloo Public Library
Pages 34-35: Chris Hughes
Pages 50-51: Chris Hughes
Pages 68-69: Chris Hughes
Pages 90-91: Chris Hughes
Pages 106-107: Chris Hughes
Pages 128-129: UWA/M. Barber
Pages 131, 137: Pirak Studios Limited
Pages 152-153: Chris Hughes
Pages 174-175: Chris Hughes
Pages 196-197: Chris Hughes
Page 212: KWR
Page 219: UWA/M. Barber
Page 236: (Top) UWA/M. Barber
        (Bottom) UWA
Page 237: (Top) UWA/M. Barber
        (Middle) UWA/M. Barber
        (Bottom) UWA
Page 238: (Top) UWA/M. Barber
        (Middle) UWA
        (Bottom) UWA/M. Barber
Page 239: (Top) UWA/M. Barber
        (Middle) UWA/M. Barber
        (Bottom) KWR
Page 240: (Top) UWA
        (Middle) UWA/M. Barber

Contents

Foreword

by Lois Claxton

The story that Ken McLaughlin tells so skilfully in this book will engage everyone who has an interest in higher education in Canada, for it is the story of the founding of one of Canada's most successful post-war institutions. For alumni of the University of Waterloo and others who were or are associated with it as faculty, staff, or volunteer supporters, however, the book will make other, more personal claims.

As an alumna of the university who for the past eighteen years has worked at UW, first as a librarian and more recently as corporate secretary, my own interest was taken hostage as I read Ken's narrative, and memories, emotions and pride were stirred. I am honoured to have been invited to contribute this foreword.

It was Easter break, 1953. I was six and excited. My cousin, fifteen years my senior and in her final year at Waterloo College, was about to treat me to a glimpse of college life. My footsteps kept pace with hers as we hurried along the sidewalk, slushy with the spring melt. Quick footsteps but careful, because I had been warned not to splash. And I was prepared to be good, very good, because being with her was always special, particularly that day, going to college. As we turned onto the grounds and up the steps at Willison Hall and into the warmth of the building, there were chatter of voices and greetings and pleasant smells. There were also rooms of dark wood and thick carpets and high ceilings and heavy drapes. Hallowed halls. And beautiful young women — for they dazzled me — with pastel-coloured pullovers and strings of pearls and, what I so desperately wanted myself, saddle shoes. I had seen college.

Easter break, 1961. Another damp day with an overcast sky; snow that had become tired; slush that invaded galoshes. Another cousin, another institution and this time, parents, his parents, overcast like the day itself. We stood at the edge of the city, at the edge of Waterloo, looking out over a razed landscape from which two buildings protruded starkly. A sign in the mud read: University of Waterloo. That it appeared neither hospitable nor inviting nor inspiring was of no consequence to my sixteen-year-old cousin. He was committed to engineering and Waterloo was engineering — co-op engineering — and that was what he would do. That the grey desolation spread out before his parents on that April day should serve their son as halls of higher learning was not the stuff of their dreams. But what they didn't know, couldn't know, was that Waterloo was both the stuff and product of dreams.

Early in the century, Waterloo College had located in Waterloo, and notwithstanding local pride in that institution, educational and societal demands in the post-war era made it increasingly clear that the college was no longer viable as constituted. To no one was this more apparent than to Gerry Hagey, a Waterloo College alumnus who, by the early 1950s, had assumed the mantle of college president, and was faced with the daunting dilemma of insufficient resources to meet growing educational demands.

If Waterloo College were to be viable in the second half of the century it needed provincial funding and that funding could be secured only for a secular institution. Hagey saw the opportunity and seized it — an opportunity to create a secular arm, devoted to the sciences, affiliated with the college and generating government grants. An opportunity for coexistence, for synergy: the religious with the secular, the arts with the sciences. An opportunity that would preserve the Lutheran identity of the institution — of major importance in this Lutheran community — while allowing new educational ventures and garnering vital secular funding. That opportunity became the Associate Faculties of Waterloo College.

If Hagey was seized with the opportunity, so too were the board he assembled and the faculty he hired to realize the dream, a dream turned nightmare at times as choices and dilemmas hurtled them at warp speed into their future. A destiny was planned; but the destiny realized was reshaped by an amalgam of politics and personalities and possibilities, an amalgam which would engender some division and discord but would, in the end, produce a unique and uniquely successful university.

That Waterloo's first hallowed hall was a temporary hut was entirely symbolic. So too its campus of perpetual mud. This was frontier country and a chance to make it. The University of Waterloo was a community project, and the players were writing the script as they played the parts, doing what had never been done, doing it against the odds, doing it despite high-placed obstruction-ism. Faculty, freer than colleagues elsewhere of the constraints of academic tradition and bureaucracy, had licence to invent. Students, enabled by co-op, demanded more of their professors and them-selves. And the university, thrust onto the national scene, seemed cocky in its self-belief.

Not for everyone, the Waterloo frontier. Academic style and grace would have to wait. Faculty and students, in shirt sleeves, swatted flies in the heat of summer, sweated over drafting tables in temporary buildings, and drank beer together at the Loo. The camaraderie was born of a shared dream and the energy to make the dream happen. Failure was not an option.

With failure ruled out, success came early — with enrolments blasting through the most optimistic projections. Students. Everywhere. And the scramble to accommodate. The atmosphere was charged: no campus had ever developed so quickly. For the next decade Waterloo was a construction site, the noise of heavy equipment an accompaniment to every lecture, and mud-spattered shoes, stockings and trousers a signature of Waterloo students. Faculty recruitment was intense. Recruiters had so much exciting to tell about Waterloo, sell about Waterloo — after they answered that inevitable first question: "Where's Waterloo?"

Where's Waterloo? It's a question that doesn't get asked much these days. Doesn't have to. People know. Around the world.

Two universities stand on University Avenue, the result of circumstances which few have understood. The one to the west is Waterloo. No temporary buildings now. No mud. No recognizable similarity to what was there in 1961. Save this — it's still the stuff of dreams.

Acknowledgments

Presidents Douglas Wright of the University of Waterloo and John Weir of Wilfrid Laurier University granted access to the files relating to the universities housed in their respective university archives. This privilege was continued by Presidents James Downey and Lorna Marsden. I am grateful to them and to the staff at the university archives at Waterloo and Laurier, as well as at St. Jerome's College and the University of Western Ontario for assistance in dealing with so many diverse archival sources. I would also like to thank the more than one hundred individuals who agreed to be interviewed as part of the University's Oral History Project as well as those who also donated personal files and archival holdings. Provosts Alan George and James Kalbfleisch provided financial support from UW's Academic Development Fund for research assistance. David Biller, Melissa Belkwell-Garrat, Suzanne Bormann, Shaun Browne, Ross Fair, Jennifer Green and Brent Hergott were admirable research assistants. This project has also been supported by funds from the university's SSHRC grant and by students in my History 491 seminar.

At St. Jerome's College, in the midst of a busy schedule, President Douglas Letson cast his critical editorial eye on parts of the manuscript; Carolyn Dirks produced archival files and my colleagues in the history department, Gerald Stortz and James Wahl, kindly permitted me to read their manuscript on the history of St. Jerome's College. I am also grateful to the Board of Governors for the sabbatical leave which permitted me to organize the University History Project and to complete this book.

The university archives is a marvellous repository of information relating to the university and its people. Without the enthusiastic support over many years of Susan Bellingham, Jane Britton, Rose Koebel and Dianne Seager in the University Archives and in the Special Collections department of the Dana Porter Library, this history could not have been written. My colleagues in UW's history department in particular — John English, Geoffrey Hayes, Patrick Harrigan and Heather MacDougall — have encouraged me in this research project as has Dean Michael Higgins at St. Jerome's College and the deans of arts at UW, Robin Banks and Brian Hendley. Douglas Wright has been a constant source of support and a fund of knowledge and James Downey has added insight and wise counsel, making this a better book. Gail Heideman, the long-time secretary of the history department, abandoned her well-earned retirement to turn my jumbled script into measured prose; Lois Claxton read all of my words and corrected many of them as well as providing the foreword for this book; Diane Mew, my favourite editor, caught many inconsistencies and her assistance was invaluable.

On the day that the *Gazette* announced the inception of the university history project, I received a call from Marjorie Barber. She and her husband, the late A.S. Barber who had done so much to shape Waterloo's co-operative education program, wished to see me. Not only did they have fascinating memories of the university, but Marjorie had also been an avid and excellent photographer. Her photographs have captured images of Waterloo in the early 1960's that I had thought were forever lost. She has graciously permitted us to reproduce many of these photographs whose strong visual images bring UW's history alive. I am most grateful to her as well as to Chris Hughes, whose contemporary photographs of UW life have captured the continuing vitality of this university. Chris McCorkindale and Sue Breen have combined these photographs and other images to create an exceptional portrait of the University of Waterloo. They have been a delight to work with.

I want to acknowledge the support over the last thirty-five years of Paul Cornell — as a professor and colleague, and especially as a friend. My wife Elizabeth and my daughters Nicola and Janet once again have been there for me — to listen and sympathize but never to criticize. Nicola and Janet typed seemingly endless drafts of the final version of the manuscript and were always willing to help me cope with the vagaries of my computer. They did so with unflagging patience and good humour. I thank them most sincerely. In this study, as in all such projects, any errors are mine alone.

Waterloo, 1997
Kenneth McLaughlin

CHAPTER ONE

The "University Idea"

When the members of the Lutheran Synod met in Toronto to consider the possibility of establishing a seminary in Canada, little thought had been given to creating a separate university. Previous attempts to sponsor a seminary to train students for the Lutheran ministry had always failed because of divisions within the Synod and lack of financial support from Lutheran congregations located more often than not in small rural communities in Ontario and in Nova Scotia. While other denominational colleges had joined in affiliation agreements with the University of Toronto, the Lutheran Church was one of the major Protestant denominations conspicuous by its absence. In 1910 two Canadian Lutheran synods — the Synod of Central Canada and the much larger, German-speaking,

Canada Synod — met together and the likelihood of an agreement with the University of Toronto seemed more feasible than at any time in the past.

Everyone had expected the new Lutheran seminary to be in Toronto. No thought had been given to locating it in Waterloo, a small, predominantly German and Lutheran town, in southwestern Ontario. Waterloo's bid for the seminary, however, had been strongly encouraged by local Lutheran businessmen. The campaign was led by J. Charles Mueller, a prominent industrialist whose company made the barrels and kegs for Joseph E. Seagram's distillery. Mueller had also been a member of Waterloo's town council in 1904 and 1906, and chairman of its board of works. In 1911 he was the president of Waterloo's Board of Trade which offered to donate five acres of land to the Evangelical Lutheran Synod to locate the seminary in Waterloo.

The offer of free land was a considerable inducement, although it was not the only factor that led to the decision to reconsider a Lutheran seminary in Toronto. The president of the Lutheran General Council was also concerned that the "unionistic focus of a common Christianity," found at major universities such as Toronto, would weaken the students' "Lutheran principles."[1] A seminary in Waterloo, by contrast, would tend to strengthen their Lutheran identity. The members of Waterloo's Board of Trade were probably quite oblivious to these implications as they voted unanimously to subscribe $1,750 for a five-acre seminary site. The mayor, the president of the Board of Trade, and three prominent community leaders conducted the campaign to collect subscriptions. Three members of the council of the Board of Trade remained as trustees of the property until 10 July 1924 when the title deeds were handed over to the seminary.[2]

The seminary board had also been able to purchase a large home, the Devitt house, for $6,000. The original class of four students and two professors ate, slept, and studied in this one building. In 1914 the first expansion program began when the nearby orchard was cleared and a small classroom and student residence was constructed. The Devitt house then became a residence for the seminary professors. Shortly after a high school division began operation and by 1924 plans

The stern faces of the official delegates attending the opening of the Lutheran seminary on 30 October 1911 are in marked contrast to the inquiring, curious faces on the youngsters in the right corner of the photograph.
WLU

A crowd of 1, 500 Waterloo notables gathered on the lawn and veranda of the former Devitt house for its inauguration as the Waterloo Lutheran Seminary.
WLU

were afoot to open a college of arts. Dr. Alex Potter, the first dean, recalled that all was in readiness on 17 September 1924 when the first students registered: "We felt our hopes had been justified and our labours recompensed when sixteen students registered for the first year's courses, and six for the second year's courses, while two part-time students registered for a few courses. A total of twenty-four!"[3] In this way, Waterloo College was on its way to becoming a community institution. Its influence would be enhanced the following year when the college entered into an affiliation agreement with the University of Western Ontario whereby students graduating in Arts would qualify for a degree from Western.

The decade of the Great Depression played havoc with the finances of colleges and universities throughout Canada, and Waterloo College was no exception. Church support declined dramatically; debts mounted as enrolment dropped; professors' salaries went unpaid; hardship and privations were common. The very existence of the college and seminary was in question when the local business community in 1929 stepped in to save it. W.D. Euler, Charles Greb, and E.F. Seagram raised $30,000 by an emergency fund-raising campaign among the residents of Kitchener and Waterloo — barely enough to prevent the college and seminary from closing. They had intended to raise $100,000, but the onset of the Depression meant that many of the pledges could not be honoured. The college would survive but the memories of its near demise would linger and would cast a long shadow over plans for expansion at a later date.[4]

When the Second World War ended in 1945 there was throughout Canada a renewed interest in universities. The technical skills and leadership provided by the universities in Canada's prosecution of the war had demonstrated that universities had a vital role to play in the modern nation, and for the first time, both politicians and society believed that universities were of national importance. As one indication of this, Ontario's new premier, George Drew, announced that "every child in this province will have an opportunity to be educated to the full extent of their mental capacity, no matter where they live or what the financial circumstances of their parents may be."[5] Of the million men and fifty thousand women who had served in the Canadian armed forces during the war, 175,000 chose to improve their education as they returned to civilian life, with more than 33,000 entering universities. Waterloo College's enrolment tripled overnight from forty-two students in 1941 to 159 in 1947. The opportunities and the challenges created by these circumstances would come to have a profound effect on this small southwestern Ontario community.

In 1947 a Waterloo College Twin Cities Committee requested that the denominational relationship of the college to the community be defined, "in view of the fact that funds are to be solicited from all sources."[6] Additional support beyond the Lutheran Church was required to meet the increased enrolment, and questions inevitably arose about the adequacy of the college campus, its lone and somewhat dated building, and its clerically dominated governing structure. The college's new president, Dr. Helmut Lehmann, an ordained Lutheran minister and a native of Manitoba, arrived in 1944 from Wittenberg College in Ohio.[7] Lehmann launched a Waterloo Expansion Program in 1947 "calling upon the Canada and Nova Scotia Synods to raise $100,000 for a new teaching building."[8]

Students attending Waterloo College were caught up in the ferment of the postwar years.[9] In January 1947 Grant Kaiser published a lead editorial in the Waterloo College student newspaper, *The Cord*, declaring that the time was right for an expansion or even a relocation of the college campus. Now that the war was over, the former Canadian Women's Army Corps Training Centre at Knollwood Park in Kitchener could perhaps be available as a possible college campus.

The Cord's bold headline captured the sense of relief as funds were pledged to keep the college open. Little more than $30,000 of the more than $112,000 in pledges was collected as the onslaught of the Great Depression devastated the local economy.
UWA

For several years people have been talking about the post-war expansion programme of Waterloo College. Rumours were flying thick and fast but no one seemed to have any authentic knowledge of what the future plans were. The conjectures varied all the way from simple additions ... to several new structures which would leave the present one in the background and would involve tearing down houses, buying property and ending up with a landscaped site similar to that of the mother college at London. How much truth there was in any of these reports, we are not prepared to say, but of one fact we are certain: Waterloo College does need to be expanded!

By March 1947 the debate about a future expansion of Waterloo College had intensified. "To move or not to move?...that is indeed the question," began *The Cord's* lead story: "Our Alma is having growing pains, $200,000 worth, and she needs 'lebensraum,' 30 acres worth. The big problem is whether to expand on the present property or to move to new scenery." *The Cord* noted that many

prominent Waterloo citizens, outstanding contributors to the College, have stated that the removal of the institution to Kitchener would definitely affect the mobility of their purse strings ... At any rate something has to be done. Dear Alma is already bursting at her seams ... Waterloo College is growing, both in size and most important, in prestige. Kitchener-Waterloo will soon rank in glory with the other university towns, and it may well be, in our time, as students, that this will come to pass.

This later photo of student life illustrates the growing vitality of the college under Gerald Hagey's presidency.
WLU

In April *The Cord* conducted a survey of Waterloo College students about the possibility of relocating the college to Kitchener.

Fred Little, a college freshman and son of a seminary professor, the Reverend Carroll Little, was opposed: "I'm against it. What will they call it? There are people in Waterloo who have contributed to the upkeep of the college and we shouldn't let them down." While a majority of the students quoted in *The Cord* seemed to share Little's point of view, others felt that Kitchener was a more dynamic community and that the college would be better off there.

One such energetic Kitchener businessman, C.N. Weber, a prominent Lutheran lay leader and college board member, altered for ever the speculative nature of the debate about the future of the college when he proposed that the board take out an option on an 87 acre farm, the Shantz property, near Victoria Street in Kitchener. With the concurrence of President Lehmann, who also wanted to see an end to this debate, a special meeting of the board of Waterloo College met on 4 September 1947 "to discuss the question of re-location and to make a decision on the Shantz property."

Dr. Lehmann began by urging the Board of Governors to move the college from its restrictive Waterloo site. Increased enrolment had made relocation imperative, he believed, and the plan by the Synod to raise $100,000 made it urgent that a new site be acquired before construction could begin. Attempts to involve the Town of Waterloo had met with disinterest, and as a result, the Board of Governors had passed a resolution favouring relocation. The board had also been approached by Mr. Shantz and negotiations had been commenced which appeared favourable to the college.

Lehmann's enthusiasm was shared by Weber, who presented an outline of the Shantz property, making clear his commitment to this project. Although there were some in Waterloo who remained opposed to the move, the board was assured that sufficient funds were available. The Church Committee on Social Missions could retain the existing college site and building as a "Lutheran Home" and the Church's connection with Waterloo would not be lost. Dr. John Reble, president of the Evangelical Lutheran Synod of Canada, recalled that "the question of relocation had been before the Synod for 2 years, and that the Synod at the last convention gave the Board the authority to relocate if advisable and if the necessary monies are available." "Local people are interested and ... throughout the Church the people are also interested; ... money can be raised by people willing to do their share but they are not desirous of more debts." Then he added ominously: "People prefer to have the college remain in Waterloo and believe that something can be made of our present location." When the vote was called, however, the decision to purchase the Shantz property was unanimous.

"We have made history," President Lehmann triumphantly announced. Information about the college's decision was sent immediately to all the churches of the Synod and the Relocation, Property and Finance Committees were instructed to complete the negotiations for the purchase of the new campus site. They were also instructed to meet with the Committee on Social Missions to work out the details for retaining the college building for a Lutheran home. The arrangements seemed complete; a new and more spacious campus would be acquired.

This decision was greeted with enthusiasm in the student news-

C.N. Weber's initiative in 1947 to move the college campus to a larger site began an intense debate about the future of Waterloo College in the post-war years. The decision to remain in Waterloo would lead to Weber's resignation from the Board of Governors; in 1962 he would be seen as a "founding member" of the rival University of Waterloo. WLU

paper. "The 'New Look' of Waterloo College will become a reality within the next few years," proclaimed *The Cord:*

> High hopes are held that building will commence in 1950 ... The future Waterloo College will be situated on the Guelph highway and will be surrounded by forty acres of landscaped grounds. If present plans prevail, the buildings will include a teaching building for the College and Seminary, a Library and Chapel, and residences for men and women.[10]

The new building was planned to accommodate two hundred and fifty students and the emphasis of the college would be on Arts and Business subjects. It was expected that the college would receive $200,000 from the United Lutheran Council's education fund collected from congregations across Canada and the United States.

The post-war expansion of St. Jerome's College to full university status was seen as a threat to Waterloo College. Bishop Joseph F. Ryan is laying the cornerstone for a $1 million building project on the college's new Kingsdale campus. In the background is Father (later Bishop) Bernard Murphy and on the right is Father C.L. Siegfried who as rector of St. Jerome's College would play an active role in the development of the University of Waterloo.
SJC/KWR

When there seemed to be little progress on the development, students began to suspect that something was amiss. In November 1949 Helen Taylor, editor-in-chief of *The Cord*, ran a full page editorial: "WHEN ARE GOING TO MOVE? When we entered Waterloo College as Freshmen two years ago we expected to graduate from a new building on a new campus," she lamented.

> At that time the site for the college had been purchased, the design for the new building was considered, and enthusiasm for the expansion program was at a high peak. With graduation only six months away, the new site remains untouched, definite plans for a new building have not materialized, and enthusiasm for the project has cooled. Who is to blame for this lack of progress?

In fact, the Lutheran Church fund-raising drive had not provided nearly enough money or pledges to complete the project. Also, the traditional rivalries between Kitchener and Waterloo had divided local supporters. The truth was, the Lutheran Church simply could not afford to launch so major a university project.

The frustration about the continuing delays led to new concerns that many students were choosing not to attend Waterloo College because of its minimal university facilities. In 1951 com-

plaints were also expressed that many more potential students were being turned away because of the college's crowded facilities. In the meantime, Vernon Bauman, the mayor of the City of Waterloo, presented a belated and meagre proposal from the city to try to keep the college in Waterloo, offering a small section of property of approximately three acres and a $2,000 subsidy to support the college in its bid to acquire the right to purchase additional property from private owners.

The Board of Governors agreed to continue meeting with the city, but a second motion, moved by C.N. Weber, called for a committee to review the buildings and plans for both sites, including the Shantz farm in Kitchener. Three members were appointed, two of whose paths would cross in the future over another land purchase — Gerald Hagey and Reverend Albert Jacobi.

When the Synod met in June there was little progress to report other than to ask the city to extend for one year the option for the college to purchase the available lots on Dearborn Street. At the same time, Gerald Hagey, a graduate of Waterloo College and a lay member newly elected to the board, asked the board to authorize the committee to have building plans drawn up "for the present site from the point of view of geographical location by architects who specialize in College plans."

In March 1951 a special meeting of the Board of Governors of the Evangelical Lutheran Seminary was convened to deal expressly

The future president of Waterloo College and the University of Waterloo, Gerald Hagey, is seen here as a Waterloo College undergraduate at the top right of the pyramid, circa 1927.
WLU

23

Dr. Helmut Lehmann (left), president of Waterloo College, receiving a cheque for $128, 000 for the college building fund. With him is Dr. Albert Jacobi (centre) and Dr. Gould Wickey (right) executive secretary of the United Lutheran Church in America. Jacobi and Wickey would play major and sometimes opposing roles in the determination of the college's future relationship with the University of Waterloo.
KWR

with the "College question." In attendance was Reverend Dr. Gould Wickey, the executive secretary of the Board of Education of the United Lutheran Church of America, who had come from Washington for this meeting. He brought with him his own report, "Study of the Expansion Problem at Waterloo College," prepared for the ULCA's Board of Education. After he presented the report, attention once again turned to Gerald Hagey, the chair of the Fact Finding Committee. An energetic and convincing speaker, Hagey proposed that the matter finally be resolved and that "the Board of Governors recommend to the Evangelical Lutheran Synod of Canada that Waterloo College be directed to proceed with its development program on the present site."[11] The college would remain in Waterloo after all.

As a result of this decision, Gerald Hagey's career was about to undergo a fundamental change. So, too, was Helmut Lehmann's. In October 1952 President Lehmann announced the proposal to build a new teaching and administration building and dining hall on the Waterloo campus, to begin in the spring of 1953. In response, the editor of *The Cord* printed a sardonic review of the expansion and relocation debacle. "Gone will be, we hear, our crowded classrooms, that are as jammed as cattle gathered around a tree in a thunderstorm ... The delay will have served to make the triumph more appreciated. Let joy be unconfined. Let praise be given where praise is due, AND LET'S SEE THE BULLDOZER."

The decision to remain on the Waterloo campus would effectively end the participation of C.N. Weber in college affairs just as it would also end the presidency of Helmut Lehmann, who resigned shortly after. For his role, however, Gerald Hagey would be elected vice-president of the board of Waterloo College and Seminary. His leadership on the campus question led many to see him as a possible successor to Dr. Lehmann, ending the tradition that the college president be an ordained clergyman. The board initiated a committee "to make a comprehensive administrative organization of the College and Seminary and all related subjects."[12] As vice-president, Hagey submitted a five-page report designed to lead the college into the future. On 25 June 1953, after endorsing Hagey's proposals, the board offered him the presidency of Waterloo College to commence on 16 July 1953.

This decision by the conservative, clerically dominated Board of Governors would set in motion a series of events that would alter forever the history of Waterloo College. It was Gould Wickey of ULCA who had first approached Hagey about accepting the presidency. The board, subdivided into two groups, clerical and lay members, had met separately to consider the appointment of a new president. Wickey, meeting with the lay members, suggested that, "if possible, the next president should be a graduate of Waterloo College with business management experience; if at all possible he should also be a Lutheran, well-known and respected in the community with experience in public relations and he should be a promoter."[13] Only one man fitted this description, Gerald Hagey.

After the meeting, Gould Wickey spent two hours alone with Hagey trying to persuade him to consider the presidency. To Hagey's objection that he lacked the academic qualifications, Wickey replied that "with a good Dean of the College, you need not worry about that part of the operation." Two Lutheran businessmen, Edward Heimpel and Harvey Ziegler, commissioned by the board, arrived at Hagey's home the following Sunday to invite him to become president of the college and administrator of both the college and the seminary.[14]

The "ground-breaking" for the college's administrative and teaching building included a crowd of local municipal, provincial and federal politicians: Dr. S.F. Leavine, fourth from the left, standing next to the federal member of Parliament, Norman Schneider. Dr. Helmut Lehmann is at the far right. KWR

This was a major career decision. Hagey went to two people who had served as his mentors: Dr. Nils Willison, the seminary's first graduate and now a senior Lutheran pastor who had also been principal of Waterloo College School, and Ira Needles, with whom Hagey had worked closely at B.F. Goodrich for eighteen years. One of Hagey's most compelling reservations about accepting the presidency was the Lutheran Church's general inability "to provide sufficient funds to adequately support the College."[15] He had wondered about other sources of college income and even about developing a scheme which would employ students to conduct survey interviews for various advertising projects for which the college would tabulate the results, thereby generating earnings both for the students and for Waterloo College. Hagey knew that this scheme had been used by B.F. Goodrich in the United States where it was known as the Robinson Plan.

At the very least, if Waterloo College was to succeed in the future, new sources of financial support would be necessary. The Board of Governors also sensed that a time for change was at hand. Dr. Willison and Pastor Datars moved an expression of "sincere appreciation to Mr. Hagey for his alertness, thoughtfulness and resourcefulness in promoting our institution and ... we heartily endorse his efforts." With this, Hagey formally accepted the offer of the college presidency.[16]

For the next two years Hagey worked to raise the college's profile in the community and to increase its enrolment. Along with Reverend Lloyd Schaus, newly appointed as full-time dean and also its registrar, Hagey was occupied revising the college's academic program as enrolment increased from 220 to more than five hundred. The new dining hall was opened and the cornerstone for the new teaching and administration building was laid on 20 September 1953, presided over by the former Kitchener businessman and member of Parliament, L.O. Breithaupt, the Lieutenant-Governor of Ontario. A fund-raising campaign was initiated, ancillary services were reorganized, and student activities encouraged. For example, the Purple and the Gold variety show had played for three evenings in the Kitchener-Waterloo Collegiate Auditorium. Applications to the college were up. Clearly, a new vitality had overcome the sleepy little Waterloo campus.

By 1955 President Hagey realized that neither the needs of the college nor those of the community could be met without the addition of a science curriculum. The Lutheran Church had been as generous as it could be with its financial support, but its congregations were not expanding. Furthermore, the Lutherans in Canada had never embraced the university tradition as, for example, many Scottish Presbyterians had. As a result, a majority of the students attending Waterloo College were non-Lutheran and, in the face of the college's limited programs, most of Ontario's Lutherans attended universities other than Waterloo College. Whichever way he turned, Hagey realized that change was inevitable if the college was to continue to flourish.

The college's new teaching and administration building was almost at its limit of three hundred students when it opened in 1954. Plans to expand through increased enrolment would be unlikely if the college could not find a way to finance additional buildings. Hagey had done his best to reorganize the business practices of the college and by and large he had been successful, but he had a long way to go. One of the more interesting examples

of previous practice had been a boarding club run by the students who collected vegetables from local farmers. As Hagey later recounted, "On a fixed date Lutheran farmers within a radius of about 60 miles of the College, took whatever vegetables they could spare to their church. Then the following week the students rented a truck, visited the churches and collected the vegetables, which were then stored in a root cellar at the college until needed."[17]

This example, one of many, indicates the problems as the college began to alter the scale and scope of its residential and academic requirements. In the face of the Lutheran Church's likely inability to support the future expansion of Waterloo College "to serve adequately the needs of the community,"[18] Hagey turned to the example of McMaster University in nearby Hamilton, where he had grown up and where his family still lived. The Baptist church which controlled McMaster University had faced a situation similar to that of the Lutheran Church at Waterloo College.

The Second World War had made it necessary for McMaster to expand its science curriculum and it had also demonstrated that state assistance would be necessary for this kind of expansion. The principal of McMaster, Dr. George Gilmour, would later recall that "it was a matter of survival even more than of expansion, because salaries were desperately low, pension provisions were precarious and [the] academic reputation in danger."[19] Gilmour had worried that without an expansion of its science offerings McMaster's existence was in jeopardy, and "in the higher education scene in Ontario, McMaster could have disappeared and no one would have noticed."

The "boarding club" at Waterloo College marks an interesting transition in the development of college life, while also providing a tangible expression of support by local Lutheran farmers for their "Lutheran" college. WLU

In 1945, with the support of Hamilton's business community, McMaster University had created Hamilton College, a non-denominational science college located on its campus, with representation on the University Senate, to be responsible for McMaster's science programs.

Hagey could empathize with George Gilmour's dilemma. He realized that a physical expansion was necessary if Waterloo College was to survive. The urgency of locating the Arts Building on the restricted Waterloo campus rather than moving to a larger site had been partly conditioned by this consideration. To have provided money for relocation, he later explained, "would have required at least twice the amount that was available. Had the building program been delayed until sufficient money was available for relocation, the institution would have been obliged to continue both Seminary and College instruction in the old building [Willison Hall], which was totally inadequate." The probable result "would have been disastrous ... the College would have degenerated to the point where its continuance would have been questionable."[20]

The Roman Catholic Assumption College in Windsor, which, like Waterloo College, was affiliated with the University of Western Ontario, was balking at the restraints on the development of its own separate engineering program imposed by Western's president. Just at the time when Hagey was considering the presidency of Waterloo College, Assumption had announced its decision to end its affiliation with Western. Premier Leslie Frost's adamant refusal to make an exception for funding denominational colleges, despite Assumption's newly-claimed independent university status, led to the creation of Essex College on 14 July 1954 as a corporation without share capital under part III of the Corporations Act. A new institution, to be known as the University of Windsor, a name strongly endorsed by Premier Frost, was created. Essex College would operate the science program, and Assumption University College would then affiliate with the new university.[21]

Hagey had visited McMaster University and with this experience and the precedent created by the establishment of the University of Windsor very much on his mind, he began seriously to consider ways of making Waterloo College eligible for provincial funding. In March 1955 he met with W. J. Dunlop, Ontario's minister of education. Hagey had already explained to Dr. Edward Hall, the president of Western, that he "desired to participate in provincial grants to universities and colleges even if this meant an organizational separation of the Theological Seminary and Waterloo College and eventually placing Waterloo College under non-denominational control." Dr. Stanley Leavine, the Conservative member for Waterloo in the Ontario legislature, had also suggested to Hagey that "Waterloo College might, if it was to receive provincial government assistance, have to obtain degree-granting powers in its own right," although Hagey indicated to Hall, "that as far as he could see at the moment, there was no serious thought of discontinuing the affiliation with the University [of Western Ontario]." These were clearly debating points, but in the light of Assumption's break with Western, Hall wondered if Waterloo would not be far behind."[22]

After meeting with the minister, Hagey presented a detailed report to the Board of Governors, inviting them to consider the role that they wished the college to play in education in Ontario. What was needed, he suggested, "was a university college of arts, science and commerce ... The need for a college larger than Waterloo now exists and will become greater as the population in this district increases." The challenge, he said, was whether or not "the Lutheran Church will enjoy the privilege of sponsoring the college that will eventually serve the needs of the community."[23]

Hagey used the examples of McMaster and Windsor to explain how Waterloo College could become eligible for provincial grants to fund expansion into a full science program. "A group of prominent citizens would apply for incorporation of a non-denominational Board of Governors under the Companies Act to operate a non-profit corporation to be known as Waterloo College of Science and Commerce." When established, he continued, "the new College Board would apply for affiliation with Waterloo College of Arts."

The board's first reaction was to defer a decision until 30 May. This time a positive recommendation was passed and forwarded to the annual convention of the Canada Synod of the Lutheran Church meeting in Ottawa in June. In his presentation to the Synod,[24] Hagey again reviewed the needs of the community, the stature that would be accorded to the Lutheran Church if it were to sponsor these new courses, as well as the prohibitive costs of offering a science program. He also introduced the notion of creating a Waterloo University, suggesting that Waterloo College's relation to it would be similar to that which it had with the University of Western Ontario, but with a much stronger presence in the new university.

As Hagey explained to the Synod:

Yearly [provincial] grants [for capital and maintenance] make it possible for new community colleges to quickly provide facilities that compare favourably with the longer established universities. They also make it practically impossible for denominational colleges to compete independent of government support — unless they have large endowments, or have the facilities of a large university campus readily accessible to them.

This was the problem, but according to Hagey, there was also a solution:

> Fortunately, the provincial government has accepted a programme that makes it possible for established denominational colleges to retain their identity and continue the purpose for which they have been established by their churches ... and at the same time provide funds for the expansion of facilities on their campuses.

The benefits to Waterloo College would be great, the risks minimal. Waterloo College would continue to operate its College of Arts, the seminary, residences and dining hall, and, of course, "retain the rights to present buildings and the land on which they are located."

This "new" Arts and Administration building opened in 1954 (facing toward Dearborn, later University Avenue) would soon be overcrowded with students wishing to attend the college. President Hagey's new Cadillac automobile, parked outside his office, is at the far left.
WLU/Bochsler

There would be several financial benefits to the college, without compromising the position of the Lutheran Church. Waterloo College, Hagey explained, "would charge the non-denominational college for whatever of our services or equipment is used. These might include — administration, teaching, registration, business management, etc." The college "would retain complete control of the courses taught and all activities in the liberal arts faculty and Seminary." There were also denominational reasons for Lutheran Church support. The board, Hagey added, "would have more opportunities to extend the work of the Church through education. Such a programme would provide the requirements for further expansion without additional cost to the Church."

There were some very pragmatic concerns which Hagey felt necessary to address before the Synod, and some of these issues were those which had been at the back of Dr. Gould Wickey's mind when he had persuaded Hagey to accept the presidency. "If we are realistic in our future planning," Hagey reminded the Synod, "we have these facts to face: The unlikely possibility of the Lutheran Church in Canada being large enough to support the further expansion of Waterloo College ... (2) The likelihood of a non-denominational college being established in this community — in affiliation with another college [St. Jerome's] if not this one. (3)

The difficulty (or possibly the inability) of this college to compete with a non-denominational college that is not affiliated with us." There was also the very real possibility "of encountering financial difficulties that might lead to the Church losing its entire investment in this institution. (4) That prompt action toward the establishment of a non-denominational college on this campus may enable it to become a 'faite [sic] accompli' before it becomes a political issue with denominational pressure [from the Roman Catholics] being brought to bear on the government."

In retrospect, Hagey felt that the threat of St. Jerome's establishing a non-denominational science and business-oriented college had been the deciding factor.[25] It was no secret that St. Jerome's, the Roman Catholic college established in Berlin/Kitchener in 1865, was restive since its affiliation with the University of Ottawa in 1947 and that its 1952 building program on its Kingsdale campus was a major impetus for growth. Two years earlier St. Jerome's had announced its intention to offer courses in science and business, "as soon as conditions warrant." Hagey was worried that if Waterloo College did not act promptly, St. Jerome's would.

> It was with the threat that I had of St. Jerome's adopting a program such as I had suggested [he later recalled] that I was able to get the Board of Governors to approve it ... I strongly recommended that we do it or we might find ourselves as an affiliated college with St. Jerome's. That, of course, seemed very — you might say, offensive — to Waterloo College.[26]

With Synod's approval, Hagey returned to Waterloo and set about gaining support in the community for the development of a non-denominational science college to be associated with Waterloo College. Preliminary discussions in the late summer and early fall resulted in a meeting of interested citizens on 16 December 1955 in the boardroom at Waterloo College. Filled with enthusiasm for the idea of developing a university in their community, this group of prominent business leaders began putting in place the preliminary steps necessary to establish a science faculty. A sub-committee was formed, including President Hagey, to work with the college's legal advisors, Messrs. Smyth and Mank, to develop plans for legal incorporation following the precedent of Carleton College in

ANNO VICESIMO-NONO ET TRICESIMO

VICTORIÆ REGINÆ.

CAP. CXXXIV.

An Act to incorporate the College of Saint Jerome, in the Town of Berlin.

[*Assented to* 15*th August,* 1866.]

WHEREAS His Lordship the Right Reverend John Farrell, D. D., Roman Catholic Bishop of Hamilton, Eugene Funcken, Edward Glowalski, Francis Breitkoff, Louis Funcken, Ludwick Ellena, and other persons of the County of Waterloo, have, by their petition, represented to the Legislature that for some time past a College has been established in the said County of Waterloo, for the education of youth in the usual branches of a Collegiate Education, and have prayed that corporate powers may be conferred on the said College; and in consideration of the great advantages to be derived from the said establishment it is expedient to grant the prayer of the said petition : Therefore, Her Majesty, by and with the advice and consent of the Legislative Council and Assembly of Canada, enacts as follows :

Established in 1866 in Berlin, Ontario, as a college "for the education of youth in the usual branches of Collegiate Education," St. Jerome's College played a major role in the drive toward university status in Waterloo. In 1960 St. Jerome's College became a "founding college" of the University of Waterloo. SJC

Ottawa. The sub-committee also sought to establish terms for the affiliation of the new science college with Waterloo College. These terms would have to be presented at the next meeting of the Evangelical Lutheran Synod held in June in Port Colborne.[27]

With the somewhat ponderous title of "The Waterloo College Associate Faculties" chosen to represent the central role of Waterloo College, and with the support of prominent Lutheran business leaders, Gerry Hagey approached the meeting of the Port Colborne Synod with a growing sense of confidence. All of these plans were coursing through his mind as he set out to persuade this very traditional church council to move forward with his plans for Waterloo College. Hagey had rehearsed his arguments and he emphasized that his plans would make it possible for "more Lutheran students to avail themselves of what the Church provides at Waterloo College" by being able to also take additional courses not now available at the college, while also relieving the Lutheran Church of "the cost of Science courses and other costly specialized courses." "With Provincial Government grants (for which the Associate Faculties) is eligible," he went on, the Associate Faculties propose to erect buildings "on land adjoining Waterloo College." This latter phrase would be significant. The Associate Faculties would have to acquire additional lands adjoining the college rather than build on lands actually owned by the college. This arrangement, Hagey explained, will "make it possible for a university to be located adjoining Waterloo College ...," and "it would follow a programme that has proven satisfactory to church colleges in the Federation of Toronto University and the University of Saskatchewan ..." With their approval in hand, the university idea was one step closer to reality.

Even though he had argued that Waterloo College should remain on its original site, Gerald Hagey was aware of the need for additional land and buildings. In a comprehensive Special Report to the Board of Governors of the Evangelical Lutheran Seminary of Canada in 1955,[28] he explained the need for a chapel, a library, an athletic building, and an addition to a newly completed arts and science building. Waterloo College also needed an auditorium, faculty and staff offices, as well as storage and work rooms.

The college library, the centre of a liberal arts education, was sorely in need of replacement. According to Hagey, the present library can be considered "only as temporary accommodation, for the quiet necessary for study is almost impossible with the library located in a residence building and over top of a gymnasium."

The college required more than buildings. Additional land would have to be obtained and the president forecast that the college "will soon be required to take up the option on the lots fronting Dearborn Street that now are being held for us by the City of Waterloo" as part of its 1950 proposal to keep the college in Waterloo.

The lands surrounding Waterloo College were not easily attainable, however attractive they might have looked on a city or college site plan. The owners of the adjoining lands had been both obdurate and recalcitrant. In the face of this impasse, Hagey sought the assistance of Norman Schneider, the member of Parliament for Waterloo North, asking for his intervention "in an effort to procure land adjoining our campus."[29] A sizable plot of land across Dearborn Street, later University Avenue, was owned by the Central Mortgage and Housing Corporation on which there was a series of townhouses mainly rented to veterans. As the land was located in a district "surrounded by low-cost wartime housing houses," Hagey suggested, "it is not desirable land for a medium or high cost housing development." Not only did Hagey want to claim this land, he also wanted an arrangement "whereby the land could be made available to Waterloo College without an immediate capital investment":

> For the next ten years all of the money that Waterloo College and Associate Faculties will be able to procure from provincial grants and fund-raising campaigns will be needed for the construction of buildings required by the [two] institutions. Whatever money will be required to purchase land will limit the availability of funds for needed buildings.

As the land questions were being endlessly debated, the academic plans for the Associate Faculties curriculum moved forward at a rapid pace. The demand for this program, Hagey told Schneider, "will necessitate a more rapid expansion on this campus relatively as compared to other colleges."

The campus was in the shape of a rectangle within a single city block of thirty-five acres. "The land in this rectangle," Hagey confidently predicted, "will probably be sufficient for expansion during the next ten years."[30] No single statement could have been further amiss; few other comments would cause President Hagey more discomfort.

The campus of Waterloo College as it appeared in 1956 before the beginning of attempts to expand its boundaries. The CMHC lands are at the top right. The college "rectangle" was limited to a line not far beyond the perimeter created by Willison Hall and the new Administration and Arts buildings. A playing field, the 1928 Seagram memorial field, was located behind Willison Hall. KWR

CHAPTER TWO

The Waterloo Plan

St. Andrews-by-the-Sea, New Brunswick, with its magnificent harbour, verdant green lawns, white clapboard homes and eighteenth-century New England buildings, seemed an unlikely setting as a companion piece to the rolling agricultural countryside of Waterloo County. In 1956, however, the confluence of events destined to reshape Canada's industrial and educational future would come together in these two communities. Nowhere would the effect be more profoundly felt than in Waterloo, Ontario.

The possibility of developing a university in Waterloo, based on Waterloo College, had been debated on and off since the end of the war and by 1956 had begun to acquire a new momentum. The alarming accounts of the massive industrial development of the

Soviet Union and the fear that Canada was faltering and falling behind had now become part of an intense national debate. So much so that in 1956 Canada's leading businessmen, scientists, and educators were preparing to convene a National Conference on Engineering, Scientific and Technical Manpower at St. Andrews to discuss the extent of Canada's manpower shortage in these critical fields and "to consider and recommend remedial action."[1]

The conference heard from eminent Canadian industrialists and political leaders such as Crawford Gordon, president of A.V. Roe, Dr. O.M. Solandt, vice-president, research and development, Canadian National Railways, and J.D. Barrington, president and managing director of Polymer Corporation. Even C.D. Howe, the minister of trade and commerce and minister of defence production, was there. Barrington made the case that industry in Canada had a major responsibility relative to education, and "if industry is to lead, then industries' leaders must be in constant touch with the universities and not just about money, but about all the problems that assail the ... universities." "Take us into your councils, my friends in the universities," he exclaimed, "and we will help you to the best of our ability, for our own good and for the good of the nation."

The delegates meeting at St. Andrews felt the sense of crisis shared by many in Canada in that summer of 1956. In their concluding resolutions, they announced that:

> ... it is their duty to warn the people of Canada that the problem of universities has become an emergency of grave national concern to the certain disadvantage of our progress as a nation, and can only be solved by energetic and immediate assistance and cooperation of all governments in Canada, of business and industry and of private benefactors.[2]

On 27 August, two weeks before the St. Andrews conference had been scheduled to begin, Ira Needles, president of B.F. Goodrich Canada and chairman of the Board of Governors of the newly-created Waterloo College Associate Faculties, rose to speak at his local Rotary Club in Kitchener-Waterloo. The timing was no mere coincidence. On that hot summer day Ira Needles chose this occasion to announce what he called the "Waterloo Plan." This was to be a new type of education, "a Co-operative Plan of Education for Engineers and Technicians."[3] Offered on a co-operative basis,

conference proceedings

national conference on engineering, scientific and technical manpower

Algonquin Hotel St. Andrews-by-the-Sea, New Brunswick | Sept. 7th, 10th and 11th, 1956

The National Conference on Engineering, Scientific and Technical Manpower, a blue-ribbon gathering of many of Canada's leading industrialists and educators, captured the worried mood of the nation and was a fitting introduction for the "Waterloo Plan" of co-operative education.
UWA

Ira Needles was a commanding presence on behalf of the "Waterloo Plan." A forceful personality, "when Ira Needles spoke, people listened," recalled one contemporary at B.F. Goodrich.
UWA

The Algonquin Hotel at St. Andrews-by-the-Sea, New Brunswick was the gathering place for Canada's leading industrialists. Its imposing, dignified setting belied their uneasiness about the future of Canada.
Courtesy Algonquin Hotel

Needles explained, "means that industry co-operates with the college in training the student who spends one quarter of a year in college and the next quarter period of training in industry." Success in both the academic term and the work term placements would be prerequisites for continuation in the program, while the alternating academic and work terms would also make it possible to admit twice as many students. As one group of students was in the work place, an alternate group would be admitted to a second term in the classroom. By this means, he suggested, university teachers and classrooms would be in use on a year-round basis.

"The advantages of the Waterloo Plan are many," Needles explained, "and in our opinion, it supplies a considerable number of answers to the problem of three vital groups, the educators, the students and the future employers of the students." The plan has been "developed and guided with the co-operation, counsel and assistance of people in industry and in the fields of both university and technical education ... Leaders of industry and the Ontario department of education are keenly interested," he said, "and reality is just a matter of time."

The announcement of the Waterloo Plan of co-operative education with Canadian industry had taken many by surprise. This was not the program that the Evangelical Lutheran Synod or the Board of Governors of its Lutheran seminary had anticipated when they had approved an affiliation agreement with Waterloo College. Many Waterloo College faculty members had learned of the program only when they read about it in their local newspaper. Edward Hall, president of the University of Western Ontario, the university with which the Associate Faculties hoped to affiliate, was more than surprised. He was considerably annoyed, fearful that this program, which had never been submitted to Western's Senate, would damage Western's reputation and that of its fledgling engineering program.[4]

Hall was perfectly correct to be angry. These concerns, however, were weighed by Needles against the agenda of the St. Andrews conference, called to deal with the problems arising from an inevitable expansion in enrolment in higher education and, more specifically, "to consider in what way business and industry, in co-operation with educational institutions, governments and professional associations might make a contribution to their solution."[5] Ira Needles could hardly have penned a better introduction to his Waterloo Plan.

The conference had concluded by creating an Industrial Foundation on Education, with Stanley Deeks, chief of engineering administration at Orenda Engines, as its executive director.[6] The selection of Deeks augured well for the future of the Waterloo Plan, for he had actually intended to propose a similar program, and he had insisted that Ira Needles announce the Waterloo Plan in advance of the conference.[7] As the newly appointed executive director, Deeks distributed copies of Needles's speech to his directors, the presidents and chief executive officers of Canada's most powerful corporations, making the Waterloo Plan and its sponsor, Waterloo College Associate Faculties, known throughout Canada.

If the Associate Faculties had not previously been known to them, Ira Needles most probably was. Needles had been with B.F. Goodrich in Canada since 1925, responsible for developing the company's Canadian operations when they had taken over from the Ames Holden Rubber Company in Kitchener. He had also been part of that remarkable group of business leaders who had been summoned to Ottawa during the Second World War and who had volunteered their services to the Canadian war effort. From February 1942 to March 1944 Needles was in Ottawa as "Technical Advisor to the Rubber Controller of Canada," assisting in the coordination of the rubber industry in a highly mechanized war. He was listed simply as an "employee of the Department of Munitions and Supply."

The experience of the war years had a profound effect on Needles and on that generation of Canadian industrial leaders who had worked together in Ottawa. Not only were important friendships established, but also a sense of urgency and a belief in the destiny of the Canadian nation became a fixed part of their resolve to build a better future for their children. These feelings and attitudes were an integral part of the intellectual ferment that engulfed Canada and Canadians in that summer of 1956.

The 1956 brochure of the Co-operative Plan ... for Technicians and Engineers generated considerable interest among Canadian companies; it also caused confusion, particularly over the proposal to train technicians and engineers in the same preliminary program. Ultimately the training of technicians would be abolished (1957) and the idea of co-operative education with industry would take precedence. UWA

A Co-operative Plan of Education for TECHNICIANS and ENGINEERS

An entirely new plan of higher education for Canadian students . . . to provide more well-qualified technicians and more broadly-educated engineers.

Developed by . . .
WATERLOO COLLEGE ASSOCIATE FACULTIES
Waterloo, Ontario

Newspaper reports praised the steady growth of Canada's economy, its employment opportunities, and a standard of living envied throughout the world. The educational system was caught up in this surge of optimism. Canadian parents were determined to provide opportunities for their children which they themselves had not had through nearly two decades of economic and military turmoil.

This would be a different era. Education was to be a priority, but it would not be the elitist and restricted university experience of the 1920s. In a national Gallup poll two years after the war's end, Canadians sought to identify "educational training to pragmatic ends."[8] Perhaps this was not so surprising, but a decade later educational training would still be very much linked to the goals of personal security and industrial progress.

Ira Needles's talk to the Rotary Club had opened with the provocative declaration: WANTED: 150,000 ENGINEERS — THE WATERLOO PLAN. The bold headline was not Needles's own, but taken from the 3 July editorial in the Toronto *Globe and Mail* as Canadians had celebrated their Dominion Day holiday. Edward Sheffield, an advisor to the federal government, had already predicted that university enrolment would double to 120,000 within the decade, sending shock waves to university leaders, businessmen, and politicians throughout Canada.[9]

Ira Needles and his colleagues at Waterloo College Associate Faculties were aware of these concerns and of the opportunity that they offered for the creation of a unique and radical experiment in university education at Waterloo. The Associate Faculties had been incorporated under the Companies Act on 4 April 1956 with a Board of Governors consisting of twenty-two prominent citizens "representing major industries, professions, and religious denominations," mainly selected by Needles in concert with Gerald Hagey, the former national public relations and advertising manager for B.F. Goodrich and now president of Waterloo College.

The decision to establish the Associate Faculties had been begun by Gerry Hagey in the summer of 1955. At a dinner meeting on 19 July with Dr. Stanley Leavine, he asked Leavine to arrange for Dr. Dunlop, the minister of education, to visit Waterloo College.[10] One week later, Dunlop and Dr. Beattie, the director of education, as well as Dr. Hall, were in Waterloo to discuss the provincial government's interest in "expanding the opportunities to study Science." At the meeting, Hagey was assured of the government's "probable support for a junior College of Science," organized by a non-denominational governing board, but which could become a "Faculty of Waterloo College."[11]

The excitement of post-war university life is captured on the faces of these first year students in 1947 as they are about to be "initiated" into Waterloo College. This tradition has survived in the University of Waterloo, as has the annual photograph of the dousing and it has become part of the folklore of the university.
WLU

After trying unsuccessfully to persuade Dr. Leavine to serve as pro tem chair of a group of community leaders in support of the university idea, Hagey turned once again to Ira Needles, his long-time friend and mentor. In September a group of six "prominent citizens" of Kitchener-Waterloo met to suggest the names of those whom they would identify to serve on a possible board of governors for a Waterloo College Affiliated Faculty. The six men with whom Hagey met were themselves a cross-section of local and national business interests: Ira Needles, president of B.F. Goodrich; Carl Pollock, president of Dominion Electrohome Industries; Carl Dare, president of the Dare Biscuit Company; Dr. Stanley Leavine, former mayor of Kitchener and the former member of the Legislative Assembly; A. M. Snider, president of Sunshine (Waterloo) Company; and E. J. Shoemaker, president of the McBrine Baggage Company. [12]

Hagey had prepared a brief outline of the historical developments surrounding the idea of creating a university, to explain "why and how this affiliated faculty is being formed" as well as "a brief story of what the function of the Board of Governors would be and what the duties and time requirements are likely to be." In turn, each of the members selected names on a larger list and agreed to call those whom they knew best. The names on the list were all prominent business and professional men from the surrounding communities. Not surprisingly, almost all of the proposed board members were well known to the organizing committee. Carl Pollock indicated his willingness to call any or all of them; Ira Needles identified those whom he knew best and others he would call if no one else had indicated they would do so; Carl Dare's list was similar and Shoemaker expressed the feelings of the group when he added this postscript to his list: "Gerry: You will doubtless get many duplicates from the 6 of us. I'll take whatever you decide." [13]

The project was very much regarded as Gerry Hagey's. The initiative had been his and he was the one who had kept it moving forward. Without this community support, however, the university idea would have been stillborn. Three months after Dr. Dunlop's visit to Waterloo, Hagey was proudly reporting to the minister of education the names of potential board members in support of the proposal to create what might ultimately become a Waterloo University. [14]

At 4:00 p.m. on 16 December 1955, in the boardroom of Waterloo College, a meeting of the first provisional Board of Governors was called to order. In attendance were: Gordon Chaplin, Carl M. Dare, Carl Gruetzner, Lewis Hahn, P. R.

University of Waterloo Founders

From 1957 to 1962 the following served on the University's Board of Governors. It was during these formative years that decisions and plans were made that set the direction for what the University has become.

J. S. Bauer	H. J. Heasley	J. E. Motz	K. J. Shea
C. R. Bronfman	G. R. Henderson	I. G. Needles	E. J. Shoemaker
J. G. Brown	P. R. Hilborn	H. Paikin	J. K. Sims
G. J. Chaplin	A. W. Hopton	A. Paleczny	A. M. Snider
C. M. Dare	K. R. Hymmen	C. A. Pollock	H. C. Templin
F. Dreger	A. R. Kaufman	D. H. Porter	O. W. Titus
W. H. Evans	H. C. Krug	A. I. Rosenberg	J. P. R. Wadsworth
W. F. Franke	F. S. Kumpf	J. Sanderson	H. E. Wambold
K. H. Gruetzner	H. M. Lackner	L. M. Savage	C. N. Weber
H. L. Guy	S. F. Leavine	M. M. Schneckenburger	L. J. Whitney
J. G. Hagey	R. B. Marr	J. W. Scott	H. J. Ziegler
L. W. Hahn	J. Meinzinger	N. R. Shaw	

A. K. Adlington (Secretary to the Board 1958 - 1962)

Hilborn, A. W. Hopton, A. R. Kaufman, Henry C. Krug, Dr. Harry Lackner, Dr. Stanley Leavine, John E. Motz, Ira G. Needles, Carl A. Pollock, E. J. Shoemaker, J. Kenneth Sims, A. M. Snider, and Dr. Hugh Templin. Regrets were received from J. G. Brown, W. F. Franke, Harry L. Guy, Bruce Marr, and J. W. Scott who were "sympathetic to the purpose of the meeting, but unable to attend due to previous business meetings."[15]

At Hagey's suggestion a temporary chairman and secretary — Ira Needles and Carl Dare — were elected. The purpose of the meeting was expressed in a motion by Carl Pollock, seconded by A. M. Snider:

> Those present agree that they will serve as charter members of a Board of Governors for a Faculty of Science to be affiliated with Waterloo College and that they will record their agreement by affixing their signature to this motion ...

The motion was unanimously approved.

Carl Pollock, J. K. Sims, Dr. Harry Lackner, Ira Needles, and Carl Dare were appointed to work with legal counsel, "for the purpose of incorporating under the Companies' Act a Board of Governors for a Faculty of Science to be affiliated with Waterloo College." This committee was also asked to meet with a committee from the Board of Governors of Waterloo College and its legal counsel "to prepare an Agreement of Affiliation of the newly-incorporated Faculty with Waterloo College." The decision had

The Founders Plaque recognizes those who served on the Board of Governors between 1956 and 1962 when the formative decisions and plans were made that set the future directions of the university. Photo by Chris Hughes (plaque) Pirak Studios Limited (paper weight)

43

Board members
C.A. Pollock (2nd from left)
and P.R. Hilborn (3rd from
left) along with Physics
Professor Arthur Cowan
at the first meeting of the
Industrial Advisory Council.
In 1956 Hilborn had been
instrumental in introducing
C.L. Emery, the principal of
the Provincial Institute
of Trades in Toronto, to
President Hagey at Waterloo
College. Out of this meeting
grew the commitment to
develop the co-operative
education program later
described by Ira Needles as
" The Waterloo Plan."
KWR

been made. A new, non-denominational Faculty of Science would be brought into being. On 4 April 1956 the incorporation of the Waterloo College Associate Faculties was completed.

The participation of leaders from the business and professional interests in the community was considered to be a sine qua non by Premier Frost and his colleagues at Queen's Park. The prestige that they brought to the university, the money that they might be expected to raise and contribute, and the influence that they held in political and corporate circles were especially important in the social acceptance of a new university. Those who agreed to serve on the Board of Governors of the Waterloo College Associate Faculties represented a wide range of interests and backgrounds. Of no small importance, radio, television, and the print media were represented by Carl Pollock, John Motz, and Hugh Templin. Old family money was present with A.R. Kaufman on the board, while the chief executive officers of both Canadian and the newer multinational firms were well represented. Religious diversity as well as a geographical and a regional balance had also been a guiding influence. With members coming from Hespeler, Galt, Preston, New Hamburg, and Fergus as well as Kitchener and Waterloo, representing the major religious denominations, the new board was assured of more than a local or singular religious identity.

The first priority of the board had been to ensure that its relationship with St. Jerome's College, the Roman Catholic post-secondary institution in Kitchener, had not been compromised. Hence its first resolution was that "it would be for the welfare of the community for the facilities provided by this Board to be available to St. Jerome's as well as Waterloo College."[16]

Hagey was also interested in the provincial government's plans to establish schools offering technical training, suggesting that Waterloo be considered as a possible site. Carl Pollock, too, had seized the initiative, suggesting to the minister that the government's interest "in the establishment of schools providing several years of advanced technical training and some extension of the basic arts and letters beyond high school" was to be encouraged. "The location of such an institute in the Kitchener-Waterloo area, closely associated with Waterloo College," he continued, "would provide a most practical and useful arrangement."[17]

The timing could not have been more propitious. In October 1955, when J.G. Althouse first took office as the chief director of education for the province, he had predicted the need for major changes in Ontario's system of education. Echoing the statistical projections of E.F. Sheffield, he predicted that by 1965 the university population of 21,000 would likely have doubled. For the first time, the universities were being criticized for their unwillingness to cope with these changes.[18] At the same time, Althouse resisted the suggestion of free-standing junior colleges as a way to meet the enrolment crisis, believing that they "would be incapable of providing the 'training' for leadership required in the industries, in business and in the professions":

> A junior college cannot attempt specialized or professional training; the best it can offer is a sort of second rate general education. The professional schools must remain in the Universities; if these do not increase their accommodations substantially, Canadian industry, business and professions will be short of leaders despite a heavy expenditure on junior colleges.[19]

Althouse strongly urged the government to take greater initiatives to meet both the expected enrolment and the social needs of the professions. Without universities, Ontario would be ill-equipped to meet the future.

These same sentiments were echoed in Ontario's submission to the 1956 Royal Commission on Canada's Economic Prospects, stating quite dramatically, that "the advance of higher education is essential to Canada's development as a modern industrial power. Without large numbers of university graduates, neither industry nor the government, nor the educational system, nor the medical

WATERLOO PRESENTS!

A NEW UNIVERSITY

A CO-OPERATIVE COURSE IN ENGINEERING

EXPANSION IN ARTS AND SCIENCE

services can be expanded as the growing structure of the nation requires."[20] Neither Ontario's premier, Leslie Frost, nor his co-ordinator of higher education, wanted to see the unlimited creation of new universities. They preferred that existing universities or colleges such as Waterloo College or Lakehead Technical Institute in Fort William, with strong community support, expand their existing facilities. Waterloo's request for financial support to increase its course offerings, especially in the scientific fields, was precisely the kind of initiative that Frost favoured.

The first official statement of the "thinking that has been done in the interests of the future of Waterloo College Associate Faculties," prepared by Ira Needles, Carl Pollock, A.M. Snider, Percy Hilborn, and Gerry Hagey went well beyond what the premier may have had in mind. They proposed to chart a radical course for the Associate Faculties. Arising out of their concerns about the inadequate training of many graduate engineers, as well as their own experience of the Canadian economy and the challenges facing Ontario's universities, their document clearly challenged the status quo. Hagey obviously regarded it as very sensitive. While distributing it to the executive of the Associate Faculties, he suggested, for good reason, that "at the present we would be well-advised to keep this confidential."[21]

Although incorporated "primarily as a College of Science," the Associate Faculties was "at liberty to offer a large range of courses" and was actually the "beginning [of] a new university"— and one, they predicted, that would play "an important role in the future continued development of our province and nation." The innovative programs soon to be identified with Waterloo College Associate Faculties were not far removed from the committee's nascent ideas about the needs of a new university.

The world had moved "into a technological era," they suggested, which had "radically changed the demand from industry for labour, technicians, and engineers." Many of the board members had faced these problems in their own companies and had resorted to recruiting skilled technicians from Europe. They were also alarmed at the failure rate in science courses at universities and in the high schools. Some companies had begun to consider setting up their own training schools, while private ventures in other cities were offering programs which President Hagey suggested were "likely to turn into 'rackets' unless universities take leadership in providing adequate technological higher education."

Hagey was also concerned that in the past technological education had paid little attention to the humanities, yet as technicians assumed new levels of responsibility, this cultural background

By 1958 Waterloo had shifted its emphasis from a relationship with the University of Western Ontario to becoming A NEW UNIVERSITY with a co-operative course in engineering and an expansion in arts and science.
UWA

would be essential. Waterloo, he suggested, was in a position "to formulate a curriculum that combines science, technology and the humanities." They were setting a course that looked to the future, rather than one that was based on past university precedents. Hagey and his colleagues felt confident they could do it, even if the older universities could not:

> Major changes in established universities are difficult. Many of the major changes that have been made in higher education programmes during the last century have developed through new colleges rather than through previously-established universities. Consequently, Waterloo, in organizing a new university, is challenged to develop courses in line with our country's present and future needs.

Waterloo "has an opportunity to do something about the present and future needs quickly," Hagey concluded, "through established universities, radical changes would be materially more difficult."

The first proposal was to extend the first year of honours science at Waterloo College to second year, thereby making it possible for a general arts student to major in science. Pre-science courses would also be offered, along with an introduction to technology. To enhance the traditional engineering programs given at other universities they planned to introduce the humanities and a clearer integration of technical and theoretical instruction. This would add a fifth year to the degree program, but it would also allow a student to transfer from Waterloo and proceed towards a degree at other universities without repeating the subjects already taken at Waterloo. Hagey conceded that "this suggestion would involve a radical change and consequently should only be adopted when adequate research has indicated its desirability, its feasibility and its possibility."

In the meantime, along with some other members of the board, Hagey was making preparations to meet with Percy Hilborn and a group of businessmen from South Waterloo who were interested in establishing a polytechnical institute in Preston. Hagey wished to determine whether they could combine their mutual interests. A meeting "of interested men from both groups" had been scheduled for 24 May. Needles, Pollock, Hagey, and Snider, the executive members of the board, planned to meet with Hilborn and his group, following the noon Rotary luncheon at the Kress House.

The Management Committee of the Associate Faculties also proposed a meeting of "top management representatives and leading Canadian companies" to explain Waterloo's proposed program and to determine their interest and whether or not they would underwrite "a thorough survey of present technical and applied science education — the possibilities of organizing and proceeding with such a course," as well as finances, student demand, and other concerns. Hagey suggested that the survey "should be under the direction of a graduate Engineer who has had experience in both technical and applied science fields ... and should include a study of advances in this direction made by institutions in other provinces, ... in the United States, and possibly Great Britain." As fate would have it, the meeting in South Waterloo would bring Hagey and the Associate Faculties into contact with the one man in Canada who would bring these elements together in a way that would reshape the system of education at Waterloo. That man was Charles Leslie Emery.

A new design for higher education involving students, faculty and industry in a co-operative venture had become Waterloo's "credo," differentiating the future University of Waterloo and its programs from those of Canada's older universities. UWA

CHAPTER THREE

Co-op: The Waterloo Experience

C.L. Emery, a graduate of Queen's University, was brimming with energy and enthusiasm as he reviewed the possibilities in the field of education. Emery was the principal of the Provincial Institute of Trades in Toronto, a school established under the Department of Education primarily to provide the academic complement for students who were employed by industry in the trades or as apprentices. What Emery wanted, however, was to create a more advanced technical institute in Ontario similar to the Ryerson Institute of Technology in Toronto. By coincidence, the group of businessmen in South Waterloo, headed by Percy Hilborn, had approached the Department of Education with general plans for an institute in their community that might serve a similar purpose. When Emery and Hilborn met in Preston, Hilborn, a charter board member of the Associate Faculties, also suggested that Emery might wish to talk to President Hagey at Waterloo College about his ideas for a new university.

Emery travelled to Waterloo and the meeting with Hagey was timely and fortuitous for both of them. The two men had much in common as they talked about their concerns for the development of education in Ontario and about the advantages that were being lost at so many of Ontario's universities and especially for those students who had fallen by the wayside, not quite fitting within conventional programs. At the Provincial Institute of Trades, Emery had first-hand experience of the concept of alternating industrial and technical training within a high school academic program. Emery immediately suggested to Hagey that this concept, somewhat amended, might be useful at Waterloo, especially for Hagey's proposed option for the training of technicians. It would certainly answer many of the criticisms which Hagey's own board members had expressed about the lack of practical experience of many of the young engineers and technicians whom they employed. Hagey was excited by the possibilities. He invited Emery to attend the next meeting of the Board of Governors on 19 June 1956.[1]

Several items of interest were on the board's agenda that evening, although none would have more significance than the one presented by Emery. Before Emery was introduced to the board, however, Hagey reported that the Associate Faculties' agreement for affiliation with Waterloo College had been approved by both the college board and by the Canada Synod of the United Lutheran Church; the application for financial assistance for the Associate Faculties from the province needed to be to the minister by mid-July, and Lloyd Schaus, dean of Waterloo College, had agreed also to serve as dean for the Associate Faculties. Hagey was especially pleased to have Emery there, for this was the meeting when the Management Committee's draft of the Waterloo College Associate Faculties Development Plan would be debated.[2]

An air of excitement and anticipation filled the room as Hagey outlined this report which challenged the Associate Faculties to set a course for the future of the new university that would be different from the older Ontario universities. At the end of Hagey's report, Emery then "outlined to the Board possibilities for developing a combined Technical and Applied Science Course." Emery's interest in combining technical training and applied science was the primary proposal presented to

Photos like these were used to illustrate the benefits to students and industries from participation in Waterloo's co-operative education program.
KWR

53

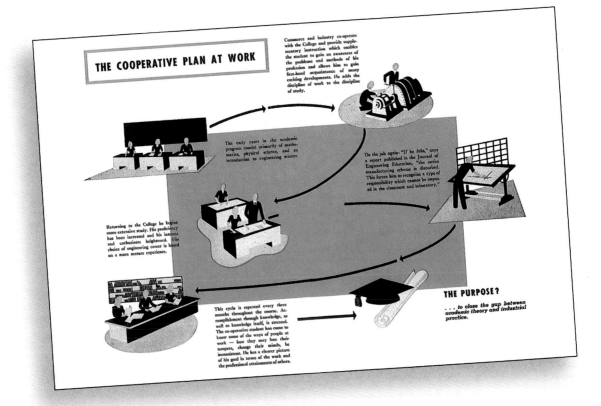

THE COOPERATIVE PLAN AT WORK

Commerce and industry co-operate with the College and provide supplementary instruction which enables the student to gain an awareness of the problems and methods of his profession and allows him to gain first-hand acquaintance of many exciting developments. It adds the discipline of work to the discipline of study.

The early years in the academic program consist primarily of mathematics, physical science, and an introduction to engineering science.

On the job again: "If he fails," says a report published in the Journal of Engineering Education, "the entire manufacturing scheme is disturbed. This forces him to recognize a type of responsibility which cannot be imposed in the classroom and laboratory."

Returning to the College he begins more extensive study. His proficiency has been increased and his interest and enthusiasm heightened. His choice of engineering career is based on a more mature experience.

This cycle is repeated every three months throughout the course. Accomplishment through knowledge, as well as knowledge itself, is stressed. The co-operative student has come to know some of the ways of people at work — how they may lose their tempers, change their minds, be inconsistent. He has a clearer picture of his goal in terms of the work and the professional attainments of others.

THE PURPOSE?

... to close the gap between academic theory and industrial practice.

The simplistic diagram of the co-operative education plan belies the intensive political debate that would soon question the "educational" value of this program. Under the astute leadership of A.S. (Bert) Barber as director of co-ordination and placement these objections would be overcome in 1958. The Waterloo Plan emphasized the significance of the university-level education provided to the students as part of their work experience.
UWA

the board that evening. It had a special appeal to those board members whose companies were chronically short of skilled technicians as well as to those others who had difficulty attracting and retaining professional engineers in the face of competition from Toronto and other larger manufacturing centres.

Almost lost in Emery's proposal was the possibility of offering this program in co-operation with industry, although this, too, seemed especially well suited to the industrial leaders and company owners who sat around the board table that evening in Waterloo College. Emery's own institute had been incorporated to provide the academic training for those already engaged in apprenticeship programs in various trades. It seemed reasonable to consider this method of alternating work and study terms, especially in the training of technicians, but perhaps it could also be developed as part of an applied science program for engineering students. Out of this formative meeting, followed by discussions with Dean Schaus, Hagey later reported to the board, "we eventually developed our original plan for Co-operative Education ... This led to Mr. Emery being added to our staff, first as Planning Engineer and later as Principal of the Co-operative Applied Science Course."[3] Emery's practical experience as well as his self-assured optimism, along with the board's expressed determination to chart a radical educational program, set in train one of the most significant educational experiments in Canada in the twentieth century.

Within a week of his meeting with the board of the Associate Faculties, Emery was writing to the secretary of the Department of Health, Education and Welfare in Washington, requesting information about American colleges and universities which were offering programs in applied science and, in particular, those that offered it by means of "co-operative education." What Emery received was Circular No. 463, which outlined the origins, development, philosophy, and implementation of co-operative education in the United States as well as a list of all the universities and colleges that offered co-op programs. Some of the names were impressive: the Massachusetts Institute of Technology, Northeastern University, Purdue, Cornell, the University of California at Berkeley and at Los Angeles, the University of Michigan, Antioch College, the University of Cincinnati, the University of Detroit, and Northwestern University.[4]

Of the forty-three institutions listed, Ira Needles was particularly interested in three. Since his graduation, Northwestern, his own alma mater in Chicago, had adopted the co-operative plan for its engineering courses; so, too, had the General Motors Institute in Flint, Michigan, and the University of Detroit from which B.F. Goodrich in the United States had student placements. Needles wrote directly to his colleagues at the Goodrich headquarters in Akron, Ohio, asking for the names of other American companies participating in co-operative programs, as well as the names of those that operated in Canada. From his colleagues at B.F. Goodrich he learned that they not only employed co-op students, but that Goodrich "even prepares literature of its own to encourage young people to procure their education under this system."[5] The answers were reassuring, identifying a list of prominent companies.

Hagey and Dean Schaus arranged to meet with the president of the Engineering Institute of Canada and were reassured that their proposed program had merit when the general secretary, Austin Wright, explained that not only was he familiar with co-operative courses in the United States and Great Britain, but that he was keenly in support of them. "There is much to be said for them," he reassured Hagey and Schaus. "The reactions which I

The General Motors Institute held a particular fascination for Ira Needles, whose experience at Northwestern University in Chicago and in his professional career as president of B.F. Goodrich (Canada) had been closely associated with the automobile industry, and for A.S. Barber, Waterloo's director of co-ordination and placement, who had attended the General Motors Institute.
UWA

MANUAL OF COORDINATION

FOR
GENERAL MOTORS UNITS
PARTICIPATING IN THE
GENERAL MOTORS
COOPERATIVE ENGINEERING
AND
BUSINESS ADMINISTRATION
PROGRAMS

have had in both countries have been quite favourable and personally I do not see why such practice should not be equally as successful in Canada."[6]

The deadline for applying for the Associate Faculties' first ever provincial grant was fast approaching. It was imperative that the idea of a co-operative program in engineering be discussed with the minister of education before a grant request was submitted. Although Hagey was a consummate optimist, even he must have felt some anxiety about proposing so radical a change from what he had suggested to the minister when he had visited Waterloo College the previous summer. There seemed so little time and so much to do.

On 13 July 1956 Hagey was at Queen's Park to outline to Dr. Beattie, the assistant to the director of education, Waterloo's "contemplated Co-operative Plan of Education for Technicians and Engineers." Dr. Beattie, Hagey recalled, "expressed a keen interest in this programme and thought it had possibilities of filling a worthy need." Now, of course, Hagey also explained to Beattie that "if we were to add the Technical and Engineering Course an additional $200,000 would be required," along with the original request for $800,000 for the science building. He assured Beattie that the Associate Faculties had already contacted several large industries, including Shell Oil, Minneapolis-Honeywell, and General Electric regarding their support for the "proposed new plan of education."[7]

Although Waterloo College Associate Faculties had made a commitment to the co-operative plan, Hagey emphasized to Dr. Beattie "the need for a very complete study of this proposal before reaching a decision to proceed with the Plan." "I stated," he recalled,

> this study would involve the employment of people, travel to U.S. Colleges now using similar plans, many personal contacts with companies employing engineers and technicians, as well as a sampling of high school students' opinions of it to determine enrolment possibilities.

The following week Hagey met with Dr. J.G. Althouse, Ontario's co-ordinator of education, presenting him with a complex outline of the co-operative education proposal which they discussed in detail. Dr. Althouse "seemed much interested in it, stated that he thought it had possibilities, and somewhat jokingly asked how I expected to live with the [other] university presidents after making this plan known."[8]

The speed with which this draft of the Co-operative Education Program had been prepared is truly remarkable; it is also a testimony to their commitment to making it succeed. Hagey had asked Dr. Althouse "whether or not we were free to discuss the proposed Co-operative Plan publicly and with members of the government" and he had been assured that "once the Minister had seen Waterloo's petition the following Monday, we were at liberty to discuss it openly." Hagey's relief must have been evident, for the Associate Faculties were already having "a description of the plan printed and proposed sending it to a selected list of industrial companies [by] the middle of the following week."

This meeting with Althouse was a turning point with regard to the proposed technical institute in South Waterloo. The capital grant submission asked for more than Althouse had anticipated, but he had included an appropriation for a grant "for a trade school in South Waterloo." If the South Waterloo group was willing, this money could be reallocated to the Associate Faculties. Percy Hilborn agreed to take this proposal to "the South Waterloo people," who concurred with his recommendation to support the development at Waterloo College, "even if it meant delaying the procurement of a trade school for them."[9] Ray Myers, the Conservative MLA for South Waterloo, agreed to convey this decision to the Department of Education. Another major hurdle in the development of the Co-operative program had been passed, but many more were still to be overcome. In some ways, this first was one of the easiest.

The proponents of the Waterloo Plan hoped that they would not arouse the ire of other Ontario universities with existing engineering programs, pointing out that the "primary purpose of this Plan is to supplement and complement the presently established engineering and technical courses, not to compete against them." It was anticipated, however, that the plan had the possibility of "graduating more engineers and training more well qualified technicians." Urging support for the Waterloo Plan, its proponents (Needles, Hagey and Emery) assured the minister that their proposal had been checked with "several presidents of large companies using many engineers and technicians ... [and] their interest in it has been almost spontaneous."[10] They also had studied the Co-operative Plan which had been in use at the University of Detroit since 1911 in which B.F. Goodrich in the United States had participated.

In July, Needles conceded that at least "another six months of exploratory work will be done before deciding to proceed." This exploratory work, he suggested, would be under the direction of "Les Emery, a well qualified man who has had more than ten years of experience in the field of Applied Science and Technical instruction." Needles felt confident about Waterloo's co-operative education program, since all the industrial leaders that he had spoken to made comments such as "It is inevitable," and "you could not stop its development now, even if you wished to do so." Now it was necessary to explore "below the surface of enthusiasm," and the Associate Faculties were requesting a $25,000 grant for a feasibility study.[11]

While Needles readily admitted that support of the plan would be a courageous move, it would also be one that was "in harmony with demands that are now being made by industry and in the public press." It is also, he suggested, "the type of programme that makes news and, once approved, would be widely publicized." If ever there was a self-fulfilling prophecy, this was it.

Wider discussion of the Waterloo Plan still seemed somewhat premature at this stage. The detailed studies had yet to be undertaken; visits to universities in the United States were several months away; no thought had been given to an actual curriculum or to the relationship of Waterloo's courses to those taught in the faculties of engineering at other Canadian universities, let alone the teaching of technicians and engineers in the same program. These last points certainly troubled Edward Hall, the president of the University of Western Ontario. Hagey and Dean Schaus had met with Hall on 14 August to discuss the plan with him. Hall was less than encouraging, but he was also biding his time, and his thoughts were undoubtedly on Western's own newly developed engineering program.

The public announcement of the Waterloo Plan on 27 August had not been done to spite Edward Hall, although he might easily have seen it that way. Just days before, Stanley Deeks, who had been the chief organizer of the St. Andrews conference, informed Hagey and Dean Schaus that the results of his research were almost identical to their observations "relative to the engineering and technical manpower shortage." One of Deeks's proposals, Hagey later explained to Hall, "was the establishment of a course almost identical to the one we were contemplating." For the protection of the Associate Faculties, Deeks suggested that the Waterloo Plan should be "registered publicly"— otherwise Waterloo might have been accused of being plagiarists or opportunists.[12] It would not be the last time these epithets would be linked to Waterloo.

The executive of the Associate Faculties decided immediately to mail a description of the Waterloo Plan to an extensive list of the top management in leading Canadian companies. They also hoped to announce the plan at a meeting where the press would have an opportunity to hear it "and publish it if they so desired." And publish it they did. The *Financial Post* printed a laudatory editorial and G.C. Bernard, manager of the Ontario division of the

This calendar of the Waterloo College Associate Faculties co-operative course has the Waterloo College Arts and Administration building as its centrepiece, and identifies civil engineering as "structural" engineering. This would be rectified in the 1958 Faculty of Science and Engineering calender.
UWA

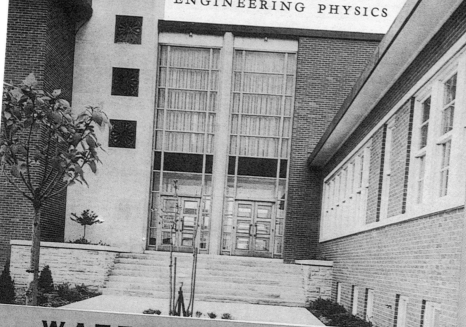

Canadian Manufacturers' Association, asked for copies of Needles's Rotary speech for all of the members of the CMA's Special Committee on Education and Manpower. Two of the committee's leading members would not need any additional copies — Carl Pollock was intimately acquainted with it, and Stanley Deeks, whose own announcement had been pre-empted by Needles's presentation of the Waterloo Plan, would remain an avid supporter of Waterloo's co-operative education idea.[13]

The Royal Commission on Canada's Economic Prospects echoed these sentiments, including the danger of "falling victim to Soviet 'ecumenical ambitions'" and in his 1956 budget speech the treasurer of Ontario, Dana Porter, worried aloud about the incredible advances that the Soviets had made "in various branches of science and technology" as he pledged his government's increased support for universities.[14] Dana Porter's support for the Waterloo Plan would be critical as opposition from the traditional universities would be heard from every quarter. To be fair, those who questioned Waterloo's proposed co-operative program and the combined training of technicians and engineers had good reasons to be sceptical and the plan itself would undergo major amendments before it could be offered for university credit.

As the minister of education and then as treasurer of Ontario, Dana Porter oversaw much of Ontario's university development in the post-war era. Porter's support for Waterloo's innovative co-operative education plan was responsible for its continuation in the face of formidable opposition. Few other politicians in the Frost government had the political influence wielded by Dana Porter.
Ashley and Crippen

In October of 1956, Hagey, Les Emery, and Alan Adlington had met with Daniel Sunday, vice-president of G.A. Brakeley & Company, one of Canada's foremost fund-raising organizations. Brakeley's was asked to conduct a survey to evaluate the support for the idea of Waterloo's proposed university and especially of its co-operative plan of education for technicians and engineers. Such a survey was essential to assess local and provincial support and perhaps ultimately to develop a major fund-raising appeal. Without such support, the university idea would never be the reality that so many hoped it would become.

The preliminary findings from the Associate Faculties' original review, based on the $25,000 grant from the provincial Treasury, had been presented to the Department of Education on 27 December 1956. In this internal report the Associate Faculties suggested that "basically the plan is practical, feasible and desirable" and that "Waterloo is capable of developing and offering the plan."[15] Co-operative education was also described as "a means through which more people, with the ability to procure a college education, will be motivated to give their education the application required for successful progress." The report also revealed, however, that there were those who were opposed to the Waterloo Plan: "the word 'technical' being associated with the plan," they suggested, "has caused a small group in the fields of higher education to be openly critical of it [the Plan] without even having a knowledge of the proposed course of studies."[16]

The survey conducted by Brakeley's in the beginning of 1957 indicated that there was significant opposition to co-operative education from the existing universities that could not be dismissed simply as prejudice against a small college trying to offer an innovative program. The Waterloo Plan, Brakeley's reported, was unproven and Waterloo College's own record as an institution of higher education was restricted to a general undergraduate program in the liberal arts, and even then it was not well known.

Hagey understood some of the reasons for this reluctance. Since its founding, the college had graduated only 615 students, most of them either as teachers (25 per cent) or as ministers of various Protestant denominations. None of Waterloo College's senior administrators was known outside of the local community, nor were any of its faculty members "known nationally for outstanding contributions." In the past, students wishing to study science or business had been unable to complete these courses at the college and as a result had graduated from other universities. In circumstances such as these, Waterloo College had never developed an effective alumni association or established a reputation among prominent business and commercial leaders in Canada. Many of those surveyed by Brakeley's genuinely doubted the ability of Waterloo College and the newly created Waterloo College Associate Faculties to develop a full engineering program, let alone one that seemed to require a more complex form of education, combined with a non-university program of technical training.

It was not just the other universities who were unimpressed with Emery's proposal to train technicians and engineers in a joint program. The Brakeley survey which had sent an outline of the plan to a selected group of industrialists in an effort to gain their support, had inadvertently created the impression "that the program ... was directed toward the training of technicians rather than engineers." While most industrialists agreed that there was a shortage of both technicians and engineers, many felt that the engineering shortage was "a matter for [the] established engineering schools."

Co-operative education, too, was not without its detractors in other Canadian universities. Some explained that they did not consider the Waterloo co-operative education plan to be good education, either from the point of view of the student or the faculty. They also predicted that it would be very difficult to recruit qualified faculty members to a college such as Waterloo, yet this would be essential before Waterloo College could be allowed to register students in such a program. Finally, these "leaders in the educational field" agreed "that a technical school closely allied, either geographically or from the point of view of faculty, with a school of engineering will inevitably have a detrimental effect on the quality of teaching in engineering."

These concerns were undoubtedly serious. But more perplexing were the criticisms about the program's proposed relationship with industry. Terming the plan "interrupted education," its critics predicted that, "a shallow and disordered program of work is the end result for the student, and consequently he may be an inferior engineer." They also predicted that Waterloo College could not carry out the proposed plan on its own without the co-operation of other engineering schools, and it was doubted that they would accept the program "as comparable to that now being given at Canadian engineering schools." Instead, those universities interviewed by Brakeley's suggested "that there is a fine opportunity in the Waterloo area for another technical

The University of Waterloo mace was presented to the university in 1965 in memory of the late Dr. S.F. Leavine, a former MLA and founding board member of the Associate Faculties. The mace was designed by Eric Aldwinckle and produced by Harold Stacey.
Photo by Chris Hughes

school along the lines of the Ryerson Institute in Toronto." Brakeley's concluded that there was "heavy opposition" from established university circles "on the ground of endangering academic standards" and the initial emphasis on the training of technicians through the plan "remains in the minds of the public."

In the face of this opposition, Hagey turned to the task of writing his first annual report to the board of the Associate Faculties in March 1957.[17] He set out to recall the events of what had been the most remarkable twelve months of his life: "This past year nearly everything has had to be done under more pressure than [is] desirable," he began. "This has necessitated bypassing many channels that should normally be followed." "Frankly," he admitted, "the job has been running your administrators, rather than vice-versa." And he conceded, "We are certainly conscious of the need to correct this situation as quickly as possible."

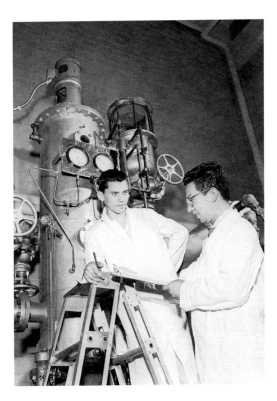

By 1958 the co-operative education program had spurred interest in Waterloo from newspapers across Canada. As Ira Needles had predicted in August 1956, it had caught the Canadian imagination. KWR

It was difficult to recount all that had happened during the year, let alone place it in perspective. A radical new program of education had been suggested and adopted. By August 1956 the Ministry of Education had been informed and a national campaign to announce the Waterloo Plan had been initiated. A dramatic confrontation with the president of the University of Western Ontario had been avoided, and Western's Senate had approved the principle of affiliation of the Associate Faculties through Waterloo College. Neither the college's courses nor its co-operative education program had been fully vetted by Western. This trial was still to come and it, too, would not be without its difficulties. In September 1956, charged with energy, full of enthusiasm for the applied studies program, C.L. Emery had left the Provincial Institute of Trades in Toronto and joined the Associate Faculties. Meeting regularly with Hagey and Dean Schaus, Emery began to flesh out a design for a co-operative education program.

The Associate Faculties had weathered an attack on their program led by the deans of engineering and applied science at two prominent Ontario universities who had told the minister of education that, while the Waterloo program should be a good course for the production of technicians and engineering assistants, "it is quite out of the question for the training of Engineers."[18]

It all nearly ended there. In the face of such adamant and

unqualified opposition from two of the province's leading universities, the minister began to have second thoughts about Waterloo's ideas. He assured the deans, as well as others who had written to him about the Waterloo program, that no decision had been made on the grant request and that the matter was still pending, and so it was.

It was the intervention in December 1956 of Dana Porter, the treasurer of Ontario, who had been called upon to review the education portfolio, that tipped the balance. Porter was perhaps the only cabinet minister who could have intervened directly. He had taken a personal interest in the Waterloo file, requesting that A.M. Moon, a member of the Department of Education, accompany Hagey and Emery to the United States to assess the validity of co-operative education.

Moon was already aware of the concept of co-operative education and somewhat sympathetic to it, since Emery's Provincial Institute of Trades and Emery himself had reported to him at the Department of Education. After attending the meeting of the Co-operative Education Division of the American Society for Engineering Education at Northeastern University in Boston on 10 and 11 January 1957, Moon returned to Queen's Park reporting in support of Waterloo's co-operative program. When read alongside Dana Porter's statements as treasurer regarding Ontario's need for engineering education, Moon's recommendation was indispensable in moving Waterloo's program forward. This was all the more so, for Moon's recommendations were written in the face of pressure to bring in a negative report regarding the Waterloo initiative.

A.M. Moon's positive recommendation in January 1957 to the Department of Education in favour of co-operative education at the Waterloo College Associate Faculties was indispensable in assuring provincial support for this embattled program.
UWA

The board of the Associate Faculties was alarmed by the opposition to Waterloo's co-operative program from other universities, and they asked Porter to assign Moon to act as a liaison from the government, "relative to the relationship of our course to the overall higher education programme of the Province."[19]

The events of 1956 and 1957 had taken place at a hectic pace, but at the same time the shape of the Waterloo Plan continued to move forward in the face of this formidable opposition. In January 1957 the President's Committee had announced that not only would the Associate Faculties "be operated co-operatively with Industry as opposed to the conventional engineering courses," but also that "no conventional courses [would] be operated as alternatives to the co-operative course in applied science or technology."[20]

The Associate Faculties had moved one step further toward creating a unique university environment. This process continued to move away from the traditional university programs as the Department of Co-ordination took shape in February 1957, when George Dufault began work as the first head of the department. He was faced with the herculean task of recruiting both employers and students for the co-operative education program which it was hoped, with "every effort," would be able to commence operations in July 1957, less than five months away.

Dean Schaus and Les Emery began preparing a report "on needs and plans for faculty and instructional staff." They also set about designing a general curriculum and seeking staff and potential faculty members from positions in industry and research as well as from other universities, inviting them to come to Waterloo to participate in a new and somewhat risky adventure. George Dufault and Les Emery recruited Ron Bowman, Ron Davies, and Don MacPherson from Orenda Engines, and Arthur Cowan of the National Research Laboratories in Ottawa and persuaded them to come to Waterloo.[21] Ralph Stanton had recently left the University of Toronto to come to Waterloo College to start a new university and Ted Batke would soon leave a career that had included teaching in the University of Toronto and senior level research in industry to travel to Waterloo. In the meantime, Paul Meinke had followed Emery from the Provincial Institute of Trades and was anxious to begin his career with the Associate Faculties. Perhaps the university idea would still be possible.

In March 1957 the application forms for students applying for entry to the "Applied Science Division" had been agreed upon when President Hagey made an announcement that would fundamentally alter the philosophy of the program. He recommended that the option for the training of technicians be cancelled and he intended to place before the Board of Governors the motion "that they withdraw from the program of studies the Third Year of Technology," thereby ending it before it had begun.[22]

The proposal to train technicians and engineers in the same program was too controversial. The reasons for Hagey's recommendation were many. The board of Waterloo College and many of its faculty members had seen the inclusion of the technicians' program as a diminution of their status as a university college. Other universities and engineering institutes had suggested that the training of technicians was incompatible with the goals of an engineering program. For his own part, Hagey acknowledged "a reluctant acceptance of the fact that the institution was not strong enough to introduce both a Co-Op. system of education and a Technology education at the university level all at one and the same time."[23]

This decision precipitated the beginning of what would become

Faced with the daunting task of recruiting both students and industries to participate in Waterloo's innovative co-operative education program, George Dufault joined the Associate Faculties in 1957. Although the pace was hectic and gruelling, Dufault later recalled these days as some of the happiest of his life. WLU

a major philosophical rift between President Hagey and Les Emery, newly designated as principal of the Associate Faculties, as to the direction taken by the Associate Faculties. Hagey's commitment was to the university program and he had made this his priority. Emery's background and his own experience led him to favour the option for technicians. Emery was reluctant to let go of his idea, proposing instead,

> that we lose no time starting to work with the Waterloo South Group and the Lakehead College, to establish in conjunction with them a desirable type of Technology Institute ... if such a development was not possible under the circumstances of this campus we should seek its development in close association with this institution.

Hagey was unwilling to be side-tracked, arguing "that we should not let anything interfere with the urgent need to get on with the establishment of the Co-op degree course." This major difference between the two men was now in the open and was perhaps the first step in the decision by the Board of Governors in May to grant Emery a leave of absence to undertake an M.Sc.

degree in engineering at Queen's. He would not return to Waterloo, although his influence would continue to be felt across the campus.

Looking back at the hurried pace of events during the first year of the Associate Faculties, President Hagey frankly admitted that "This is probably the shortest time in which a major education project such as this has been organized; except in times of war emergencies."[24]

During this past year, this institution has received more national publicity than many of our large universities. The development of our co-operative course is probably being followed with more interest than any other course in Canada ... As a relatively small institution, we have undertaken a programme ... the magnitude of which, in relation to our size, is probably without precedent. One might say that we have staked our claim in an area with a large known potential. Now our job is to develop that claim and most of our energies should be directed toward that objective during the coming year.

The task was daunting. If anything, the pace of development over the next few years would increase. It was an immensely exciting time to be involved in university life, the likes of which would not likely be seen again.

CHAPTER FOUR

A New Campus

On 2 July 1957 seventy-four students arrived on the campus of
Waterloo College to begin classes with the Associate Faculties.
Two hurriedly constructed temporary buildings, built by Ratz
Lumber, had been erected immediately behind Willison Hall.
These temporary quarters, known as Annex 1 and Annex 2, provided space for offices, classrooms, and a laboratory. Almost immediately they became part of the folklore of the new university-to-
be. Soon to be dubbed Annex Alley, this became the centre of university life for the Associate Faculties.

Along with the excitement of university life and discussions
about professors and courses, textbooks and assignments, a distinctive university jacket, with pockets for both a slide-rule and a

whisky flask, was added to campus life. Amidst this excitement the very real need to provide permanent classrooms and laboratory space for the students in the applied science program was increasingly apparent.

With so many new students in 1957 the campus was crowded. Waterloo College had barely enough land for its own needs. Everyone expected the Associate Faculties to acquire additional lands adjacent to the existing college campus. With access to provincial funding, the Associate Faculties might also be able to acquire land from the federal government on the other side of Dearborn Street or privately owned land adjacent to the college. No one thought that the land purchases would be easy. Expropriation was always a possibility, but as the recent experience at Queen's University had demonstrated, it was cumbersome and expensive and would not endear either Waterloo College or the Associate Faculties to the local community. As the college students in the regular arts courses began arriving for classes in September, it was obvious that something had to be done.

Nothing had changed since the spring when President Hagey had written to Norman Schneider in Ottawa about the Canada Mortgage and Housing Corporation lands near Dearborn Street. Other negotiations, including those for the six-acre Wolfe property, where cows still grazed outside President Hagey's office, and which also had an orchard and cider mill at the corner of King and Dearborn, had gone from bad to worse. The Associate Faculties had offered $45,000; Mr. Wolfe believed that his property was worth twice that amount. Wolfe had hired a new lawyer who, without success, was attempting to arrange a new round of negotiations. The unsanitary conditions under which an adjacent property was being kept led the city health inspector to intervene, hoping to pressure the owner to sell it to the Associate Faculties. But the amount of land was of little consequence and valued at only $8,000.[1]

The other major land owner, Swan Cleaners, was prepared to sell his property fronting on King Street, but would require a financial incentive to relocate the business. "The only other location the owner will consider," Hagey reported, "is the Snyder property on the south-east corner of King and Dearborn which would be available to the Associate Faculties, for a price of $36,000." The total cost to the

The movement of the temporary Annex buildings to the new campus marked a dramatic beginning to the university year in 1958. President Hagey had insisted that these buildings be moved to the new campus before the students returned in September. And so they were.
KWR

The construction of the two Annex buildings in 1957 on the campus of Waterloo College behind Willison Hall marked the beginning of the Associate Faculties when the first students arrived in July. Crowded and hot, without air conditioning and with roofs that leaked when some enterprising students sprayed water on them in an attempt to reduce the summer heat, these buildings symbolized Waterloo's hurried drive for university status.
KWR

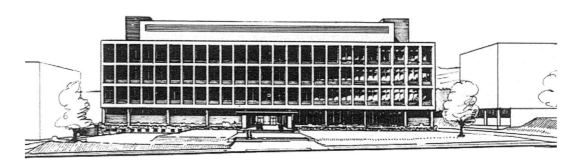

Associate Faculties, including the relocation of Swan Cleaners, would be in excess of $100,000; and time was running out. The provincial government had announced a $500,000 capital grant to the Associate Faculties for a new Science Building. As the autumn term began in 1957, a definite sense of urgency had descended on the campus.

Preliminary plans for the new Science Building were staggering. The estimate was $1 million for a structure "approximately twice the size of the Arts Building."[2] Its location and that of future Applied Science buildings would be critical for the development of the campus. Excitement and a sense of uneasiness overcame the campus at the prospect of so large a building and the creation of a campus that would be so very different from the size and scale of the Waterloo College of the past. Some of the more traditional members of the faculty at Waterloo College began to sound the alarm. It was all happening so quickly — too quickly, some were saying.

In the next estimate, the cost for the General Science Building had increased to $1.5 million. The Faculty Advisory Committee was urgently meeting "to discuss the whole problem afresh,"[3] hoping for a solution that would allow the board to proceed "with an adequate building, if possible within the original estimate." The committee suggested a new proposal. Perhaps the Associate Faculties should consider erecting "a specialized building rather than a general science building." A Chemical Engineering Building to accommodate the full six years of undergraduate work in chemistry and chemical engineering would be first. This could be done within the budget and it could be in use by September 1958.

Although no one foresaw it, this recommendation would drastically alter the plans for the development of the lands adjoining Waterloo College. As the committee began to set out the likely arrangement of other buildings, it became clear that a much larger university campus would be required. A specialized Physics and Engineering Physics Building ready for the start of classes in

September 1959 would be next. In September 1960 a Mechanical Engineering Building with one wing devoted to power laboratories for electrical engineering would be needed. A fourth building for September 1961 would house civil engineering laboratories and general engineering. By September 1962 laboratories for special sciences such as botany and geology would be required.

In light of the Associate Faculties enrolment of one hundred first year students each quarter, by 1961 this would provide only "a reasonable margin of safety"[4] in the timing of Waterloo's expansion. Unlike more conservative universities such as Queen's or Toronto, where expansion and rapid growth were resisted, the Associate Faculties was eager to press forward. Waterloo was destined not to be a university like the others.

For the first time the size and scale of the new university began to acquire a physical reality. The previous architects of the General Science Building, Wright and Jenkins, had been replaced by the firm of Shore and Moffat, who had recently designed buildings for the University of Saskatchewan and the University of Toronto. In September 1957 Shore and Moffat developed a plan for the Waterloo College campus, proposing to build a new Administration Building that would be "in a dominant location off Dearborn Street and between the Arts and Engineering Buildings." In this way, "the theological school and [a new] chapel would dominate the campus from a central location." The symbolism of Lutheran predominance represented in Shore and Moffat's first depiction of the proposed campus is significant. It represents Hagey's view of the university that he hoped would be developed around Waterloo College. It also represents a university that was not to be.

The Annex behind Willison Hall is visible on the left. In the foreground of this carefully staged photograph two young Waterloo students walk across the campus toward the ivy-covered walls of Willison Hall. This strong rendition of collegiate life and university tradition is enhanced by the stylized "engineering" on the college jacket.
UWA/Bochsler

The theological school and chapel had a symbolic presence. The physical reality of six new Science and Engineering Buildings, however, created a dramatically different orientation to the campus, one in which the nineteenth-century conflict between the beliefs of science and religion would be juxtaposed. The impetus to create this new university threatened to lead inexorably to a clash of values and interests, and of methods and beliefs. These architectural plans suggested perhaps more than the architects intended and implicitly forecast a debate that many hoped to avoid.

The creation of Waterloo's new university moved one step closer to fruition on 15 October 1957 when the Building Committee of the Associate Faculties submitted the plans for the Chemistry and Chemical Engineering Building to the Board of Governors, who recommended that the architects proceed with the preparation of specifications for tendering. In the midst of this euphoria, something went amiss. The president's senior Academic Advisory Committee called for a reconsideration of the decision to establish the campus of the Waterloo College Associate Faculties on the "present campus site."[5]

The Academic Advisory Committee, the most influential committee of the Associate Faculties, comprised the heads of the departments of Physics, Applied Physics, Mathematics, Chemical Engineering, and Chemistry, and it had the responsibility for the academic program and the curriculum for the applied science courses. At the very moment when tenders were going forward for their building, why would they question the fundamental decision to locate this building on the Waterloo College campus? From Hagey's point of view, their timing could not have been worse and their advice was not what he wanted. He did his best to block their proposal. The committee's insistence that it be allowed to present its case for a relocation of the campus to the Board of Governors of the Associate Faculties precipitated a major crisis. The Advisory Committee suggested to Hagey that they did not want a break with Waterloo College and that the vision that they sought to capture was based on his own forecast of possible enrolment at Waterloo:

> 1,400 in Engineering, 1,100 in Arts, and possibly courses in Science, Architecture, Business Administration, Home Economics, Music, Physical Health Education, and others; Schools of Medicine and Law had been mentioned for the long range future. The number of students expected on campus would be about 4,000, with faculty and administration numbering more than 400.

If this were to happen, the Waterloo College campus would be too restrictive in size and too expensive to expand.

The committee was touching on a long-standing problem. The shortage of land on the existing campus site and a proposed relocation of Waterloo College had resulted in the resignation of Hagey's predecessor as president of Waterloo College and Hagey had staked his own career on building a university with Waterloo College as its centrepiece.

The Academic Advisory members reminded him that the campus of Waterloo College "envisages a maximum of 30 acres of which less than 20 acres are available for the expansion of the Associate Faculties. Besides the space problem it appears that the present area is very expensive and much of it cannot be procured except through expropriation." If Waterloo is to be a university of the first order,

> Enough room must be left between [the] Applied Sciences buildings for future expansion or additions for programmes such as nuclear reactors or computers, ultrasonic tunnels, etc. which might be required in future engineering. Any other expansion into full university educational coverage will be impossible if any green spaces are to be left between buildings. Also there is at present no space for student dormitories which lose much of their value if they are off-campus.

The committee also had a solution. They pointed to the availability of a large tract of land nearby which had previously been offered as a possible university site for $1,000 per acre. This would be a much more prudent choice that would provide an attractive and spacious campus less than half a mile from Waterloo College. The cost would be much less than expanding piecemeal along Dearborn and Bricker streets. Instead, in a wonderful turn of phrase, credited to Ted Batke, one of the committee members and a future vice-president academic, the committee's memo suggested that:

This dramatic photograph of the construction of the Chemistry and Chemical Engineering Building rising out of the mud of the former Schweitzer farm would be a portent of things to come. Over the next decade, nineteen buildings would be added with $80 million in capital expenses and a campus that extended to 1,000 acres.
UWA/Shore Tilbe

It is our opinion that if a University of Waterloo is to be built in the backyards of Waterloo College and adjoining houses [as they later phrased it, on the backyards of Bricker Street], the citizens of Ontario, whose money is being used, will cite the project as a prime example of limited vision. The government, the Board of Governors, and the faculty will be jointly responsible for a patchwork of congestion in the heart of one of Ontario's most attractive regions ... If the views of this committee are found valid, then immediate steps are necessary to obtain a new site and arrange for the Chemistry Building to be erected on it by the Fall of 1958.

CONTRACTOR:
Ball Bros. Ltd.
Waterloo College
Associate Faculties
CHEMISTRY BLDG.

Hagey's response was one of impassioned opposition. He rejected the proposal and sought to dissuade them from taking it to the Board of Governors.[6]

"It is understandable," he said, "that your concern is for the Associate Faculties and its future as a university in this community." And Hagey conceded, "Thinking of the Associate Faculties as starting from scratch and seeking a site, it is logical to assume that this site might be where there is an abundance of low cost land available ... The Associate Faculties, fortunately, has not been obliged to start from scratch. It has been given a running start by being sponsored and organized by, and with the assistance of Waterloo College." Even as he made his case, Hagey had to face the inadequacies of the resources of Waterloo College to operate a university program, admitting, for example, that, "It was the concern of the Board of Governors of Waterloo College that the [Lutheran] Church would not be able to adequately finance the total needs of this community for higher education which led the Board to encourage the development of the Associate Faculties."

Although he conceded that the procurement of land next to the Waterloo College campus would be more costly, "there are reasons of expediency that need to be taken into consideration," and he added ominously, "These can very easily affect the very life of the Associate Faculties."

In truth, Hagey feared that the move to another campus would endanger his own leadership and all that he had worked for to bring Waterloo College into full university status. He also faced the opposition of those at Waterloo College who disliked the idea of the Associate Faculties and its co-operative education program and who preferred the exclusive Lutheran identity of their liberal arts college:

> From the above information describing the history of the decision of Waterloo College to stay at this site, and realizing the emotions of the community that are related to this site, plus the presentations of the ability of this site to accommodate future expansion that have been made to the Provincial Government ... I believe it would be easy for you to understand that many months would be required for inter-Board, Church, and community discussions before the Board of the Associate Faculties might dare to venture a decision in favour of relocation.

"At this stage in our development," Hagey intimated, "a delay in the Chemistry Building programme could be crucial."

Desperately, he hoped not to become embroiled in this new campus relocation scheme, recalling "although the previous [campus] decision was made about six or seven years ago, there are still some people who are continuing to fight this battle, just as there are those in the United States who are continuing to fight the battle of the Civil War." Without a full knowledge of the facts, he opined, "it is easy to conclude that a mistake was made at that time. Factually, I think that history will indicate that the decision was in the best interest of the extension of higher education in this community." President Hagey seemed almost a tragic figure caught between the pull of the future and the priorities of the past.

There was even more to it than this. He also feared that the committee may have had a separate agenda that was fraught with danger for his plan to keep the Associate Faculties and Waterloo College in tandem. He broached the topic carefully and with a note of resignation, especially after his review of the moral and political support previously provided by Waterloo College.

"In reading your brief," he continued, "I sense that the suggestion to relocate involves more than your concern about the present site. Possibly my thoughts are unfounded, but I have the feeling that your Committee which exists between Waterloo College and the Associate Faculties [is] ... concerned lest this relationship involves a handicap (financial or otherwise) for the Associate Faculties ... Should there be such a concern," Hagey challenged, "I would think it would be desirable for it to be brought out into the open."

Hagey also had to confront the committee about the role in all of this of Les Emery, whom he saw as a rival for the leadership of the Associate Faculties and who, at the time, was on a paid leave of absence at Queen's University. In a community the size of Waterloo, rumours abounded. Hagey was quite correct on at least one point: the idea of a possible location for the new campus had in fact been Emery's. He had led the trek to scout out the vacant lands and he had also been in touch with Abram Wiebe, the president of Major Holdings, whose company had recently acquired the former Schweitzer farm. This alone had angered Hagey and aroused his suspicions about Emery's role. Finally he confronted the committee directly:

I assume that the brief has resulted from the discussion within your committee at its meeting with Mr. Emery this past Saturday afternoon. Should you wish to have your brief presented to the Board, I suggest that it should clearly indicate the individuals whose views it expresses. It should be stated clearly

Why is the word BEER emblazoned on Waterloo's 500,000-gallon water tower? "It's there for the honour of engineering," said Waterloo College Associate Faculties engineering students on 4 June 1958. Two engineering students, Bill Stephen and Mike Matthews, posed with their handiwork the next day while engineering students, lying on the grass at its base, spelled out the words "Eng 63" as an airplane hired by the students took their picture. The highly-publicized "Beer Tower" incident generated national publicity for Waterloo and its students.
KWR

whether it is the view of your committee and Mr. Emery only or whether this subject has been discussed with the whole faculty and expresses the majority opinion of the faculty.

In private meetings, Hagey was unable to suppress his displeasure, advising some of the committee members that he had been making business decisions when they were still in knee pants and that he did not appreciate their interference or that of Les Emery in the running of the university. They were, after all, merely a committee to advise him. It was not their responsibility to involve themselves in areas of jurisdiction that rightfully belonged to the president and the Board of Governors.

The Academic Advisory Committee again requested to be present at the next meeting of the Board of Governors.[7] They suggested to Hagey that their recommendation was not to abandon the campus of Waterloo College; nor should the "unfortunate controversy" of the past be part of this discussion:

There has of course been no suggestion that the present campus be abandoned by the College — but rather that the site should remain for the development of the College and Seminary. The prominent and dignified setting appropriate to a liberal arts college and its chapel ought certainly to be retained.

"The University," however, "should preferably be built on an adjoining site to the west." It was difficult to deny their request "to build the best possible university within the limits of [the] available resources."

When the Academic Advisory Committee appeared before the Board of Governors on 12 November 1957, Hagey and the chair of the board, Ira Needles, were unfailingly polite, but neither seemed impressed by the proposal. Without this support, the members of the committee feared that their ideas were destined to fail, but each time the discussion seemed about to end, one of the younger board members, Carl Pollock, kept it alive.

Pollock was not a typical industrialist, although his company, Dominion Electrohome Industries, was one of the largest employers in Kitchener and Waterloo. A graduate of both the universities of Toronto and Oxford, Carl Pollock had always had a keen interest in universities and a strong sense of what was involved in university life. In fact, at one time he had

Carl Pollock's fascination with universities and university life was sustained by a creative and imaginative intellect. A graduate of and scholarship winner at the universities of Toronto and Oxford, he would play a major role in the development of the University of Waterloo, serving as a member of the first Board of Governors, ultimately as its chairman, and as the university's beloved chancellor from 1975 to 1978.
Belair

hoped to follow a career in university research rather than in business, but while working on a postgraduate research project at the University of Toronto, he returned to Electrohome in the face of his father's illness.

The university idea, however, had always remained part of his dream. Perhaps this was his chance, or at least the chance to build a university in his own community. Pollock was prepared to take what fate had offered. This was an opportunity not to be missed. His own confidence began to tell on one other board member: A.R. Kaufman. When Kaufman spoke in favour of acquiring this new land, the debate was over.

While recognizing the desirability of not crowding buildings too closely together, the board felt that, in the interim, the Chemistry and Chemical Engineering Building should be located on the existing Waterloo College campus. This was clearly a compromise to save face for Hagey, and in its own way, this decision, too, would have a profound effect on the look of the new campus when this first building designed for the Waterloo College campus, at the last minute, was relocated to the new university lands.

The decision to move forward with the development of Waterloo's university project was clear. In its next resolution the board empowered the Academic Advisory Committee "to study the possibilities of this institution procuring a degree granting charter." "Assuming that students registered in our engineering courses are acceptable for transfer to other universities," the board advised, "there is no urgency to rush a development toward a degree granting university." Still, the negotiations for a new campus continued at a hurried pace. The impetus to settle the question of the location of the campus was carried forward three weeks later when the management committee received a letter from Major Holdings offering to sell an attractive parcel of land containing 183.8 acres, just west of the Waterloo College campus.

The committee worked tirelessly to review the proposed purchase and to negotiate terms that would ensure both probity and frugality. So important a land transaction would attract considerable attention and the board could not afford to err, for much more was at stake than the purchase of what had once been part of a

The inevitable rivalry between arts students and engineers was symbolized in this procession. Led by Engineering Society President Bill Lennox, a future UW dean of engineering, the engineers erected their own sign "Arts, Science and ENGINEERING" at the corner of King and Dearborn (later University Avenue). UWA

Mennonite farm. On 30 December an offer from Abram Wiebe was dispatched to President Hagey. The Board of Governors was called into session on 9 January 1958.[8]

President Hagey was reluctant. Once again, his report began with an assessment of the value of properties previously considered and immediately adjacent to land owned by Waterloo College. At the very least, he was protecting himself from undue criticism from within the college. The fate of these lands was doomed when the city assessor indicated that the minimum cost of land within the campus rectangle would be between $300,000 and $400,000. To develop a campus within the other CMHC lands, as Hagey had proposed, would be between one and two million dollars. On learning this, negotiations with Major Holdings had been renewed, but not before procuring the advice and a positive recommendation from Kaufman and his personal real estate advisor. This latter point was crucial; it had been the moral suasion as well as the overwhelming economic and social influence wielded in the community by Kaufman that had carried the board at its November meeting.

Before the vote on the land acquisition was taken, Hagey presented an emotional report of the Associate Faculties' moral obligations to Waterloo College, again urging "that factors outlined in his report merited consideration previous to a decision for the Associate Faculties to relocate."[9] His emotional commitment to Waterloo College jumps off of every line. Yet, there is no record in the minutes of any further discussion of these issues. Kaufman, seconded by Preston businessman Percy Hilborn, simply moved that the president's report be accepted and "that he be authorized to convey to the Waterloo College Board this Board's acceptance of the principles stated in his report." Carl Pollock moved that "Mr. Kaufman, with the Administration, be authorized to negotiate an approved agreement with Major Holdings Limited and, subject to the approval of the Waterloo College Board, commit this Board to the purchase of one hundred and eighty-three acres of land as outlined above."[10] And that was it. The motion carried unanimously. The meeting adjourned.

Major Holdings' offer was appealing. The land provided the possibility of developing a campus on the scale of major Canadian universities, and even larger than the University of Western Ontario. The terms of the purchase agreement were designed so that the Associate Faculties would obtain access to the entire tract of land while paying in the first year for only a 50-acre portion of it. The purchase price of $344,240.50 for the total 183 acres was significantly less than the amount necessary to develop the restrictive Waterloo College rectangle.

Despite the euphoria surrounding the purchase of these lands, Hagey remained concerned about the impact on Waterloo College. This decision, he had said, "may well be considered to be one of major importance in the development of a university at Waterloo." In words that would be prophetic and in ways that he could not have anticipated, he forecast that "the decision for or against moving to a new site has possibilities of exerting an influence much beyond that of making possible a picturesque or scenic campus for a future university."

For its part, the board of the Associate Faculties unanimously accepted the principles relating to the "moral obligations" to Waterloo College. The following week Hagey presented the same memorandum to a joint board committee of Waterloo College and the Associate Faculties. At that time, it seemed that the problems he faced as president of both Waterloo College and the Associate Faculties were unduly daunting. Starting a new university was one thing; somehow holding these disparate interests in tandem on separate campuses would be quite another, and it was not over yet. There was also the Lutheran Synod to consider. Its original commitment to the university idea was cautious and qualified and its denominational interests were rarely the same as those of the Associate Faculties.

Not wishing to replicate the "Beer Tower" incident, the next class of incoming engineering students hung a banner on the front facade of the Waterloo Hotel. The president of the Engineering Society was commissioned to distract the police officer at the corner of King and Erb Streets as the banner was put in place, and the Waterloo Hotel was officially re-named Annex Five. A complicit management allowed the banner to remain for several weeks.
UWA/M. Barber

It is not surprising that Hagey feared that the battle lines about moving to a new campus might be drawn again, and he was right. Emotions would always run high on issues such as these. Not everyone at Waterloo College shared his commitment to creating a university and certainly not one based on the Associate Faculties. Their opposition would not be easily silenced. As a graduate of Waterloo College's Arts Faculty, Hagey had retained a passionate feeling for the college which had done so much to shape his own life. He wanted especially to be reassured that the relocation to the new campus would not adversely affect Waterloo College as the Arts Faculty of the proposed

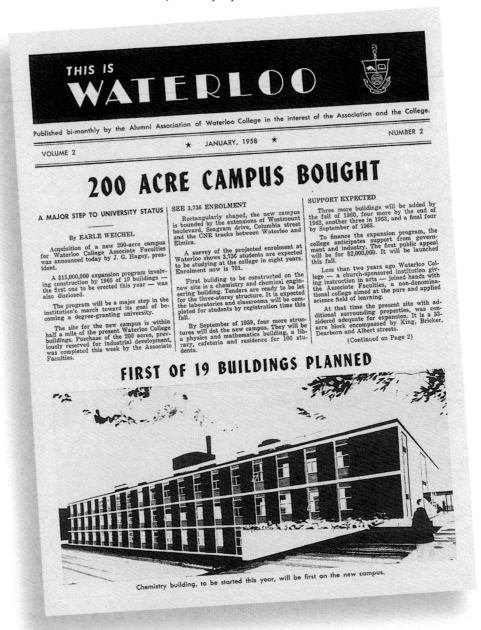

THIS IS WATERLOO

Published bi-monthly by the Alumni Association of Waterloo College in the interest of the Association and the College.

VOLUME 2   ★ JANUARY, 1958 ★   NUMBER 2

200 ACRE CAMPUS BOUGHT

A MAJOR STEP TO UNIVERSITY STATUS

By EARLE WEICHEL

Acquisition of a new 200-acre campus for Waterloo College Associate Faculties was announced today by J. G. Hagey, president.

A $15,000,000 expansion program involving construction by 1965 of 19 buildings — the first one to be erected this year — was also disclosed.

The program will be a major step in the institution's march toward its goal of becoming a degree-granting university.

The site for the new campus is within half a mile of the present Waterloo College buildings. Purchase of the 200 acres, previously reserved for industrial development, was completed this week by the Associate Faculties.

SEE 3,736 ENROLMENT

Rectangularly shaped, the new campus is bounded by the extensions of Westmount boulevard, Seagram drive, Columbia street and the CNR tracks between Waterloo and Elmira.

A survey of the projected enrolment at Waterloo shows 3,736 students are expected to be studying at the college in eight years. Enrolment now is 701.

First building to be constructed on the new site is a chemistry and chemical engineering building. Tenders are ready to be let for the three-storey structure. It is expected the laboratories and classrooms will be completed for students by registration time this fall.

By September of 1959, four more structures will dot the new campus. They will be a physics and mathematics building, a library, cafeteria and residence for 100 students.

SUPPORT EXPECTED

Three more buildings will be added by the fall of 1960, four more by the end of 1962, another three in 1963, and a final four by September of 1965.

To finance the expansion program, the college anticipates support from government and industry. The first public appeal will be for $2,000,000. It will be launched this fall.

Less than two years ago Waterloo College — a church-sponsored institution giving instruction in arts — joined hands with the Associate Faculties, a non-denominational college aimed at the pure and applied science field of learning.

At that time the present site with additional surrounding properties, was considered adequate for expansion. It is a 33-acre block encompassed by King, Bricker, Dearborn and Albert streets.

(Continued on Page 2)

FIRST OF 19 BUILDINGS PLANNED

Chemistry building, to be started this year, will be first on the new campus.

university or that Arts would have an equal voice with that of the Science Faculty in establishing future academic policies.

It was more than this. Hagey also wanted to ensure that Waterloo College would be the dominant Church college in the new university, even though, as he put it, "There was good reason to believe that Churches other than the Lutheran Church will wish to become associated with the University of Waterloo."

In this regard, Hagey suggested that it would be appropriate to recognize the symbolic and historical role of the Lutheran Church by reserving the natural knoll, the highest point on the campus site, for a Lutheran chapel, "if Waterloo College wished to construct one." He had earlier hoped that the Lutheran Church might have provided a chapel on the Waterloo College campus, "through which Christian services might be made available to students of all denominations." This might still be possible on the new campus. The Lutheran presence could still be a dominant feature on the campus.

The move to the larger campus acquired a renewed sense of urgency when the joint board committee met on 16 January to gain the approval for the land purchase from the Waterloo College Board of Governors.

On 22 January Reverend A.J. Baetz, secretary of the Board of the Evangelical Lutheran Seminary, wrote to the pastors of the Canada and the Nova Scotia Synods to explain the recent events relating to Waterloo College and the seminary and to provide them with accurate information as to the board's action before it was reported in the Canadian media.[11] Of particular interest, he said, was the unanimous recommendation:

> That the Board of Governors of the Evangelical Lutheran Seminary of Canada go on record as being in favour of relocating our Arts College on a campus mutually acceptable to the Board of Governors of Waterloo College Associate Faculties and the Evangelical Lutheran Seminary of Canada.

A joint Campus Planning Committee, with the president of the college as an ex officio member, was established, with the priority of determining "definite sites being assigned to Waterloo College for the erection of its buildings." This was a major commitment by the college board and one that suggested that the Lutheran Church stood firmly behind President Hagey.

Pastor Baetz believed that there were distinct advantages in the seminary having a location "which is physically separate from the future university," just as there was "much to be gained by our

Church College in being territorially closely related to the [educational] facilities provided to the university through government grants." The relocation of the Arts College, he suggested, also "opens up the possibility for the expansion of our Seminary on its present site."

Baetz assured the members of the Synod that the "probable development of our Church Arts College within a university was discussed and steps were taken to assure the continuance of the plan as outlined in the Agreement of Affiliation between Waterloo College and Waterloo College Associate Faculties." On this he was quite specific: "This is to the effect that the Church College of Arts will become the Faculty of Arts for the university. It was further agreed by both Boards that relocation should in no way interfere with the fulfilment of the Agreement." Three days later, on 25 January 1958, the story became front-page news in the *Kitchener-Waterloo Record*, describing the new 200-acre campus as "a major step in the institution's march towards its goal of becoming a degree granting university."

The joint board meeting had recommended a significant change in the development plans for the university. In the last minutes of the meeting, the decision was made that the Chemistry and Chemical Engineering Building would not be located on the Waterloo College site, but that it would be the first building on the new campus. This would create its own problems as the design of the building for a location on the Waterloo College campus was well under way. A new site was chosen where the contours of the land closely matched those at Waterloo College, near the original farmhouse and barn of what had once been the Schweitzer farm. For a time at least, the historic farmhouse would provide temporary office accommodation for eager young faculty members anxious to be part of a new university.

The entire debate, approval, and purchase had taken only three months. This breakneck pace would characterize much of Waterloo's development in the early years. The problems created by this decision would live on and they would come to haunt the president of Waterloo College, Joseph Gerald Hagey.

On the day that the purchase of the land was announced, the Reverend Albert W. Lotz, president of the Board of Governors of the Evangelical Lutheran Seminary of Canada, met with the faculty of Waterloo College to outline the "official Lutheran position" and to reassure them about future plans for Waterloo College:

> Our Board enthusiastically and unanimously approved the
> desire of the Associate Faculties to acquire land for a new

campus site. For many years our Board has recognized the desirability of having more land than we now own ...Our new association with the Associate Faculties helps us to enthusiastically look forward to the continuing development of our church college.[12]

Lotz went on to explain, "when Waterloo College becomes the Arts Faculty of the new university, the heads of the Arts departments would automatically be the university department heads for the instruction of the Arts."

Lotz belittled the idea of a competitive Arts College being established by the Associate Faculties, although he was not unaware of the rumours within Waterloo College about this possibility. Some critics predicted, "that the availability of large government grants to a non-denominational arts College would give it a superiority in faculty and Faculties which in turn would relegate the Church arts College to an inferior position within the university," or "that the Associate Faculties Board of Governors' interest in Science might result in the Arts curriculum being unbalanced." It had not taken long for those who opposed the development of the Associate Faculties to begin to organize a movement against the proposed university.

Pastor Lotz believed that there were no grounds for their fears, for under the affiliation agreement, a rival Arts College could not

The Schweitzer farm house — alone and forlorn as construction detritus litters its lawn — was soon home for faculty members' offices and later the university's Graduate Club. Its once staid surroundings would resound with the sounds of student conversation, laughter and debate.
KWR

be established without the approval of the Waterloo College Board of Governors. "With our Boards harmoniously co-operating with one another," he added, "I am confident that we have no reason to fear the development of a non-denominational Arts College that would be detrimental to Waterloo College."

The official announcement of the land acquisition and the steps towards university status had been made jointly by Ira Needles, chairman of the Board of the Associate Faculties, and J. G. Hagey, president of Waterloo College and Waterloo College Associate Faculties. In it they carefully referred to both the arts and science programs of the proposed university. "The building program envisioned by governing bodies of both arts and engineering faculties of Waterloo College stretches over eight years and requires an estimated capital outlay of more than $15 million for land, buildings, libraries and special equipment." While attention was called to the "high degree of acceptance already accorded Waterloo's new co-operative educational program," Hagey especially emphasized the arts program: "No one who supports this new engineering program has forgotten the origins of Waterloo College as an arts centre of learning."

In his remarks, Hagey expressly pointed to the importance of an arts education:

The humanities call now — as always — for the attention of all who work towards a fuller Canadian life ... During the past five years, the enrolment of arts students at Waterloo College has increased at an average rate of 18% per year. Admission rates have now been raised. As a result of this, it is anticipated that the future increase will be approximately 10% per year.

Waterloo's new programs were ambitious, and "in harmony with both the demands and our country's needs," concluded President Hagey. The winds of change were blowing and Waterloo College and the Associate Faculties would feel their effects. On that January day in 1958 it would have been impossible to predict the direction of that change. No one could have anticipated that two separate universities would be created out of the turmoil that had begun that Saturday in October when five young faculty members, most of them newly arrived in Waterloo, had trekked across the muddy fields of the old Schweitzer farm, lured by its open spaces, burbling stream, and picturesque rolling hills.

CHAPTER FIVE

Waterloo and Western: Troubled Waters

Along with Sidney Smith at Toronto, F. Cyril James at McGill, and Larry MacKenzie at the University of British Columbia, George Edward Hall, the president of the University of Western Ontario, was one of a distinguished group of university leaders who played a crucial role in reshaping their universities as well as Canadian society. These were the years when "university presidents actually presided over their institutions," ruling until old age retired them.[1] A decorated officer in the Second World War, a distinguished research scientist and former dean of medicine at Western, Edward Hall revelled in the authority bestowed upon him as a university president. He felt confident that he could withstand the pressures for change that seemed to assault him and his institution from all directions, as the world of the 1950s with its fixed, Christian, and middle-class values faced changes in Ontario's universities that were at times threatening and disruptive.

From Edward Hall's point of view, the ferment occurring at Waterloo, one of Western's oldest colleges, highlighted all of these issues. He had realized early on that it was perhaps inevitable that Waterloo College would separate from "the mother university,"[2] and to a degree he encouraged it. That the separation would be so controversial and fraught with emotion that he would intervene in the internal affairs of the college and urge the removal of its president, however, was a step that no one could have anticipated.

The appointment in 1953 of Gerald Hagey as president had meant that Waterloo College was administered by a man with unusual drive and determination, but with little of the academic training and experience which many regarded as prerequisites for university leadership. At first Edward Hall had been little concerned about Hagey's unorthodox advertising background, for the new president of Waterloo College was deferential and respectful of Western's academic reputation and its traditions. The first inkling of a very minor problem arose out of Hagey's desire to have Waterloo College make more effective use of its buildings for summer school and extension course offerings — two sources of revenue closely guarded by Western at the expense of its colleges.

In 1955 Hagey first suggested to Hall that other changes were in the making and that at some time in the future, Waterloo College might wish "to participate in provincial grants to universities and colleges." Hagey was aware that this might even necessitate the separation of the Lutheran seminary from the college and "eventually placing Waterloo College under non-denominational control." He had been discussing Waterloo College's financial problems with the local member of the provincial Legislative Assembly, Dr. Stanley Leavine, who had felt that "Western's charges for affiliation were too great, and that Waterloo College might, if it was to receive provincial government assistance, have to obtain degree granting powers in its own right."[3]

President Hall was not terribly surprised by any of this; more than a year earlier, in 1954, he had commented "to the effect that one of these days Waterloo College would wish to become independent of the University of Western Ontario."

Ira Needles's announcement of the Waterloo Plan during his carefully orchestrated Rotary Club speech was the first severe test of the relationship between Hagey and Hall, but even it had been resolved. At the time, President Hall was extremely vexed and he

Gerald Hagey, always an energetic and dynamic speaker, in a happy moment at Waterloo College. Mrs. Minota Hagey is seated on his right.
WLU

told Hagey so. "The announcement of your [Waterloo's] proposed course in engineering and technology as made by Mr. Needles yesterday [27 August 1956]," he wrote, "came as a distinct surprise to me. The public announcement of your proposed courses was, I feel, most unfortunate."[4]

Hagey replied immediately, registering some surprise since he had not anticipated "any irritation on your part to the newspaper reports of Mr. Needles talk at the local Rotary Club."[5] Needles's talk, he explained, became necessary because of the threat that another institution was intending to announce the inauguration of an alternating work-study plan which would have pre-empted Waterloo's reputation in this innovative and pioneering educational concept.

Despite this minor contretemps, on 28 September 1956 Western's Senate formally approved the request of Waterloo College for the affiliation with Western of Waterloo College Associate Faculties and, at the same time, Edward Hall wrote to Hagey thanking him "for the very acceptable explanation of the desirability of the early release [in Needles's speech]" of the information about the "Co-operative plan of education." "Now that the Associate Faculties had been affiliated through Waterloo College, with the University," Hall added, "I would like to assure you again of our sincere interest in the plans and future development of Waterloo College and its Associated Faculties."[6]

As president of the University of Western Ontario, Edward Hall played a significant and surprising role in the development of the Waterloo College Associate Faculties and in their ultimate separation from Waterloo College. UWO/London Free Press Collection of Photographic Negatives

Hall also accepted Hagey's suggestion that students who enter Waterloo College Associate Faculties for the co-operative plan in their preliminary, non-university years, not be registered in the university. This idea "is indeed an excellent one" which, he admitted, he had not realized. Only when the detailed plans for the first year of engineering at university level were developed would they have to be presented to the Senate, and following the approval of the curriculum by the Senate, the students in that year would be registered with the university. With the assurance that those students who completed that year "would have the privilege of applying for admission, on transfer, to the second year of engineering at this or other universities," Hall expressed his "sympathetic understanding of your plans for the growth of Waterloo College and the Associate Faculties."[7]

It seemed that the relationship between Waterloo and Western and Presidents Hagey and Hall would be cordial. Certainly Hagey thought so. He told W.J. Dunlop that autumn that he had every reason to believe that "a good working relationship had been established between the two of them" and in October he confidently reported to Dunlop that "the major problem has been satisfactorily solved in an agreement with the University of Western Ontario whereby Waterloo's offering this [applied science] course meets with their approval."[8] Not only had he and his colleagues discussed their course outline with the Engineering Faculty at Western, but, according to Hagey's understanding, "it was favourably received and we anticipate that the Western Faculty Academic Committee will recognize it for the approval of the students to transfer on an individual basis." As soon as this approval was formally received from Western the curriculum would be presented to the faculty at Queen's and Toronto," the two other Ontario universities that had faculties of engineering, since at that time Waterloo intended to offer only the first year of a university engineering program.

In the spring of 1957, along with Dean Schaus and Les Emery, who had been responsible for developing Waterloo's curriculum in applied science, Hagey met with Hall and the head of Western's engineering program. Again they came away from the meeting feeling that "our outlined program was satisfactory to Dr. Hall" and to Western's Faculty of Engineering, and "as we were not planning to offer the third year of our engineering program [Year I] for at least one or two more years, Dr. Hall suggested that there was no immediate urgency to bring this before the Senate [at Western]." In fact, Hagey reported, Dr. Hall had remarked that, "possibly by the time we are ready to offer the third year, we might have our own degree-granting charter."[9]

The relationship of the proposed co-operative engineering program to that at Western's, however, soon resulted in another flare-up between Edward Hall and Gerald Hagey. In a letter to the high school principals of Ontario, Hagey had announced the development of the co-operative education program at Waterloo. He also stated that although Waterloo College Associate Faculties intended to seek independent university status, it was "continuing its affiliation with Western."[10] Hall was alarmed that this letter would attract students to Waterloo at the expense of Western, especially since its own engineering program had barely begun. He was also annoyed by yet another example of Hagey's apparent lack of understanding of proper university protocol.

This open competition between universities was just not done. Western's reputation was also at stake. In a fit of pique, Edward Hall read the contents of Hagey's letter into the minutes of the Senate at Western, and he demanded that Hagey redraft the offending letter, especially so as to clarify the relationship of the

Associate Faculties with Western.[11] When Hagey did this, from Hall's perspective the new letter now had too much of a "sales angle." The primary purpose of the second letter was to indicate that these courses were not being recognized by Western, and it did just that, but then Hagey also described the excitement engendered by Waterloo's co-operative education program and the new faculty members whom they had recently appointed to teach in it.

Hagey was blissfully unaware that this letter, too, had created renewed hostility towards him at Western. In October he thanked Dean Frank Stiling for his assistance in co-ordinating a meeting of college faculty members with those teaching in Western's science program. He also understood from Waterloo College's dean, Lloyd Schaus, that Frank Stiling would now present Waterloo's request for recognition of its applied science curriculum to Western's Faculty Academic Committee.

The first cause for alarm came in December when Dean Stiling rejected Hagey's request that Western accept transfer students from the Associate Faculties to complete their engineering degree at Western. A meeting of the faculty of Stiling's University College passed a resolution stating "That no general arrangement be made with Waterloo College on the matter of transfer from their engineering course to the course at University College, but that their students should be considered individually on their own merits as those from other colleges and universities are."[12]

The matter was now out in the open. Waterloo's engineering students could not expect simply to transfer to Western as arts students had done over the past thirty years. There was much more to this decision than was at first obvious; it was more than merely an academic guideline. In an exasperated personal letter to Edward Hall, Dean Stiling announced:

> The time has come I think, when the name of the University of Western Ontario should be dissociated from that of Waterloo College. I feel very strongly that the reputation of the University is adversely affected by the academic adventures of Waterloo College and the information about this institution which has been published in the newspapers. I am thinking especially of the alternation of the academic work and industrial work in the engineering programme of the Associate Faculties of Waterloo.[13]

Stiling had done more than complain privately to Hall. At lunch the previous week with the minister of education he had asked if the provincial government would feel unkindly towards

Faculty wives often met informally even as debate within the college and the Associate Faculties intensified. Seen here are (left to right) Mrs. J.W. Dyck, Mrs. D.C. Fraser, Mrs. T.L. Batke, Mrs. J.B. Saunders, and Mrs. Robert Langen (as identified in the style of the day in the Kitchener-Waterloo Record). KWR

Western if the university terminated its affiliation agreement with Waterloo College. According to Stiling, the minister "did not answer my question but said, 'I think you have to in order to protect yourselves.'" I recommend, said Stiling, "that we terminate the affiliation agreement as soon as possible."[14]

Although this letter was clearly marked personal, Stiling had shared his opinion with several others, including at least one dissident faculty member from Waterloo College who clearly wanted to see Hagey removed as president. In confidential meetings both Hall and Stiling made their position clear, "either Hagey will be out or the federation agreement will be cancelled." Rumours of this travelled quickly to Waterloo where the board of the Evangelical Lutheran Seminary of Canada, the corporate body controlling Waterloo College, was informed of Hall's and Stiling's intense displeasure with both Hagey and Waterloo's co-operative education program.

The forces seemed to be gathering against Gerry Hagey and the Associate Faculties. Gould Wickey, the executive secretary of the Board of Higher Education of the United Lutheran Church in America, who had first recruited Hagey for the presidency of Waterloo College, had come up from Washington to review the impending crisis.

Arriving unannounced, Wickey held confidential meetings with unhappy faculty members, a private meeting with Hagey at the Walper Hotel, and separate meetings with lobbyists who waited for Hagey to leave the hotel and then arrived unannounced at

Wickey's room to persuade him to their point of view. By the end of these meetings, there was no doubt that Wickey was taking sides, and the side that he was taking was not that of Gerry Hagey or of the Associate Faculties. Although this had not been the impression that Wickey had left with Hagey, the threatened diminution of Waterloo College's Lutheran identity seems to have entered the debate as an extension of the criticisms of the science-oriented and secular leadership of the Associate Faculties.

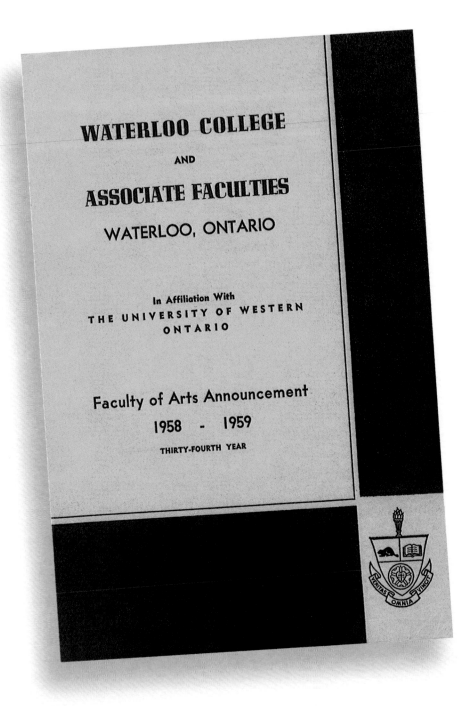

WATERLOO COLLEGE

AND

ASSOCIATE FACULTIES

WATERLOO, ONTARIO

In Affiliation With
THE UNIVERSITY OF WESTERN ONTARIO

Faculty of Arts Announcement
1958 - 1959
THIRTY-FOURTH YEAR

A report circulated to the members of the Board of Governors of Waterloo College in anticipation of the board's regular meeting on 16 April set in motion a series of events that would shock the Associate Faculties, threaten their relationship with Waterloo College, and perhaps even their very existence.

The report described a visit to Western attended by Gould Wickey, Dean Schaus, and President Hagey on 14 April. Their meeting with Edward Hall had not gone well. The president had intimated that he had major concerns about the course of events at Waterloo. So serious was the perceived crisis that the board, on the recommendation of Gould Wickey, appointed a special committee, consisting of Dr. A.G. Jacobi, president of the Evangelical Lutheran Synod of Canada, and Pastors Albert Lotz, Delton Glebe, and Arthur Buehlow to meet with Dr. Hall, Dr. Allan, Western's vice-president, and Frank Stiling, the principal of University College.[15]

Conspicuously absent was Gerald Hagey. The reason for this was soon obvious. Hall led a concerted, no-holds-barred, attack on Hagey personally, on his actions as president of the college, and on the legitimacy of the educational programs of the Associate Faculties.

The report of this extraordinary committee was presented at a special meeting of the Waterloo College Board of Governors on 22 May which had been convened for the sole purpose of receiving the report of the 30 April meeting in London. What they heard may not have come entirely as a surprise.[16] Rumours of Hall's displeasure with Hagey and the Associate Faculties had been circulating on Waterloo's campus for some time, spread by Lutheran faculty members of Waterloo College who had come to distrust Hagey and who were alarmed by the plans for a new campus dominated by the Science and Applied Science faculties which threatened their Lutheran presence and influence.

The report from Pastors Lotz, Glebe, Buehlow, and Reverend Jacobi was devastating for Hagey and the plans of the Associate Faculties and, judging from the preamble, the authors had thoroughly acceded to Western's point of view. They had characterized their reception at Western as "gracious" and their conversations were described as "most cordial." In light of three pages of unremitting criticism of President Hagey and the Associate Faculties, these "cordial, candid and unhurried" conversations must have been remarkable indeed.

As it was reported to the special meeting, Hall had begun the discussion on 30 April by stating frankly "that relations between Waterloo College and Western had been deteriorating and that the reason for this lay in the refusal of our Waterloo Administration to accept the advice and counsel offered by Western University." And Hall's list of examples of Waterloo's so-called aberrant behaviour was extensive. He cited the detailed studies undertaken at Western before its engineering course was finally approved which took several years. The same procedure which involved faculty and Senate approval "applies to all colleges affiliated with the University."

Waterloo had ignored all these steps. Some members of the Waterloo committee were likely nodding their heads in agreement: "The point Dr. Hall was making was that there are orderly methods of procedure within the University and that one does not rush precipitously into establishing an engineering faculty or a university. Careful preliminary study by qualified men is essential." In fact, after three years, Western's engineering program had fewer students than the Associate Faculties intended to admit in its first year.

Not only had the actions of Hagey and the Associate Faculties been precipitous and without regard to Western's academic procedures, Hall had concluded that Waterloo's engineering program was based on a misperception of engineering needs. Western had formulated its engineering program on the "engineering sciences with an emphasis on scientific background or theory ... instead of an emphasis on technology." He further pointed out that "since Western was entering the field of engineering science they obviously could not sponsor a similar faculty at Waterloo," and he noted that "according to the affiliation agreement no professional courses could be set up by affiliated colleges. These facts were known by the administration at Waterloo."

Hall implied that the Associate Faculties' engineering program was poorly researched, doomed to fail, and unacceptable in a college affiliated with Western. He had been equally critical of Assumption College's attempt to introduce engineering courses through an arrangement with the University of Detroit, forcing Assumption to sever its connection with Western. His list of grievances against Hagey and the Associate Faculties, however, went well beyond his dislike and disdain of their engineering program. He explained that, over and over again, President Hagey had crossed the bounds of academic propriety and acted in clear defiance of Western. "The administration at Western University was surprised by the brochure put out by Waterloo College Associate Faculties [the previous summer] implying that the Science Course offered there had the backing and approval of Western University. Through this brochure the University learned that the Waterloo Associate Faculties' course in engineering was being offered. The proposed course as set out in the brochure came to them," he said, "as a fait accompli:"

President Hagey was told by Hall, Allan and Stiling (a) that it is the wrong type of course and (b) that they could not approve a second engineering course in the University. They asked themselves, Is Waterloo trying to defy the Senate or the heads of Western University, or is Waterloo trying to force the hand of Senate? Dr. Hall stated that when President Hagey was asked what interpretation could be placed on such action, he admitted that it was in defiance of Western.

As if this admitted defiance was not bad enough, Hall continued, this was merely the beginning.

The brochure, the object of Hall's annoyance, was also sent to all of the high school principals in Ontario, leaving the impression that Western approved of the Associate Faculties' course and "would give the degree." When Hagey was asked to send a clarifying letter on which Dr. Stiling had made "extensive changes," Hall complained that Hagey completely ignored Stiling's changes: "The letter was sent out as originally drafted by himself [Hagey] without incorporating the suggestions or correcting the false impression."

In the meeting Edward Hall had returned time and time again to his opposition to the Associate Faculties' engineering program and to President Hagey's methods:

> Dr. Hall stressed the fact that the engineering course of the Associate Faculties was set up, advertised and introduced in defiance of Western University and without their counsel or approval ... He also made it crystal clear that any "confusion of communications" had arisen as between Mr. Hagey and Dean Schaus in their relations to the Board [of Waterloo College] and not as between the University and its relations to Mr. Hagey and Dean Schaus.

Hall and Allan also disapproved of co-operative education and its system of quarterly courses. Western had made an extensive study

of this and warned the board of Waterloo College that this alternation of academic courses would have a dire effect on the college's own academic standards:

> He [Dr. Hall] and Dr. Allan expressed concern about the possible danger that Waterloo College would be forced to lower its standards ... Either the standards would have to be lowered or Waterloo College would eventually have to adapt itself to the in and out of co-operative system.

Hall and Allan emphasized the dangers to Waterloo College from being part of the radical, untried, and defiant Associate Faculties and warned them to reconsider their relationship or suffer the inevitable consequences. In this litany of fear, Hall and Allan sought to divide Waterloo College from the Associate Faculties:

> Dr. Hall said that it takes years to develop a university. He and Dr. Allan stressed the point that Waterloo College has a high academic standard built up over the years, that it has enjoyed an excellent reputation in the academic world, that its faculty has the best kind of standing in the University, and has always been

looked upon with great approval by Western. They assured us that they were keenly interested in our present welfare and future development. Waterloo College, because of its past record and good reputation as a first-class arts college, is, they said, in the bargaining position. The Associate Faculties, having no reputation, has little bargaining power.

In this "considered," "gracious," and "unhurried" meeting, Edward Hall was not about to give up until he had sown the seeds of discontent even further. Or perhaps, as the president of Western, he felt a duty to watch out for the interests of his colleagues at Waterloo College. Certainly he seems to have felt no hesitation about interfering in internal college affairs.

Dr. Hall added that it was his firm conviction that Waterloo College could soon be expected to take its place as a university [without the Associate Faculties] through proper procedures, of course, [and] without defiance of Western. He stated further that it was his firm conviction that Waterloo College could thrive by itself as a Church College without the Associate Faculties. He pointed out that federal and other grants at the present time are large enough, together with tuition practically to cover the costs of an arts college. He suggested that Waterloo College recover the science courses it had offered before and seek its own degree granting power as soon as possible, to be used when the time is ready.

President Hall believed "that Waterloo College would have no difficulties in obtaining such a charter on the grounds of its excellent reputation."

In closing, Hall "expressed a lack of confidence in the present administration at Waterloo," and he was quite specific about Gerald Hagey's inadequacies. His lack of university experience, Hall suggested, left him entirely unqualified and unsuited to be a university president, explaining furthermore that "one cannot deal with faculty people as one would deal with hired help in industry," implying that faculty members at Waterloo College who were not in favour of Hagey and his policies were perfectly justified in opposing a president with little or no understanding of universities.

Although they may have anticipated some of these concerns, this barrage of unremitting criticism of President Hagey and the Associate Faculties must have stunned many of the board members of Waterloo College. Only three months earlier they had announced the purchase of a new campus and their own tentative

plans to relocate Waterloo College there. The serious personal criticisms of Hagey and his actions, however, could not be overlooked. Nor could the challenge to Waterloo College's academic standing, let alone its Lutheran presence, be dismissed. These were serious matters, and if not university leaders themselves, Pastors Jacobi, Lotz, Glebe, and Buehlow were serious men, committed to preserving the reputation of their Lutheran college and seminary. Much was at risk. The Board of Governors requested an interview with the board of the Associate Faculties at its next meeting scheduled for 28 May, less than a week away.

The life of the institution known as the Associate Faculties was at stake; so, too, was the career of its president. There could be no turning back. What was at issue was not any single incident, but two or perhaps three institutions, Western, Waterloo College and the Seminary, and the Associate Faculties, each with a very different sense of the role, purpose, and place of university education in the second half of the twentieth century. The passions were intense and emotions were at a breaking point.

In a less happy moment, a beleaguered President Gerald Hagey faced a future that seemed riddled with problems and few easy solutions.
UWA

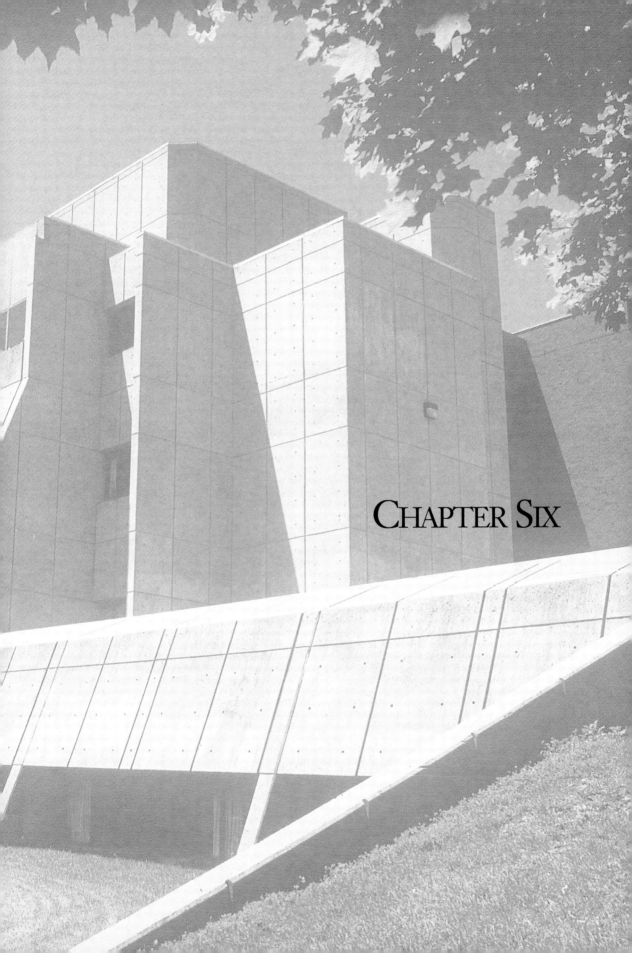

CHAPTER SIX

Setback and Renewal

Neither Ira Needles nor Gerry Hagey was altogether surprised by
Western's opposition to Waterloo's co-operative education program,
although they must have been stunned by the ad hominem nature of
Edward Hall's personal criticism of Hagey. As early as June 1957,
before the first students had enrolled in the pre-engineering class,
the report from George Brakeley and Company had outlined a
daunting task that lay ahead if they hoped to create a successful new
Canadian university.

Brakeley's had acquired a considerable reputation in the area of
university development, having conducted campaigns on behalf of
many other Canadian universities, including Toronto, British
Columbia, Western, McMaster, McGill, Queen's, and Assumption

(Windsor).[1] Drawing upon this wealth of expertise as well as advice from several of their past clients, Brakeley's report[2] outlined the myriad of problems that confronted the Associate Faculties. Professional engineering accreditation as well as their university affiliation remained unsolved. Industrial co-operation in the training of off-campus students in 1957 had yet to be assured, but the exceptional business contacts of Ira Needles and the diligence of George Dufault augered well for the future. To that would soon be added the support of A.S. Barber, who had first-hand experience of co-operative education, having attended the General Motors Institute in Flint, Michigan, and with a wide range of experience in industry in Canada.[3] Still, as Brakeley's report had noted in 1957, the program of co-operative education must stand on its own merits in Canada, and "the theory that 'because it works in the United States it will work in Canada' is unacceptable."[4]

At issue in 1958 was the future of Waterloo's engineering programs. UWA

Fund-raising appeals by other universities were also competing directly with Waterloo, but even where there was sympathy "and sometimes enthusiasm" for the Associate Faculties, "at the same time, it was apparent that the program was not well understood. To have proceeded with a major fund-raising effort [in 1957] before a fuller and more widespread understanding of the proposed program had been brought about," Brakeley's predicted, "would be to invite costly failure."

The acquisition of significant financial support beyond government funding was as necessary as it was difficult. Not only did the Brakeley report point out what both Needles and Hagey already knew, that "the capital needs of Waterloo College and Associate Faculties are extensive and may appear disproportionately large in terms of Waterloo College's present size and by comparison with other institutions of higher learning," but also that the Associate Faculties must "emphasize and re-emphasize, that the contemplated program is, in reality, a plan for an entirely new centre of learning." This was a concept somewhat at odds with Edward Hall's and to a degree Hagey's own view of the importance of Waterloo College in the development of the university.

The Waterloo Program, Brakeley's suggested, must also spell out and explain "how and where a greatly enlarged faculty will be recruited." Brakeley's cautioned that this would not be easy. Even though the development of Waterloo College and the Associate Faculties' desire to serve the immediate constituency were sound, Brakeley's had concluded in 1957 that "greater ambitions, i.e., the Co-operative Plan and degree-granting status, appear highly conditional at the present time."

Brakeley, Hagey, and Needles all shared the concern that it

would be extremely difficult to raise the funds required for Waterloo's expansion. Hagey had already conceded that "Waterloo [College] has done relatively little for its alumni" and although there was an awakening interest, there had never been any major donations. He also explained that support for Waterloo College had never engendered a strong financial commitment, noting somewhat ironically, that, "from an enrolment standpoint the experience has been that when times are good a fairly large percentage of the local students go to larger universities, and in poor times more of these attend the local college." [5] Many of those in the community who would support a university were already committed to other universities. From this point of view, the Associate Faculties was not particularly well placed in its desire to move to full university status.

Most individual donations to Waterloo College had come from members of the Lutheran Church and had been in relatively small amounts. In 1953 Hagey had conducted a direct mail campaign to 150 local companies, but the average donation had been only $2,500, raising less than $30,000 annually over the three years. Needles and Hagey now hoped that Waterloo's co-operative education program would make it possible for both Waterloo College and the Associate Faculties to expand and to achieve university status. [6]

Were they to succeed, Waterloo would occupy a unique niche in the Canadian university system. Only by means of the co-operative program, Hagey believed, would Waterloo be able to gain national support:

> I think it may be taken for granted that Industry is more willing to contribute when they can foresee their contributions directly yielding benefits to Industry. For the latter reason we believe that the interest Industry has shown in Waterloo's Co-operative plan will incline Industry to favour a contribution to Waterloo so that at least one co-operative college may be established in Canada. [6]

For good reason, Hagey was placing his hope for the future on industries beyond Kitchener and Waterloo — "The rubber and insurance companies are the only large national industries with head offices in this community. The rubber industry has not been known as a generous contributor, nor have mutual insurance companies." Instead, Hagey suggested:

> I do believe that many of the large companies who have generously supported welfare projects in the past are interested in Waterloo's co-operative Applied Science Course. While many of these have little opportunity to know much about Waterloo College, I believe they do recognize its possibility of establishing co-operative education in Canada.

Hagey's intention was for the Associate Faculties to be seen as a new university offering a clear alternative to the older Canadian schools.[7] He also recognized that the Canadian experience was shifting away from the precedents established at Oxford and Cambridge, just as since the war the Canadian economy had left behind the money markets of London and the woollen mills of Manchester.

Drawing inspiration from the earlier findings of Ira Needles and his own recent visits to the United States, Hagey reminded Brakeley's:

The $250,000 donation to the Associate Faculties by the Seagram Corporation to commemorate its centennial and that of the City of Waterloo was a milestone signifying community and business support. In the photograph (left to right): Charles Bronfman, Mayor Leo Whitney, Ira Needles, Pastor Albert Lotz, and President Hagey. Lotz and Hagey would develop a close personal friendship which would be tested and found true as the plans for the university unfolded. Charles Bronfman would later join the UW Board of Governors.
KWR

Many of our large Canadian companies being subsidiaries of U.S. companies have had an opportunity to experience the benefits of co-operative education. At the same time they are familiar with the hesitancy of our large universities to sponsor co-operative courses in Canada. Because of this they realize that the most practical way for them to encourage the development of this type of education is to support Waterloo as an established college that is willing to promote it.

Despite Hagey's optimism, George Brakeley advised in March 1957 that the time was not right to launch a financial campaign. Support for the idea of a co-operative education program did exist, but

> confidential interviews with industrialists and business men, as well as educators and the general public, clearly indicate a lack of knowledge of the plan, an uncertainty as to the capabilities of the associate Faculty [*sic*] and its Board of Governors to carry through the plan as they understand it, and the acceptance and standing which graduates of the eventual university will receive prior to and after graduation.

Hagey was not daunted.

"Frankly," he told George Brakeley, "I had rather surmised that it [the recommendation] would be along the lines you have indicated." The Management Committee of the Associate Faculties would be meeting on 14 March 1957 and Brakeley's report would be the subject of discussion. The Battle for Waterloo had begun. There would be many more skirmishes along the way, but no one, least of all Gerry Hagey, had thought of retreat as an option.

In the meantime, the acquisition of a new campus, the arrival of seventy-four students eager to enrol in the co-operative engineering program, and the successful participation of a number of Canadian industries in Waterloo's work-study experience had emboldened Hagey and Needles. Now the problems with the University of Western Ontario and their relationship with Waterloo College seemed to threaten their success. As they prepared for the meeting of the Board of Governors on 28 May 1958, President Hagey and board chair Ira Needles must have wondered about these latest threats to their dream of establishing a university that would have a special place in post-war life in Canada. Many faculty members who had come to Waterloo to share the enthusiasm for creating a university that seemed to promise an education directed towards the future rather than one based on the prejudices of the past were also unsettled by this attack on their academic integrity and they wanted an opportunity to express their views on the "university question."

The request from the Waterloo College board for an interview was not the only agenda item for the 28 May 1958 meeting. On 28 April, two days before the special committee from Waterloo College had met with the senior administration at Western to receive the blistering critique of the Associate Faculties' engineering program, the Academic Advisory Committee of the Associate Faculties had prepared its own memorandum to the Board of Governors, recommending application for a university charter by the Associate Faculties.[8]

Supported by the Faculty of Science and Engineering, they requested that President Hagey place their document before the Board of Governors. The timing of the Academic Advisory Committee's memorandum had undoubtedly been precipitated by the earlier visit to Western of Dr. Wickey, Dean Schaus, and President Hagey. The committee challenged Hall's fundamental assumptions about engineering education and his conclusions about the Waterloo program.

Chaired by Bruce Kelley, a science professor at Waterloo College since 1947, the members of the committee were aware of the rumours about a conflict with Western over their philosophy of engineering education. They strongly defended the Associate Faculties' commitment to the co-operative system of engineering education, a commitment which "was known and recognized by the

University of Western Ontario when it approved Waterloo College's request" for the affiliation of the Associate Faculties. Faculty members had come to Waterloo because of it, and they "have assumed the task of building up a first-rate academic curriculum."

It was true that the model for the curriculum was not Western's. The Associate Faculties had chosen to follow the programs at the University of Toronto and at Queen's University and they had "subscribed to the philosophy enunciated by Dean McLaughlin of Toronto, 'differentiation into well-known divisions such as Civil, Mechanical, Electrical, and Chemical Engineering is essential.'" The committee wondered aloud at the conflict of interest on Western's part as well as Western's tendency to want to interfere with Waterloo's curriculum: "Since Western's administration has, on several occasions, indicated that it is not in sympathy with the co-operative system, it is clearly undesirable that Western have any voice in the development of Waterloo's Engineering course." The two philosophies of engineering education were perhaps irreconcilable. Waterloo's program, however, fulfilled a distinctive need in Ontario. By January 1959 it was anticipated that more than seven hundred students would be enrolled; Western had 112 students in its engineering courses.[9] The strong support from government and industry, from the community and from the students, left the Associate Faculties with "a responsibility to all four groups to press steadily onward in our development," and seek a university charter. The university charter should be one that would enable the University of Waterloo to grant degrees at the bachelor's and master's levels in arts, science, and engineering, with degrees in science and engineering to be granted in time for the graduating class, "not later than October 1962."[10]

In keeping with the recognition of the importance of the Arts Faculty in the new university, the committee recommended "that the Arts Faculty of Waterloo College become the Arts Faculty of the University not later than October 1962." This would provide a definite program for future development and would "lead to better understanding and relationships among Waterloo College, the Associate Faculties, and the University of Western Ontario."

The memorandum closed with strong affirmation, "wholehearted" and "enthusiastic" support for the "Co-operative Engineering programme"; a "deep appreciation" of the effort and sacrifices by the board members in the development of the Associate Faculties, and praise for Gerald Hagey's presidency of the Associate Faculties. In light of the rumours rampant on campus about Hagey's leadership, the Academic Advisory Committee members went on record in his support, declaring:

We should like to express the firmest support for our President in his work of developing the College to University status. The enthusiasm and vigour which Dr. Hagey has displayed in the whole field of higher education, have been invaluable to the community as a whole and to the College in particular. We share his vision of a University in this community and feel that the recommendations outlined in this brief can bring this vision to fruition.

President Hagey was undoubtedly cheered by this ringing affirmation, but his problems were far from over.

Edward Hall's criticisms of Hagey's leadership had been damning, all the more so since much of it was in the form of innuendo designed to undermine both his leadership and his presidency of

Students in the Electrical Engineering Laboratory were oblivious to the intense political debate that surrounded the future of their university and its engineering curriculum.
UWA/Max Fleet

Waterloo College within the Lutheran community. None the less, it was to the meeting of the board of the Associate Faculties that he had to turn his attention.

The college board had asked for a joint meeting in less than a week after the Hall report had been presented to them. Hagey was undoubtedly perplexed. His papers contain the rough draft of his reply to Hall's allegations as well as a more subdued version ultimately distributed to the board of the Associate Faculties in time for the 28 May meeting. Taken together, these documents reveal Hagey's frustration and consternation as well as his combative instinct. In this, Edward Hall had met his match.

In his report to the Board of Governors of the Associate Faculties,[11] Hagey reviewed the legal and technical points of affiliation with Western and Waterloo's obligations to present its courses to Western's Senate for approval at such time "as it is decided that students in our course are expected to receive their degrees from Western," an assumption that was at best premature and one that had never been broached either by Hagey or by Hall. Hagey agreed that the original brochure sent to Ontario's high school principals may have led some to conclude that because of Waterloo's affiliation with Western, its engineering students would also be registered with the university, but this had long since been corrected.

There were other more fundamental issues that had to be dealt with. First "was a criticism of the President of Waterloo College and Associate Faculties as not being adequately qualified for his position." There it was. Out in the open. Now it could be dealt with. "I believe," Hagey commented, "there are two basic issues in relation to Western that require clarification":

(1) Is Western determined to prevent the continued development of Waterloo's co-operative engineering course?
(2) Is Western's President determined that he can no longer work with the President of Waterloo College and Associate Faculties, and consequently, that any continuing relationship between London and Waterloo could only be mutually satisfactory by a replacement of the latter's President?

The board was faced with several decisions, he suggested: whether to continue to develop its co-operative engineering programme, to seek its own university degree-granting charter, and finally, to establish "a means of determining the extent to which Western's President's disapproval of Waterloo's President makes any continuance of relationships between London and Waterloo undesirable."

True to his position as president of Waterloo College as well as of the Associate Faculties, Hagey also fretted about the relationship of the Associate Faculties to Waterloo College and the latter's obligation to the Canada Synod of the Lutheran Church. Any deterioration of the relationship with Western "as a result of Waterloo establishing a co-operative engineering course, in spite of Western's disapproval of this type of education," he said,"is a cause of justifiable concern by the Board of Waterloo College." In light of this, Hagey proposed that the two boards strike a joint committee to decide "on the action that is in the best interests of both Boards." The latter recommendation was one that would buy time and allow cooler tempers to prevail and this was the recommendation that was followed over the summer months.

In his first draft of this Memorandum Hagey had been far less reserved and his anger and frustration show through on every line. "The matter of disagreement over the co-operative type of education is one which needed to be brought out into the open if there was any inclination on the part of Western to interfere with the progress of this course at Waterloo," Hagey began. "Apparently, there is this intention on at least the part of its president. This intention was not known to me previous to the April 14th meeting."

The architectural simplicity of this first building on the new campus of the Associate Faculties marked a break with tradition. Ontario's universities more often than not, were built in a "collegiate gothic" style fashioned after British universities and rendered in cut stone. Premier Frost would soon wonder aloud why other Ontario universities did not follow Waterloo's architectural example.
UWA

Hagey was also angered at the way that Hall had chosen to make known his displeasure, as at no time during any of their previous meetings had he hinted at this or at his lack of respect for Hagey's leadership. Hagey felt that he had been judged behind his back: "It is unfortunate that now criticism has been registered in the way that it was, rather than in the form of a letter to the Board or [to] me." It was difficult to reply to innuendo or to comments allegedly made to a committee from which he had been excluded.

Hagey was also frustrated by the apparent willingness of Edward Hall to talk openly about him to dissident college faculty members: "It is well known that at least one member of our faculty has discussed with Western's administrative officers a concern about the administration at Waterloo. It is also understood that members of our faculty attending the Gettysburg conference [on Lutheran education] [then] made known to Dr. Wickey Dr. Hall's irritation or disagreement with the administrative policies being followed at Waterloo."

Hagey's concerns were understandable, but they would not stop unhappy faculty members or individual board members from receiving a friendly hearing from Western's president. Hagey undoubtedly realized this and these comments did not survive in his final draft. Nor did his concern that the board of Waterloo College might act to try to close down the Associate Faculties' co-operative education program. In this draft memorandum, however, he did express a fleeting concern about just this eventuality: "I presume that there is no thought on the part of the Waterloo College Board to interfere with the development of [the] co-operative engineering course. I am confident that it is the desire of the Associate Faculties Board to proceed." If this was the desire of both boards, Hagey had suggested, "then I think that this desire should be made known to Dr. Hall with the recommendation that we immediately endeavour to work out a programme with the University of Western Ontario whereby Waterloo may proceed in the development of this course without interference by the University of Western Ontario."

Although this crisis had passed for the moment, later in the summer (4 August 1958), Pastor Delton Glebe, newly elected as president of the Board of Governors of Waterloo College, was writing to Edward Hall explaining that "the Committee representing our Board of Governors, which met with you and Drs. Alan [*sic*] and Stiling on April 30, desires to continue the discussions which emanated from that meeting."[12] Hall assured Glebe that he "would be very happy to meet with your special committee again."[13] The

Designed by Shore and Moffat, architects for this phase of the university's development, Waterloo's buildings were set within the campus landscape. Not "monumental architectural statements," they nonetheless exhibited a verve and a clean design that seemed in keeping with the aspirations of this new university-to-be. Shown here is the Physics and Mathematics Building — the second university building — in August 1959, "almost ready for the influx of students in September." UWA/Shore Tilbe

process was about to start all over, but this time Glebe was undoubtedly worried more about Waterloo College and its relationship to Western than he was about Gerry Hagey or the Associate Faculties. It was important for them to rescue their college from what appeared to be a very difficult situation.

Gould Wickey, too, was once again writing directly to Edward Hall,[14] excluding President Hagey from this correspondence with Western's president. As he explained to Hall, "I have been asked to counsel with the Board of Governors of Waterloo College concerning the present situation and future developments." He hoped to visit Waterloo in September or October of 1958 and he needed Hall's information especially as to whether a university such as Hall's "would offer a degree based on work [Engineering] done at a related college, not located on the university campus." The relationship between Waterloo College, the Associate Faculties, and the University of Western Ontario remained at the forefront of Wickey's agenda as well as that of the special committee from Waterloo College.

Hall had replied promptly to Wickey's queries about Waterloo College and the Associate Faculties' likely relationship with Western.[15] By implication, he suggested that the very existence of the Associate Faculties as an affiliate of Waterloo College was highly irregular and would not be condoned in any other English-speaking university in Canada. In the first place, "there are no English-speaking universities in Canada where there is a separate faculty of arts and a faculty of science ... [and] to my [Hall's] knowledge, an affiliated or federated college does not have a faculty of science in any of the English-speaking universities of Canada." Furthermore, Hall continued, "It is understood, certainly in this University, that no affiliated college may have a professional school." And he warned, "Although I cannot speak for the Senate, I would hardly think that the Senate would agree to confer a special degree for work done at an affiliated college, if such work was not offered within the constituent University." This was clear enough. Gould Wickey was given little hope that Western would recognize the work of students enrolled in the Associate Faculties, and Waterloo College would be wise to extricate itself from its arrangements with the Associate Faculties.

Three days later, the special committee from Waterloo College met with Edward Hall and his colleagues, Vice-President Allan and Dean Stiling.[16] The committee members from Waterloo College, Dr. Albert Jacobi and Pastors Delton Glebe and Alvin Baetz, were undoubtedly anxious after their previous meeting with Western's senior administrators.

Edward Hall was one of Canada's pre-eminent university leaders and at their last meeting he had left no one in doubt that he disapproved of both President Hagey and the Associate Faculties and that the board of Waterloo College had erred in their relationship with the Associate Faculties at the expense of their long-standing affiliation with Western. Hall had been most emphatic on these points. Would he have mellowed over the summer months?

Now that a new academic year had begun, and the Associate Faculties had an even larger influx of engineering students than before, outnumbering by far the students enrolled in engineering at Western, and rivalling Waterloo College's own arts enrolment, the need for a resolution of the problems with Western and with the Associate Faculties had become more urgent than ever. The Board of Governors of Waterloo College had made several critical decisions since the previous meeting with President Hall.

Acting as spokesman, Pastor Glebe explained to Hall and his colleagues that the Waterloo College board intended to petition the provincial government for degree-granting privileges for both the college and the Lutheran seminary and that this action had already been approved by the Canada Synod of the Lutheran Church. He also indicated that the Associate Faculties board was going to petition to incorporate as a degree-granting institution, and that "Waterloo College would not exercise its degree granting privileges, if they were granted, unless it was deemed desirable and expedient so to do."

In October 1961 the Kitchener-Waterloo Record announced that "several rooms of the new engineering building of the University of Waterloo will open soon as engineering students return to classes." By 1961, however, arts students and their professors would also be camping out in these new quarters, awaiting their own building which would not be available for another year. Such was the pace of life at Waterloo.
KWR

The "public" in the Kitchener-Waterloo area had reacted "most favourably" to the idea of a degree-granting institution in their community. The board of Waterloo College, however, still felt responsible to the students now enrolled there to ensure that they could obtain a degree from Western, and they hoped that even after the university legislation was enacted, "that the affiliation with Western could be maintained for some years." Pastor Glebe conceded, however, that it was clearly necessary for the Associate Faculties to have their own charter so that the students enrolled in the co-operative engineering course could be assured of a degree. As he explained, "The course ... had been developed so far now that continuation of it was necessary. To drop it would mean much adverse publicity."

Hall and his colleagues reacted with mixed emotions. Dr. Allan questioned the feasibility of having three institutions in the same community petitioning for degree-granting status and he predicted concerns about this in the private bills committee. On the other hand, Edward Hall was pleased to rid himself of any responsibility for the Associate Faculties, reminding them that Western's Senate would not likely have approved the Associate Faculties' curriculum. He agreed, however, that Senate would "tolerate the situation with Waterloo College of Arts." Having conceded that much, Hall was not one to let the matter drop. In fact, he began once again to "stir the pot," creating new stresses for the already tenuous relationship between Waterloo College and its Associate Faculties. As Pastor Glebe subsequently reported to the board of Waterloo College:

> Dr. Hall also suggested that he felt Waterloo College was losing considerable grant money from the Canada Council because the students enrolled in W.C. Assoc. Fac. were not eligible for per student grant ...
>
> Dr. Hall [also] suggested that Waterloo College of Arts should be taking the lead in establishing a U. at Waterloo.

Hall went so far as to suggest that the board of the Associate Faculties "could and should be willing to make the money available" to Waterloo College to become the University of Waterloo, rather than letting the Associate Faculties assume the lead and the prestige of becoming "the University."

Hall was at his provocative best as he lectured to the college delegation: "He asked whether we are willing just to remain as Waterloo College in this new set-up with no control or not. He was very concerned that W.C. of Arts should teach the arts subjects since they have the prestige — have been in the business long

enough — have made a name for themselves. Also that Waterloo College of Arts also be responsible for the dept. heads ... and that Arts College promote post-graduate work."

This "most cordial" meeting concluded with Hall expressing his desire "to have conferences with the Waterloo College lawyers drawing up the University Act so that he could suggest certain things out of his own experience as the president of a U."

Two months later, on 12 December, President Hagey presented a three-page document to the Senate of the University of Western Ontario describing Waterloo's plans to proceed towards full university status.[17] Clearly Hagey did not want Edward Hall's further interference or advice. At the same time, he had no wish to exacerbate the already sensitive relations between the two institutions. He conceded that as Waterloo's engineering program developed it had become "increasingly apparent that the co-operative plan could

There may have been times when President Hagey longed for the simplicity of Waterloo College in the early 1950's, but those days seemed so long ago, almost an idyllic view of life in small-town Ontario that was once his Waterloo.
WLU

not be made to conform to Western's examination schedules and other conditions that the Senate might rightfully expect to apply to such a course offered by an affiliated college." One result of this, Hagey explained, was "the unanticipated situation of the Associate Faculties being required to immediately prepare for university status in order to continue the program it had undertaken." Hagey could hardly have been more polite or more circumspect.

It was clear for the moment at least that Hagey and the Associate Faculties had regained the initiative, even if "the steps which have led to our present position are rather unorthodox, even though they may have appeared to us as a normal development." A meeting with Dr. Hall and Dr. Allan the previous week recognized that there still may be "some difficult situations during the period of transition to full university responsibility," Hagey continued, perhaps holding back some of the anger he had so obviously felt months earlier or perhaps speaking tongue-in-cheek as he addressed Western's Senate for the last time before Waterloo achieved its own university status:

> During this time, the experience and guidance of our parent university can be especially helpful to us. The sympathetic appreciation of our problems, the practical suggestions and assurance of moral support that we received from Dr. Hall and Dr. Allan, ... was indeed reassuring to those of us who are endeavouring to chart a new and different [difficult] course.

These had been difficult and trying times, not only for Gerry Hagey and the Associate Faculties, but also for those at Waterloo College who had seen their relationship with the University of Western Ontario threatened. But there was more to it than that. Gould Wickey's apparent support for those Lutheran faculty members who opposed both Gerry Hagey and the development of the Associate Faculties would provide an important degree of credibility to those who were not in support of his initiatives for change. These would be the same people who, two years later, in 1960, would lead the Lutheran faculty against federation with the University of Waterloo. They would tour the countryside, described by some as "circuit riders," working the rural congregations into a frenzy, preaching against the evils of federation and the loss of their Lutheran identity by joining the new University of Waterloo.

The Board of Governors of the Associate Faculties had responded overwhelmingly in favour of Hagey's presidency. Their agenda now quickly shifted towards establishing an independent university. The crisis with Western had clearly advanced the schedule beyond anyone's expectations.

It was not surprising that the faculty and Board of Governors of the Associate Faculties rallied behind President Hagey, setting aside whatever differences they might have had. Most of the members of the Academic Advisory Committee had a career beyond the university, in industry or government, in particular Batke, Cowan, and Bowman. Those who did not, like Wright and Stanton, were convinced that the old universities and the old ways were not good enough. They had let Canada down; they had let Canadian students down, and Waterloo's co-operative education program offered an opportunity to move in a new and different direction.

The students at the Associate Faculties and many of those in arts at Waterloo College continued to support Hagey, grateful to have been given an opportunity for a university education. The provincial government, too, supported the Associate Faculties. After their initial reservations, they had come to approve of the "Waterloo experiment." Through it all, Hagey had the unquestioned support of Ira Needles, chairman of the Board of Governors of the Associate Faculties. Needles was not easily intimidated by Edward Hall or by the University of Western Ontario. The support of business and industrial leaders was also never in question. Carl Pollock, who served not only as president of Dominion Electrohome Industries, but also as a leading spokesman for the Canadian Manufacturers' Association, stood behind the idea of a new university in Waterloo and its co-operative education scheme. So, too, did many prominent Lutheran businessmen in the community.

Others, however, wished to keep their college as they had always known it. These differences would come to divide the very community that had seen the university idea in Waterloo as an exciting window onto the future. Ere long, the Board of Governors of Waterloo College would move to separate the presidency of the college from that of its Associate Faculties. Hagey had served as president of both, hoping in this way to bridge the gap between the two.

In light of all that had happened it was perhaps inevitable that the presidency of the two institutions would be split. In the midst of this Hagey wrote to Dr. Nils Willison, his friend, confidant and former teacher thirty years earlier. Dr. Willison had been the first graduate of the Waterloo College Seminary and had been the principal who had helped to organize Waterloo College to become an affiliate of the University of Western Ontario. He had become one of the college's first faculty members in 1924. Over the years, Hagey and Willison had become friends, and on 14 May 1959, Hagey attempted to explain his feelings about recent events to Dr. Willison.

Ever since I have been at Waterloo as President and even before accepting the appointment I have greatly appreciated your kind words of encouragement. I well recall your visit to our home a little more than six years ago in 1953 which provided me an opportunity to discuss with you the plan that I had, that I considered would make it possible for me to accept the Board's invitation to become president of the College ...The Board of Governors has accepted my resignation as President of the College to become effective June 30th of this year ... Although I did not envision the administration of the two corporations being separated at as early a date, I am now convinced that it is desirable for this to happen.

The Board's decision made it necessary for me to either remain as President of Waterloo College or resign and accept the Presidency of the University. I have decided to follow the latter course because I am convinced that it is the best interests of the College for me to do so.[18]

In many ways, Gerry Hagey's identity was still tied to Waterloo College and as he explained to Dr. Willison, he was unshaken in his belief that if only the people of his Church "could appreciate the opportunities which are being made available for the College through the development of University status at Waterloo," the future would be bright. There would still be many trying situations for both the college and the university to face. "This is to be expected because of the rapid expansion during the past two years and the necessity for us to continue to move forward at an abnormally fast pace in order to complete the programmes to which we are now committed." These were difficult and turbulent times, facing a future that often seemed to have little connection to the past.

CHAPTER SEVEN

St. Jerome's College and the University Question

When the Associate Faculties announced its decision to acquire a 200-acre campus in anticipation of the creation of a University of Waterloo, the joint statement by the board chairman, Ira Needles, and President Gerald Hagey explained that "The planned development at Waterloo is toward a degree-granting university of arts and science."[1] The previous week, at a joint meeting of the Boards of Governors of Waterloo College and the Associate Faculties, when the final decision to purchase the new campus site was agreed upon, President Hagey had also suggested that:

There is good reason to believe that churches other than the Lutheran Church will wish to become associated with the

University of Waterloo … if and when it receives a charter … If the Associate Faculties decides in favour of relocating, it might be desirable for them to include or zone a portion of the campus on which future church colleges might be located. Conceivably, this might even include a relocation of Waterloo College.[2]

Some may have been surprised by the proposal to relocate Waterloo College. Others would have been equally surprised by his suggestion of creating an area of the campus for the inclusion of church colleges other than his own Lutheran, Waterloo College. The explanation for his suggestion had long historical roots and lay at the very heart of the Ontario government's ideals for future university development in the province. It was also deeply rooted in the unusual historical tradition of Waterloo County, where the religious divisions which had so often created unrest throughout the province had not been embraced and where an unusual degree of religious tolerance had always existed. In March 1959, with the advice and support of Premier Leslie Frost and his minister of education, W.J. Dunlop, Waterloo College, Waterloo College Associate Faculties, and the Roman Catholic St. Jerome's College were granted university status. St. Jerome's College would shortly move from its Kingsdale campus in Kitchener to the new university campus in Waterloo.[3]

With the move to the campus of the University of Waterloo and the opening of Notre Dame College (in 1997 re-named Sweeney Hall), these students were able to take advantage of the opportunities for university education available at St. Jerome's College.
SJC

Many were undoubtedly pleased to see St. Jerome's, the community's oldest post-secondary institution, founded in 1865, becoming an integral part of the formation of the University of Waterloo; others, however, were less than happy — especially those at Waterloo College who saw St. Jerome's as a threat to their claim to be the Arts Faculty of the new university. From the beginning, however, St. Jerome's participation had been essential to the development of plans for a university in Waterloo.

Like Waterloo College, St. Jerome's had been poised for a major expansion at the end of the Second World War. In 1953, Hagey had acknowledged that many people in the community remarked to him that it was "unfortunate for me, that when I became President of Waterloo College, St. Jerome's was so far ahead of the Lutherans with its building program."[4] He would later claim that St. Jerome's was as much responsible for the hurried drive for university status in Waterloo as were the needs of the Associate Faculties and the crisis with the University of Western Ontario.[5]

The beginning of this move by St. Jerome's for university status began in 1937 with the consecration of Joseph Francis Ryan as Bishop of Hamilton, the diocese which included Kitchener and Waterloo within its episcopal boundaries. From the time of his consecration, Ryan had made the establishment of a Catholic liberal arts university in his diocese a personal crusade.[6] One way to achieve Ryan's goal would have been for St. Jerome's to affiliate with an existing Canadian university. The creation of a proposed Waterloo University offered a possible answer to this problem, although not necessarily the one that Ryan preferred. As a former student at St. Jerome's, Bishop Ryan took a strong personal interest in the fate of his alma mater, and he would do so in ways that were unexpected and not always helpful. But his determination and his constant pressure in this matter could not be overlooked.

In 1963 the University of Waterloo would award an honorary LL.D. to Bishop Joseph F. Ryan for his role as a Canadian educator. Ryan is seen with Chancellor Dana Porter following Convocation.
UWA

In 1943, in the midst of the war, Ryan had initiated a fund-raising campaign to finance St. Jerome's development as a full university, explaining that "in the postwar years, St. Jerome's is planning a program of expansion which will bring her to the status which is her destiny as the Catholic College of the Diocese of Hamilton ... As soon as conditions warrant after Victory, St. Jerome's, through an expansion program, will offer courses with university recognition."[7] In this campaign, conducted in all of the parishes in his diocese, Ryan had found a unique method of raising money for his college while also identifying it with Canadian patriotism.

Using the purchase of Victory Bonds as a means of collecting funds, Ryan united the needs of St. Jerome's College with Canada's future wellbeing: "It is patriotic," he said, "because all the money will be invested in Victory Bonds until a building program is possible," and individuals would receive an income tax deduction from the government for their donation.

For God and Country

| Today
Your Dollars
Fight | *After Victory*
Your Dollars
Teach |

The use of Victory Bonds as a fund-raising measure for St. Jerome's College was timely. Bishop Ryan recognized the popular acceptance of the need for university education as a national priority.
SJC

Ryan tapped into the growing acceptance of the need for university education as a national priority, explaining that St. Jerome's would be a national asset. "Our government, even with the pressing problem of financing our war effort, has concern for the preservation and extension of education. Canada wants schools like St. Jerome's to carry on during and after the war."

A series of full-page advertisements, sponsored by local businesses with a connection to St. Jerome's, announced that the campaign was "to establish a new St. Jerome's College with university recognition," adding their support for St. Jerome's to the cause of civic and national improvement. The attainment of university status was also the theme of St. Jerome's College president, Father Michael Weiler, the keynote speaker at a banquet for 350 canvassers held on 1 June 1944 at Kitchener's Walper Hotel. "The dream of a college leading youth to university degrees will be an early postwar realization," he said. "Those who give will be investing in the education of their children and their investment will provide a college that will train them to take their places in postwar Canada."[8]

Within a matter of weeks the campaign had reached its goal. Taking advantage of this success, Ryan enlarged the aims of the campaign to encompass all aspects of Roman Catholic education. When fundraising ended in 1948 contributions and pledges had exceeded $2 million. The story was not altogether a happy one for St. Jerome's. Holding the purse strings within his episcopal grip, Bishop Ryan decided that its share would be only $250,000, and these funds would be available only upon the initiation of the college's building project. This allowed Ryan a degree of control over the college's future; he could make additional funds available if the plans for the development of the college were in accord with his ideas.[9]

First and foremost, St. Jerome's expansion depended upon forming an affiliation arrangement with an existing Canadian university. St. Jerome's had earlier considered affiliation with Western even before Waterloo College had approached the university. But for reasons that are unclear they had not followed up on this initiative, even though many Roman Catholic candidates for the priesthood completed their studies in London at St. Peter's Seminary through an arrangement with the University of Western Ontario.

Carleton College in Ottawa had recently obtained its university status by means of a charter under the provisions of the Companies Act and this was suggested as an option for St. Jerome's. (This would be the route followed by the Associate Faculties in 1956.) Father Weiler, who had been meeting with the rector of the University of

The fund-raising campaign for St. Jerome's College would exceed both the bishop's and the college's expectations; by combining St. Jerome's College with the general cause of Roman Catholic education, by 1948 in excess of $2 million had been raised. The diocesan letter outlined Bishop Ryan's hopes for the future university status of St. Jerome's College. SJC

Ottawa, however, preferred an affiliation agreement with the University of Ottawa, which as an existing Roman Catholic university had much to offer. As Weiler explained to Bishop Ryan:

> We considered the University of Ottawa with its Dominion and Provincial Charters and its rank as a Pontifical University should give us standing with other universities. We also feel that the prestige of Ottawa would strengthen the credits of any of our graduates who might apply for advanced standing to schools in the United States.[10]

In April 1947 the Senate of the University of Ottawa agreed to an affiliation with St. Jerome's and the college announced that it would immediately offer the first two years of a university arts program and admit women to its courses.

Although the announcement was late in the year, four women enrolled that September. In the beginning, courses were restricted to the humanities and to those sciences which did not require laboratories, but St. Jerome's was authorized by Ottawa to organize departments and courses in "Experimental Sciences, Positive Psychology, and Business Administration, [but] only after the university shall have approved the qualifications of personnel and the laboratory facilities, in each case and for every course of instruction."[11]

In 1952 St. Jerome's acquired a prominent 90-acre site in Kitchener for its university campus, and on a bright September day Bishop Ryan laid the cornerstone of a $1 million project to build an Arts and Administration Building which would house classrooms, a new library, and an assembly hall. Plans for a men's dormitory and chapel were also ready to tender for immediate construction. The 1953 opening of the college complex, attended by Bishop Ryan and Premier Leslie Frost, coincided with a gala alumni reunion and a "state" dinner at the Walper Hotel where John E. Motz, publisher of the *Kitchener-Waterloo Record*, chaired the fund-raising campaign that would lead St. Jerome's into the future.

In the same year, Father Cornelius Siegfried was appointed as rector of St. Jerome's College, bringing the college nomenclature into accord with that used in the University of Ottawa. Siegfried's

leadership would be instrumental in guiding St. Jerome's into full university status, but not in the way anticipated by Bishop Ryan or by many of Siegfried's own colleagues.

A graduate of the University of Western Ontario with a master's degree in mathematics from the University of Michigan, Cornelius Siegfried was more pragmatic than philosophical in outlook, more attuned to Ontario's politics than to those of the Roman curia. He was considerably more comfortable with the realities of Ontario's university life than with the disputations of theologians. As he would soon discover, Ontario's politics would play an essential role in the resolution of the university question in Waterloo.

Father Weiler, the previous president of St. Jerome's College, in 1948 had rebuffed an attempt by the Kitchener Chamber of Commerce to discuss possible co-operation between St. Jerome's and Waterloo College in the development of a university program. Weiler had rejected the idea of working with Waterloo College because of the presence there of the Evangelical Lutheran Seminary. Siegfried's response would be quite different, but then much had changed in the succeeding six years.

Before becoming rector of St. Jerome's College, Cornelius Siegfried had taken an active role in the Roman Catholic Teacher's Federation and had made many friends in the Department of Education at Queen's Park. Siegfried now wrote to his contacts in the department, and especially to its director, Dr. C.F. Cannon, who also had responsibility for Ontario's universities. He hoped to drop in to see him for "a few minutes," and to ask for his advice, "on some points in our long range plan for developing St. Jerome's as a liberal arts college under denominational control."[12] Although the Ontario government was painfully aware of the need to increase access to Ontario's universities and to create new centres for learning, the policy of Leslie Frost was clear and immutable. His government would support the expansion of existing universities and colleges, but it would not provide funding for denominational institutions.

Premier Frost was present at the opening of St. Jerome's Kingsdale campus, and he spoke glowingly of the importance of religion in education. "You cannot have education without religion," he said, "you cannot have life without religion. There can be no material development without religion."[13] For all of this, the premier was not prepared to reverse a century of tradition which had denied provincial grants to denominational colleges or universities. On the other hand, he warmly approved of the arrangement at the University of Toronto and at the University of Western Ontario by which these colleges were in a federated system with a non-denominational, provincially funded university. Indeed, this was his preference and it was one which seemed to appeal to many Ontario residents as the way in which universities should be organized. In 1952, when Frost had first anticipated an application for a private bill from St. Jerome's College for independent status, he sought to defer any decision until a satisfactory arrangement could be made between Assumption College in Windsor and the University of Western Ontario.[14]

The precedent created by the establishment of Assumption University, Essex College, and ultimately the University of Windsor would have a profound impact on developments in Waterloo. In the midst of all of this, Leslie Frost's presence at the opening of the Kingsdale campus and the college's plan to expand and to offer a range of university courses, including some in science and business, was not lost on Gerald Hagey. When he approached  his Board of Governors and later the Lutheran Synod in 1955 to consider establishing a non-sectarian science college to be affiliated with Waterloo College, St. Jerome's was very much on Hagey's mind. He reminded his board and the Synod that two other Roman Catholic universities in Ontario, Ottawa and Assumption, had accepted non-denominational colleges as affiliates in order to benefit from provincial grants, and he added:

> This pattern, having been formed ... if Waterloo [College] did not quickly take the leadership in this direction, St. Jerome's might. Discussions with prominent citizens, reveal that there has been, and is, local interest in procuring for this community an independent, degree-granting university. These interests, appear to be sufficiently strong that pressure for a university in this community will be brought to bear with or without the co-operation of Waterloo College ... Should we be forced to compete against a government-subsidized college, our position would be most unfortunate.[15]

In the summer months of 1955, Hagey continued to gather information and to garner support for the possibility of creating a non-sectarian college that would lead to a community-based university. On 19 July at a dinner meeting with Dr. S.F. Leavine, the recently defeated Conservative MLA, who continued "to carry the patronage of the riding for the Ontario government," Hagey asked

Leavine to arrange for the minister of education, W.J. Dunlop, and the director of education, J.G. Althouse, to visit Waterloo College in the hope of enlisting their support for the development of Waterloo College. At the same time, Hagey talked to Leavine about the position of St. Jerome's and discussed with him "the possible interest of St. Jerome's College in a Faculty of Science at Waterloo College."[16] This seemed all the more relevant since the candidate who had defeated Leavine was John J. Wintermeyer, a prominent Roman Catholic lawyer closely affiliated with St. Jerome's.

Along with Ira Needles and Gerry Hagey, Father Cornelius Siegfried, known to his friends as "Cork," is credited with guiding the fortunes of the University of Waterloo. Siegfried was ecumenical in outlook before the idea of ecumenism took hold in Canadian society or in the Roman Catholic Church.
KWR

Leavine was as good as his word. One week later, on a scorching hot day in July, Dunlop, Althouse, and Edward Hall arrived at Waterloo College to discuss with Hagey the government's interest in "expanding the opportunities to study Science."[17] Both Dunlop and Althouse had been accompanied by their wives, and the meeting quickly adjourned to a much more attractive setting where so many important decisions were made — the terrace at the Westmount Golf and Country Club. Hagey was assured of the government's probable support for a "junior College of Science," organized by a non-denominational governing board, but which could become "a Faculty of Waterloo College." The minister, however, pointed out "that such a Faculty of Science would have to be available to St. Jerome's students wishing to take Science options." In the fairly tenuous understanding of university policies and procedures, Hagey suggested that the participation of St. Jerome's students in the science option "should not present any difficulty as Roman Catholic students are now attending Waterloo College." This may well have been the case, but it was not quite what either St. Jerome's or the minister had in mind. Nonetheless, it was clear from the first tentative discussions that a university would not be possible in the community without the inclusion of St. Jerome's College.

Two years previously, in response to the attempt by Assumption College in Windsor to acquire provincial funding, Premier Frost had made it clear that the provincial policy was "that a university in title existed in Ontario only when at least two affiliated colleges were in place."[18] This precedent would have significant implications at Waterloo as St. Jerome's and Waterloo College struggled to arrive at an understanding for the formation of a university that would serve the needs of both institutions and their students.

The Ontario cabinet, meeting in January 1956, first discussed the possibility of a separately incorporated Science Faculty to be affiliated with Waterloo College, and although no opposition was voiced in cabinet, the Department of Education would make no commitment until it could formulate a general policy to deal with increased enrolments in Ontario's existing universities. In February the minister was still delaying consideration of a draft of the petition for affiliation, but it appeared that there was an additional reason for not considering Waterloo College's application. Hagey met again with Dunlop. "It was inferred," Hagey explained, "that if the government is to provide financial assistance ... we should have popular support for it." This meant, he suggested, the inclusion of St. Jerome's. Waterloo College's proposal needed "support by the R.C.'s as well as the Protestants."[19]

Returning from an earlier trip to Toronto, Hagey had immediately sought a meeting with Father Siegfried and he wasted little time in informing Dunlop of Siegfried's response to the idea of a non-denominational college:

> This morning [6 January 1956] I discussed it [the idea of a separately incorporated college] in some detail with The Reverend C.L. Siegfried, Rector of St. Jerome's College. I found him much interested in the information which I gave him and was informed that he will discuss it with his counsel [sic] and Bishop.[20]

Hagey had also passed along to Siegfried the minister's suggestion that the rector should feel free to discuss Waterloo College's

proposal with him, "if he so wished." Siegfried, too, acted quickly. He met with Dunlop and his staff, and also with Bishop Ryan in Hamilton, then in Ottawa with members of the senior administration at the University of Ottawa, and finally, in Kitchener with the members of the Congregation of the Resurrection which administered St. Jerome's College.

These early meetings strengthened the interest of St. Jerome's College and provided the impetus for the development of an independent university in

In 1960, standing between Gerry Hagey and Wyn Rees, (the principal of Renison College), Father Cornelius Siegfried considers the future site for St. Jerome's College on the University of Waterloo campus. With them are M.R. Good representing the Mennonite community and J. Ross Morrison of the United Church. All four denominations would ultimately build colleges on the UW campus.
KWR

Waterloo. In a second meeting with Hagey, Siegfried had been very explicit in this regard. He advised him that, "If the probability of this development is expected to lead to Waterloo becoming a university in its own right, his people would support it." In developing a basis for an agreement of affiliation with the new board, Hagey reported, "the above possibility is being taken into consideration."[21] This decision would be one that Hagey would take to the board of the Associate Faculties, but it was one that he was hesitant to present to the Evangelical Lutheran Synod for fear that their support for the university idea might be compromised. This indecision on Hagey's part would cost him dearly in the end, although at the time it was perhaps necessary to retain the momentum to move the university forward.

The inclusion of St. Jerome's in the proposed university was essential both for the approval of the government and also for the members of the Board of Governors of the Associate Faculties. Within days of receiving the petition for incorporation of the Associate Faculties, the minister of education "[again] emphasized the desirability of having tangible evidence that the people of our community are supporting our efforts." To this end, Hagey reported to Dunlop that he and Siegfried "again spent some time together, at the end of which he [Siegfried] informed me that, on the understanding that it was our plan that the Associate Faculties would some time in the future become a degree-granting university with which St. Jerome's could become affiliated, they would be interested in doing so and would wholeheartedly support our efforts."[22]

Those who have seen the St. Jerome's campus only in later years could hardly envision that this sign in 1961 marked the actual site of the college and its future buildings.
SJC/KWR

The Board of Governors of the Associate Faculties regarded a positive relationship with St. Jerome's College as a primary consideration in the move towards university status. At its very first meeting on 25 April 1956 they had passed a formal motion, declaring that, "if and when university-degree-granting status is reached, this Board will entertain a Petition from St. Jerome's for an association that makes the facilities of this Board available to St. Jerome's on a favourable basis." Hagey himself was rushing to prepare a draft of terms of affiliation between the Associate Faculties and Waterloo College for discussion at the annual meeting of the Lutheran Synod in June. There was so much to do and so little time to do it.

As all of this was progressing, Dunlop sent a casual note to Hagey over a matter that in the future would become a point of dissention. On 17 April 1956 Althouse had passed on to the minister the documents which Hagey had left for him the previous day, and the minister was concerned: "The suggestion of control over academic courses [by Waterloo College]," he wrote to Hagey, "makes me wonder whether this has been agreed to by the University of Western Ontario and I wonder also whether the authorities of St. Jerome's College are in full agreement with this plan. This is a point which, it seems to me, should be discussed with all those concerned."[23] From the point of view of St. Jerome's College, however, the temporary role and influence of Waterloo College was not a problem. St. Jerome's support was on the basis that the Associate Faculties' intention was to become the university and it would be this new university that St. Jerome's would join, not Waterloo College. That this point was made so concisely in 1956 is of considerable significance. That the letter of explanation to the co-ordinator of higher education was written by President Hagey emphasizes both the significance of St. Jerome's inclusion in the university's plans as well as the clarity of the arrangement that had led to this support for the inception of the Associate Faculties.[24] It also implies that Hagey and Siegfried had begun to work closely together and from at least one perspective — that of Bishop Joseph F. Ryan — this would pose its own problems.

Throughout these formative years Siegfried's position was unwavering. He explained this to C.P. McTague, the MLA who had earlier advised the Basilian priests on similar matters relating to the relationship between Assumption College and the University of Windsor:

> St. Jerome's College is prepared to support and actively to encourage any satisfactory plan whereby the two existing colleges could cooperate with each other, with any other local body and with the provincial government to improve their educational services. It is the opinion of St. Jerome's College that the most desirable arrangement would be a federation of Waterloo College, St. Jerome's College and a third College under non-denominational control, all sharing a university charter independently of any existing university. If the principle of federation has the approval of the Ontario Department of Education, I am confident that it would receive support from the people of this area.[25]

When Hagey had been asked by Dunlop to determine whether the students at St. Jerome's College would benefit by using the facilities of the proposed Faculty of Science, Siegfried had explained that "no satisfactory arrangement for sharing facilities can be made, unless both colleges operate under the same university charter." St. Jerome's preferred that a university charter be granted to this area "simultaneously with the establishment of a non-denominational college, rather than the plan proposed by Waterloo College which

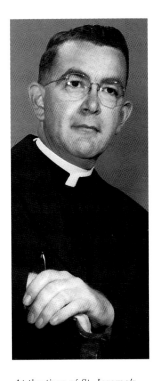

At the time of St. Jerome's federation with the University of Waterloo, Father John Finn served as dean and registrar. He would succeed Father Siegfried as president and for many years was professor of French. A humble and gentle man, John Finn was much liked by his students. In 1993 the men's residence was named the J.R. Finn Residence in his honour.
KWR

would have the new college affiliated with Western University."[26]

It was not that Siegfried was prejudiced against Western, his own alma mater, but so long as St. Jerome's was affiliated with the University of Ottawa, its students could not take science courses at another college affiliated with another university. In any case, St. Jerome's students were already chafing at the restrictions in the science offerings available to them. In Hamilton, Bishop Ryan remained ever assertive about his desire to see St. Jerome's expand to full university status. Ryan was prone to interfere, although for the moment he restricted himself only to urging Siegfried to seek "Federation in any university set up that may come into being in Waterloo County."[27]

Siegfried was in Toronto again in July 1956, meeting with Althouse to clarify the position of the government. St. Jerome's was prepared to support the formation of a university in this area, Siegfried reported, "provided that those in authority at St. Jerome's College are assured that it's [*sic*] position in the new university will be that of a federated college." "The active support and cooperation of the two existing denominational colleges," he added, "will be necessary in order to obtain universal approval and assistance from the entire community."[28]

There was the rub. Roman Catholics were the largest single religious denomination and their public support for St. Jerome's, let alone the major investment in the new campus at Kingsdale, made its claims hard to overlook by a government so carefully attuned to the political nuances of the electorate. Both Althouse

and the director of education, Dr. Beattie, were sympathetic to the college's point of view, which was also very much in keeping with the government's own policy, and they advised Siegfried that his position would be explained to the minister of education and to the premier.[29] Siegfried must have felt a sense of relief. He may have felt it even more when the points made in this letter to Bishop Ryan were confirmed by Althouse.

Over the summer months of 1956, President Hagey was also very busy, pushing ahead with the plans for the Associate Faculties. A federation agreement between the Associate Faculties and Waterloo College had been approved by the Canada Synod of the Lutheran Church at its meeting in Port Colborne on 6 June. As he now rushed to prepare the Associate Faculties' application for a government grant, Hagey wondered whether he would be free to discuss publicly the proposed co-operative plan which he was now proposing to introduce as the basis for the new university. Dr. Althouse not only gave Hagey the authorization to talk openly about the concept of co-operative education, but he also assured him that he had recently met with Father Siegfried, who had "stated quite emphatically that St. Jerome's did not wish in any way to interfere with the possibility of the Associate Faculties procuring a government grant."[30]

While the government considered its course of action on the university question in Waterloo, Father Siegfried came under renewed pressure to strengthen the position of St. Jerome's College. John Wintermeyer had a long-standing connection with St. Jerome's.

Nineteen sixty-two saw the construction of three new buildings on the university campus. In the left foreground is one wing of the St. Jerome's complex of three buildings. The cement pillars in the centre form the framework of the Arts Building (now Modern Languages) and on the right is Renison College. In the background on the left is the Physics and Mathematics Building while in the distance the Schweitzer farmhouse still gives witness to the original orientation of the land.
KWR

Bishop Ryan and Mother Loretto of the School Sisters of Notre Dame speaking at the opening of the college buildings in 1962.
SJC

As the member of the provincial legislature for Kitchener he had taken a personal interest in the university question. He also called upon Bishop Ryan, expressing concern that "no approach is being made to the Premier with respect to a university charter ... and particularly a federation agreement with St. Jerome's." Ever the politician, Wintermeyer continued, "I do not want you to think that I am pushing you at all, but it does seem to me that during the period of time that Waterloo College is in a period of setback, that we should be pushing our cause as strongly as possible."[31]

Ryan subsequently summoned Siegfried to the Chancery Office in Hamilton for a meeting concerning St. Jerome's future. Ryan had spoken again with John Wintermeyer that very morning (19 December 1956). The bishop demanded to meet with Siegfried and with all of the St. Jerome's College faculty.

Ryan was displeased with Siegfried's handling of the university question and told him so in no uncertain terms. "I am very concerned about the position that you have taken on this matter," he warned. Siegfried's growing friendship and close personal relations with President Hagey were suspect.

> I feel myself that it has been a mistake to personally and singly negotiate or talk with Mr. Hagey on this matter ... if you are going to pursue this matter any further with him ... there should always be one or two of your associates with you. I also feel that on your next meeting you should make a very forceful presentation of your position to Mr. Hagey, much more forceful than you have done on previous occasions. You should state not only what you are hoping for, but what you want, federation, an equal status with Waterloo College.[32]

Students from St. Jerome's College were the first to receive Bachelor of Arts degrees from the University of Waterloo in 1961. At UW's Third Convocation in May 1962 St. Jerome's students, shown here, process toward the stage at Seagram Stadium to receive their degrees. Among these graduands is Douglas Letson (far left), the first lay person to be dean and subsequently president of St. Jerome's.
UWA

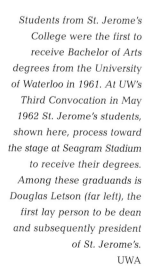

144

Siegfried had met with the board of the Associate Faculties even before the Lutheran Synod had approved their federation with Waterloo College. Had he pushed too hard, the whole university idea would have been jeopardized. His caution was prudent, but Ryan also had a point. There was more in common between the attitude of Bishop Ryan and the leaders of the Lutheran Synod than with either Hagey or Siegfried. Both Ryan and the Lutheran leaders sought to ensure the prominence of their own religious denominations within the new university, while Siegfried and Hagey were more concerned with the need for the development of a modern university in which religion would play an essential part but would not be predominant. Nevertheless, Hagey would continue to push for the role of Waterloo College as the Arts Faculty of the proposed non-denominational university and Siegfried would carefully bide his time.

Ryan's concerns echoed a refrain that would later be heard at the Lutheran Synod and they illustrate the emotion engendered by religious sentiments. He was most emphatic when he told Siegfried:

The future of Catholic education on a university status in this Diocese depends entirely on St. Jerome's. There is no other

The official opening of St. Jerome's and Notre Dame College (now Sweeney Hall) was an occasion for pomp and ceremony as Bishop Ryan, flanked by Fathers John Finn and Zachary Ralston, moves forward amidst the honour guard of the Fourth Degree Knights of Columbus.
SJC

145

Father Norman Choate at Convocation with Canadian author Margaret Atwood who received an honorary D. Litt. from the University of Waterloo in 1985.
UWA

hope for the future. [Possible arrangements with the Baptist-oriented McMaster had earlier been rebuffed on the issue of religion.] You are on the ground floor and whatever moves you make now are going to be the moves that either bring about or preclude the possibility of Catholic education on this higher level.[33]

And, Ryan warned, "I hope that no mistakes will be made in this matter."

Siegfried's position was not an enviable one. Much of what the bishop had said was undoubtedly true. Yet there were very few to whom he could turn for advice, and within his own religious community there were those who opposed his negotiations to situate St. Jerome's within a new and untried university. Others were jealous of Siegfried's leadership, while some merely feared the financial costs involved. Suspicions of the influence of the Lutheran Synod still remained much as they had in 1947.

In other ways the position of St. Jerome's was more positive than it had ever been. The postwar expansion and fund-raising had raised the profile of the college as separate from that of its high school department, while the continuing role of the high school ensured that a steady stream of graduates would be directed toward St. Jerome's College. Similarly, the active role in local Roman Catholic parishes of priests from the Congregation of the Resurrection who were faculty members at the college, including Father Siegfried, gave a prominence to St. Jerome's in the local community. The presence of "friends" of St. Jerome's as charter members of the board of the Associate Faculties perhaps made Siegfried rest more easily. Henry Krug had long supported the college. The patriarch of the Motz family, W.J. Motz, had not only graduated from St. Jerome's, he had also played an active role in college life. His son John was a charter member of the Associate Faculties' board and he had organized support for the St. Jerome's campaign in 1953 as well as at the ceremonial dinner attended by Bishop Ryan and Premier Frost.

Shortly after the January meeting with his bishop, Siegfried approached the Board of Governors of the Associate Faculties hoping to clarify St. Jerome's position in the proposed university. Siegfried sought to avoid a forced debate on the status of St. Jerome's relative to that of Waterloo College. Instead, he asked that provision be made in the original charter or act establishing the university for representation from St. Jerome's on the Senate and for the right of St. Jerome's to provide courses in harmony with its denominational beliefs as well as to offer religious worship and

UW President Dr. Douglas Wright, St. Jerome's President, Father Norman Choate, with Gerald Emmett Cardinal Carter, who received an honorary LL.D. and Chancellor J.P.R. Wadsworth at the 1989 Convocation. UWA

religious instruction for its own students. No one objected to these terms and they were unanimously accepted. So, too, was his final request, "that St. Jerome's will be consulted further in those matters that will affect its position in relation to the proposed university, before the Associate Faculties makes application for a degree granting charter."[34]

With the board's unanimous acceptance of these terms in hand, Siegfried asked Dr. C.F. Cannon, the director of education, for a meeting in Toronto, and for Cannon's advice "on some points in our long range plan for developing St. Jerome's College as a liberal arts college under denominational control."[35] Much like Gerald Hagey, Cornelius Siegfried was charting new territory and in 1957 the Ontario government was very much committed to the concept of developing Ontario's universities on the basis of existing colleges. The Waterloo proposal was exactly what they had in mind, and Cannon assured Siegfried of the government's support for St. Jerome's College.

Two years later, in 1959, Siegfried would thank Cannon for the "very personal interest" he had shown in St. Jerome's petition for university status, and in "our effort to obtain a favourable position in the University of Waterloo ... Thanks to the encouraging support we have received from men like you, the Minister and the Premier, we are now in a better position to do the job we would like to do."[36] The concurrence of St. Jerome's interests with those of the government of Ontario was a significant factor in the success of St. Jerome's College in its relationship with the university. In the future, it would be Waterloo College that would be at odds with the premier and his government. In the days of Leslie Frost, this was not an enviable position.

Amidst the breakneck pace of acquiring a new campus, developing a curriculum, and planning new buildings, a moment of respite occurred in December 1958 when the first building on the new campus of the Waterloo College Associate Faculties was opened by Premier Frost. More than any other, the premier was responsible for overseeing the growth of Ontario's universities. Seated with him at the head table were I.G. Needles, chairman of the Board of the Associate Faculties, J.G. Hagey, President, Waterloo College and Associate Faculties, Rev. D.J. Glebe, President, the Board of Governors, Waterloo College, Dr. G.E. Hall, President, the University of Western Ontario, and Rev. C.L. Siegfried, President,

St. Jerome's College. Siegfried was pleased when the Associate Faculties took advantage of the presence of the premier and so many other prominent university and community leaders to explain that the "three colleges"—Waterloo College, St. Jerome's College, and the Associate Faculties — were "working together in drafting a private bill to incorporate Waterloo College Associate Faculties as The University of Waterloo [and] preparing agreements, according to which the church-related colleges may become federated with the future University of Waterloo."

The private member's bill introduced by John Wintermeyer in March 1959 established the University of St. Jerome's College along with the University of Waterloo and Waterloo Lutheran University. A pleased Father Cornelius Siegfried wrote to the minister of education to acknowledge his support:

> We appreciate your insistence from the very beginning that St. Jerome's be given the opportunity to participate in the development of the University of Waterloo, and to benefit from the facilities established there. Your patient hearing of our point of view and your fair-minded approach will always be remembered ... Everyone at St. Jerome's is grateful to you for your support and

A Marjorie Barber photo of St. Jerome's in its early years on the UW campus.
UWA

guidance in our petition for university status in our own right, and in our negotiations for federated status in the University of Waterloo.[37]

Throughout 1958 and 1959 Siegfried and his colleagues had continued to negotiate the terms of an agreement by which St. Jerome's College would become an integral part of the proposed University of Waterloo. It was clear that Siegfried had been given considerable latitude. In the end, the clause in the act suggesting Waterloo College's "prior right to teach the students who go to the university proper" caused some hesitation, but even then the St. Jerome's Board of Governors conceded that, although Siegfried should contest this clause, if his protest would hold up proceedings, he should "drop it and submit our agreement for approval."[38]

On 23 January 1959 the Board of Governors of St. Jerome's College voted to purchase fifty-five acres of land in Waterloo, "somewhat to the north of the campus of Waterloo College and separated by Columbia Street." This would have given St. Jerome's College a large campus site, but in June the purchase was suspended when an agreement with the University of Waterloo provided land for the college on its 200-acre site. With this decision, St. Jerome's could again move forward, playing a leading role in the formation of the new university. These plans were never simple,

nor indeed would they prove to be in the future. Cornelius Siegfried must have felt thankful at what had been achieved and confident about the future of his college. It was not the Roman Catholic university that Bishop Ryan had in mind in 1937, but it was a Roman Catholic university very much in the spirit of its time. It would be ready to play its part in the ecumenism of the day, as the religious divisions of the past gave way to the challenges of university life in Ontario in the second half of the twentieth century.

In the end it was all worth while as students from the university quickly made St. Jerome's College part of university life and the college established itself as integral to the success of the new university.
UWA/NFB

CHAPTER EIGHT

A Waterloo Lutheran University

Had Gerry Hagey "had the Latin," had he attended one of Canada's major universities such as McGill, Toronto, or Queen's, his ideas about universities and their role in Canadian society might have been quite different. His university experience was Willison Hall. Its single building provided dormitory and classrooms, the college library and gymnasium, as well as administrative and faculty offices. Had his university experience been different, however, he might never have attempted the creation of a multi-faculty university based on a small denominational college in Waterloo. For certain, he would not have committed the university to so radical a scheme as the co-operative applied science program without seeking any academic advice. Just as likely, he would never have proposed juxtaposing two educational concepts with such different philosophies as those of Waterloo College, ultimately under the control of the Evangelical Lutheran Synod, and the Waterloo College Associate Faculties, governed entirely by a group of local business and professional leaders who had chosen to follow a new and radical approach to university education.

If Gerry Hagey did not have the Latin, he did have a strong belief in the Lutheran Church and its place in Canadian society. Unfortunately, there were no precedents in the Lutheran tradition for what he was about to do. There was not even anyone within the Lutheran community that he could easily turn to for advice. Nor did the oft-quoted examples of the experience of other denominational colleges or universities such as the Baptist Church's McMaster University in Hamilton or the evolution of the Roman Catholic Assumption College at Windsor offer useful precedents. What Hagey set out to do at Waterloo was different. In part, Hagey's commitment to outreach through his earlier contacts within the Lutheran community may also account for his ready acceptance of the system of co-operative education which would make Waterloo College Associate Faculties available to students who would not likely have been able to attend a traditional university program. Few Lutheran congregations were in Canada's larger cities and modern urban centres. In Ontario they were mostly in the rural communities or smaller towns with names such as Neustadt, Hanover, Walkerton, Chesley, Heidelberg, New Hamburg, and Hespeler. Most were in communities that were originally German-speaking, serving the artisans, labourers, and farm workers who had migrated from Germany to Ontario in the nineteenth century. Almost none of these people had a university background.

The lack of an educated professional class separated these Lutheran immigrants from many others who had arrived in Canada. For those who had descended from this tradition, the idea of an alternating work-study form of education would have a practical appeal, allowing them to combine their practical orientation with a university education. It also brought the cost of university education within their reach. Ironically, the very success of this program came to be seen as a threat to the singular importance of Waterloo College and the Evangelical Seminary within the Lutheran community, for the college and seminary had long been seen as a safeguard for the Lutheran tradition. For them, the

The Arts and Science (Administration) Building, seen here under construction in 1954, was to be the centrepiece in Hagey's plan to develop a new university from Waterloo College.
WLU

a.-Cash.	
German Synod.	
W. V. Uttley (Berlin)	$ 5.00
Waterloo	26.20
Normanby	1.00
Walkerton	1.00
Ladysmith	28.00
Sullivan	13.80
Conestogo	1.25
Preston (Ladies' A.)	58.62
L. Lipphardt (Waterloo)	5.00
Normanby	20.00
Tavistock	6.40
Brant	10.20
Pembroke	40.00
Waterloo	10.22
Berlin	10.12
Hanover	6.00
Wellesley	149.25
Wellesley	3.50
Hanover	2.00
Normanby	1.00
Tavistock	6.00
Heidelberg	57.90
Sullivan	13.06
Massey	10.00
Zurich	20.00

This list of donations to Waterloo College provides an interesting insight into the social and economic background of Ontario's Lutheran communities.
WLU

seminary took precedence over Waterloo College's conventional liberal arts program and they were suspicious of the initiative to create a new secular, science-oriented college.

While other Protestant denominations in Canada had debated the issues of Darwinian evolution and social reform, Lutheran congregations, even in Hagey's time, had been caught up in an internecine struggle over the use of German as the language of worship. The debate was about retaining the language of Martin Luther for a church that was not always comfortable with the modern age. The applied science program abruptly ended this isolation.

It is not likely that this was foreseen in 1955 when Hagey first approached the Evangelical Lutheran Synod about the possibility of a modest expansion of the facilities at Waterloo College. This was in a sense the mandate that he had been given as the first layman ever appointed as president of their college. Hagey was very much on his own within the Lutheran Church as he sought to develop a university program that would meet the needs of postwar Ontario, and at the same time retain the dominant influence of his church. As a president who was not an ordained minister, he was especially sensitive about his relationship with the Evangelical Lutheran Synod and concerned more than ever to establish and secure the position of the Lutheran Church in the development of the future university in Waterloo.

It is perhaps easy to understand that in 1955 his priorities relating to the rights and privileges of Waterloo College sought to limit the influence of the Roman Catholic St. Jerome's College, as well as to contain the possible growth of the non-denominational science college. The unexpected and extraordinary success of the co-operative applied science program, however, would upset this historically-conditioned vision of a small science college attached to Waterloo College.

The petition for affiliation of the Waterloo College Associate Faculties presented to the Evangelical Lutheran Synod in June 1956 described to them the desire to enlarge and strengthen "the work of Waterloo College in Science and related fields."[1] The Associate Faculties would become "an affiliated college with Waterloo College" and through it with the University of Western Ontario, "for the purpose of training and educating students in Pure and Applied Science and in all its branches, and in Business, Commerce, and other branches of learning" not competitive with those carried on and taught by Waterloo College.[2]

Although each would have an independent Board of Governors, the plan was to create a joint board, called the Board of Regents, "to serve in the over-all general interest of both colleges and any

PETITION FOR AFFILIATION

THE BOARD OF GOVERNORS OF WATERLOO COLLEGE ASSOCIATE
FACULTIES hereby petitions THE BOARD OF GOVERNORS OF THE EVAN-
GELICAL LUTHERAN SEMINARY OF CANADA, operating Waterloo College
of Arts at Waterloo, Ontario, for affiliation with WATERLOO
COLLEGE OF ARTS as a College of Science for the purpose of en-
larging and strengthening the work of Waterloo College in Science
and related fields.

In submitting this Petition, the Board of Governors of
Waterloo College Associate Faculties wishes to make it clear that
they are aware of the fact that, since 1925, Waterloo College has
been affiliated with the University of Western Ontario and has
provided opportunities to all students in Waterloo County and
surrounding areas to obtain a Liberal Arts education and has,
through this affiliation, qualified students as candidates for
degrees of Bachelor of Arts presented by the University of Western
Ontario, without having to leave the City of Waterloo. The entire
surrounding area, therefore, owes a debt of gratitude to Waterloo
College for the opportunities it has provided, but the Board of
Governors of Waterloo College Associate Faculties wishes to point
out that similar opportunities have not been available to students
seeking advanced education in scientific, professional, and business subjects and that further expansion along these lines is
desirable. The Twin Cities of Kitchener and Waterloo are, as we
all know, a growing community, and the enrolment in Waterloo
College has been rapidly increasing in the past few years and has
now reached nearly the capacity of the existing plant. It is

future affiliated faculties and colleges." With equal numbers appointed by both boards, the Board of Regents would "afford representation to municipalities and counties within the area to be served by the two colleges with due regard to the cultural, economic, ethnic and religious composition of the community being served." The failure to establish the Board of Regents would be sorely felt in 1960 when the larger interests of the community came into conflict with the competing interests of the Associate Faculties and the Lutheran Synod.

As president of Waterloo College Hagey would retain the dominant administrative leadership. With a series of interlocking committees to ensure the protection of the interests of Waterloo College, he would also be president of the Associate Faculties, while the dean of the college, Reverend Lloyd Schaus, would be its dean. As Hagey had explained to the Synod, the plan was for Waterloo College to continue all courses being offered, but to allocate its science courses to the Associate Faculties when appropriate equipment had been obtained and new faculty members hired. These new science offerings, Hagey predicted, would provide "a broader base of support for the College as a whole, and not just for the Associate Faculties." He had always hoped that many of Ontario's Lutherans who attended other universities because of the greater range of courses there might now choose to come to Waterloo College.

Looking to the future, Hagey explained, Waterloo College would have "an equal voice ... in the establishment of policies and programmes that affect the over-all development of educational facilities at Waterloo." In the application for affiliation, as drafted by Hagey and the college's own lawyers, the Associate Faculties suggested that in light of their likely ability to acquire provincial or other grants, that this would never "be used to the detriment of Waterloo College or the position of the Lutheran Church. On the contrary, wherever practical, it shall be used to improve academic standards and instructional facilities in Waterloo College."

Neither the seminary nor Waterloo College were eligible for the provincial grants which were deemed necessary for the development of the college into full university status. Admitting that it was perhaps unusual, Hagey explained that the creation of a future university would be the responsibility of the Associate Faculties, rather than that of the Evangelical Lutheran Seminary, the corporate body that had established Waterloo College. He also explained that the Associate Faculties would then change its name to "Waterloo University" and the president of Waterloo College would also become the president of Waterloo University.

An meeting of the Board of Governors (1953-1954) with President Hagey at the centre of the table. Reverend Albert Lotz is seated second from the right and next to him is Dr. Nils Willison.
WLU/Murray's Studio

The original purpose of preparing candidates for the seminary and for Christian lay leadership in other vocations, "as well as providing a Christian witness for the Lutheran Church in the field of higher education," would be enhanced within the new university, Hagey continued, hoping to assuage any lingering doubts. The relationship of Waterloo College to Waterloo University would be that of a federated college, similar to its relationship to Western, except that in the new university Waterloo College would also have "an equal voice in the management of all matters of an interlocking nature."

Therein lay the seeds of future discontent. What Hagey described may have appealed to the cautious conservatism of the Lutheran Synod, but the relationship that he described was hardly that of a federated college. And while the Associate Faculties may have been identified as the means of achieving provincial funding for the proposed university, in the minds of those attending the Synod, the university that they envisioned was very much a Lutheran university with Waterloo College at its centre.

Much of Hagey's effort over the next four years would be spent trying to create a university in which Waterloo College would emerge as equal in status with the Associate Faculties within the future Waterloo University. He would use the concepts of federation or affiliation to imply equality within a future university, not just in its founding but also in its operation as a university. The 1956 terms of affiliation outlined in considerable detail the working administrative arrangements between Waterloo College and the Associate Faculties, but they fell short in forecasting those changes that would be necessary when university status was actually achieved. And in 1960 this would be the source of unhappiness and discontent. Where changes occurred, charges of betrayal of the Lutheran interest were soon to follow.

Even before the Articles of Affiliation in 1956 had reached the floor of the Synod, the future relationship of St. Jerome's College to the newly-incorporated Associate Faculties had been considered by the Board of the Associate Faculties. At its first meeting on 25 April, 1956 they had agreed that their facilities would be available to St. Jerome's as well as to Waterloo College. From the point of view of St. Jerome's College, the terms of Waterloo College's affiliation agreement with the Associate Faculties were not an issue, for St. Jerome's anticipated "federation" with the future Waterloo University. This was also the understanding of W. J. Dunlop, the minister of education. From Hagey's point of view, however, it was better to ignore the commitment to St. Jerome's than to make an issue of it at the Synod. In June 1956, when the Lutheran Synod voted in favour of the Terms of Affiliation (101-21), the rector of St. Jerome's College, Father C. L. Siegfried, confidently announced the next day that "when the time comes ...we shall hope to become a part of the new university and to lend our full support and co-operation to its foundation."[3]

Waterloo College's restrictive campus site and the inability of the college to provide sufficient land for the new Science and Applied Science building to accommodate the programs of the Associate Faculties was the first serious indication as early as 1957 that the plan to establish a university with Waterloo College as its centre-piece might not unfold as the members of the Evangelical Lutheran Synod had expected. Although the Board of Governors of Waterloo College had initially planned to move their arts programs to the new campus, even then, Gerry Hagey's mind had been filled with memories of an earlier plan to move to a more spacious site. Then, too, the assurances from Lutheran Church leaders of additional funding to re-establish the college had not happened. What worried Hagey was the possible diminution of his college from a central position in the future university as well as the likelihood that the benefits of access to the university's facilities would be less tangible on separate campuses.

He reminded both boards in January 1958 that for as long as it was desirable to Waterloo College, "the latter would constitute the Arts Faculty of the University ... Now that there is the possibility that the two institutions may be located on different campus sites," he cautioned, "there is reason to review the intent of the Affiliation Agreement ... having in mind the purpose for which Waterloo College encouraged the organization of Waterloo College Associate

AGREEMENT FOR AFFILIATION

ARTICLES OF AGREEMENT made in duplicate the ${}$ *21st* ${}$ day

of June, 1956,

BETWEEN

   The Evangelical Lutheran Seminary of Canada,
   operating Waterloo College of Arts at Waterloo,
   Ontario, a body corporate with head office at
   the City of Waterloo, in the County of Waterloo,
   and the Province of Ontario, hereinafter called
   WATERLOO COLLEGE.

AND

   Waterloo College Associate Faculties, a body
   corporate with head office at the said City of
   Waterloo, hereinafter called WATERLOO COLLEGE
   ASSOCIATE FACULTIES.

Faculties."[4] Unspoken was the knowledge that the arts subjects required to complete the curricula for students registered in the science and engineering courses provided the income which he sought for Waterloo College. Without this support, the future of Waterloo College looked worse off than it had before the whole federation process had begun. For this reason alone, it was essential that Waterloo College continue to play a central role in the development of the new university. Similarly, without the presence of Waterloo College, the future of the Associate Faculties was also uncertain. For the moment, both sides were committed to remaining in tandem under Hagey's presidency.

 Hagey therefore sought reassurance for Waterloo College that the future University of Waterloo "will be one in which attention is given equally to all disciplines of education ... Care [also] needs to be exercised to prevent the possibility of the size of any one faculty being a factor that enables it to dominate the general academic policy-making body of the University." He specifically asked for assurance that relocation to the new campus would not affect the opportunity for the Arts Faculty (Waterloo College) "to have a voice equal to that of the Science Faculties in establishing the academic policies of the two institutions for the future university." He hoped that the Associate Faculties would also "state its willing-ness to continue the sharing of administrative costs." It was perhaps unusual for the president of one institution, the Associate Faculties, to plead the special case for another institution, Waterloo College,

Articles of Affiliation

of which he was also president. The idea of a conflict of interest seemed not to have entered Hagey's mind. Ironically, when such charges were made, they came first from Waterloo College, not from within the Associate Faculties.

Within two months of the purchase of the new campus in 1958, both Waterloo College and the Associate Faculties had decided to procure degree-granting status "at as early a date as possible." There were some at Waterloo College who had serious reservations about the future relationship with the Associate Faculties and about the possible termination of the college's long-standing affiliation with the University of Western Ontario, let alone their ability to offer independently of Western a complete arts program. Discussions about the implications of achieving university status had taken place in the Associate Faculties, in the Committee on Academic Studies at Waterloo College, as well as by the executive of the Waterloo College Faculty, the Seminary Faculty, and the Executive Committee of the Waterloo College Board. If university status were to be obtained, Waterloo College would need additional funds in order to expand library holdings as well as for new faculty appointments. So much would be required that it was doubtful if it could accomplished before 1962 and even that would be difficult.

Tension between the two institutions was heightened when the provincial budget for 1958 included a $1 million capital grant to the Associate Faculties — an amount equal to that given to Western, McMaster, and Queen's. No one at Waterloo College was prepared for this. Many were not pleased, for this was seen as an indication of the government's expectation that the Associate Faculties' request for university status would move forward quickly, creating new anxieties about the ability of the college to keep pace with the Associate Faculties and to offer a university arts program as well as to continue to meet the demands of the students registered in the co-operative program.

The extraordinary success of the co-operative education program resulted in an enrolment of 720 students in 1958, with a projected enrolment of 1,200 by 1960 and 2,100 by 1963. In June 1958, two hundred leading industrialists, scientists, engineers, banking and business executives as well as public officials had come to Waterloo from across Ontario and Quebec to attend an Industrial Conference and to discuss Waterloo's co-operative education program. Even Samuel Bronfman was there with a $250,000 pledge for the opening of Seagram Stadium, the Associate Faculties' first building. That the building had been donated to the Associate Faculties and not to Waterloo College was a foretaste of future resentments.

The creation of an Industrial Advisory Council of Canadian business leaders to advise the Associate Faculties in the continuing development of its engineering program had ensured the Associate Faculties' success by providing important economic and political support for the co-operative education program in the face of criticism from other Ontario universities. It would be impossible to turn back. By 1960 more than 250 companies were employing co-op students and another 350 companies had either expressed an interest in taking Waterloo's students or were making the necessary arrangements to do so as soon as students became available. This growth in student numbers and the surge of new buildings for the Associate Faculties which had overtaken campus life seemed all the more likely to be an enduring feature of the university experience at Waterloo.

Engineering students brought their own sense of camaraderie and enthusiasm to both campuses. It had been this way from the very first days. Joan Dufault, recalled that after her husband, George, had spent the weekdays visiting industries in the province, seeking to enlist them in the co-op plan or speaking to students in high schools, when he returned home on Friday evenings or Saturday mornings, there would be a queue of "hopeful applicants" waiting to question him on the possibility of being accepted. "This would be done in our living room of a rented house on Margaret Avenue ... They all were pretty well parked out front on a permanent basis. I would take a sandwich...into the living room, so that the maximum number of interviews could be fitted in."[5] The presence of these students everywhere on campus provided a sense of reality to the often abstruse constitutional issues that seemed to preoccupy President Hagey throughout much of 1958.

Rumours about the impressive level of financial support for the Associate Faculties had circulated throughout Waterloo College, and once again concerns were expressed about the future position

The creation of an Industrial Advisory Council in 1958 marked a turning point in the fortunes of the Associate Faculties. Some of the participants are shown here: A.S. Barber, director of co-ordination (far right), Gordon Henderson, a Sarnia industrialist who would serve on the Advisory Council and later the Board of Governors; Joseph McCulley, the warden of Hart House, University of Toronto; R.G. Stanton, chairman of Mathematics; and T.L. Batke, chairman of Chemical Engineering. Batke's high-level research in industry had served him well, while Stanton's soon-to-be published text on numerical analysis would transform the engineering curriculum at Waterloo. UWA

"Waterloo, being in the stage of developing a new university is in a preferred position to establish a co-operative course," said President Hagey.
UWA

Student guides mingled with some of Canada's leading industrialists who toured the Waterloo Campus.
UWA

of Waterloo College in the proposed university. Would Waterloo College simply be a denominational college located on a separate campus or would it remain, as Hagey had hoped, the Arts Faculty of the new university? These concerns were not unjustified, for in the organization of the other Canadian universities, the university itself reserved the rights and privileges necessary for the integrity of all of the faculties within the institution.

Hagey had come to understand this and especially the nuances relating to the position of federated or affiliated colleges within Ontario's universities. He believed that with care he could still ensure a position of equality for Waterloo College. As the university idea evolved, however, he became concerned about another issue which would have a profound impact on the future development of the University of Waterloo. This was whether a non-denominational university could grant degrees in divinity for the candidates from the Evangelical Lutheran Seminary.

George Gilmour, the president of McMaster University, had suggested "that there is a question mark on the part of the Government as to whether or not a non-denominational university has the authority to grant degrees in theology."[6] Hagey had always understood that the degrees from Western given to the graduates of the Lutheran Seminary had come by virtue of the authority of the original charter of Huron College at Western. Because of this, and the possibility that the Lutheran Seminary might extend its post graduate studies, Hagey began seriously to consider a more radical proposal — "the possibility of Waterloo College applying for a degree-granting charter."[7] This would also answer his long-standing desire to find a way to ensure the predominance of Waterloo College in the Arts Faculty of the future university.

In a memorandum to J.H. Smyth, the lawyer retained by the

college and seminary, and ironically also by the Associate Faculties to draft the University Act, Hagey proposed that:

> In order to follow through on the intent of the original [1956] agreement between Waterloo College and the Associate Faculties, it would appear in order for Waterloo College to enter into an agreement with the Associate Faculties, and subsequently the Board of Governors of the University, whereby Waterloo College is approved as the university arts faculty.

Of course these ideas were not subject to public discussion. They were confidential directives to Smyth and they had never been debated in the Associate Faculties and certainly not mentioned to Father Siegfried, of St. Jerome's College. These agreements between Waterloo College and the university, Hagey explained to Smyth, "would be purely agreements rather than affiliation or federation arrangements," and they did not preclude other arts colleges being federated or affiliated with the university or the university establishing its own "Arts College if there is a need for such."

From Hagey's perspective, these two conditions relating to the Evangelical Lutheran Seminary and to Waterloo College's role in the arts program "were basic and would require mutual agreements before even the drafting of a bill is undertaken." Much would happen after this first memorandum of 20 March 1958 and the implementation of the University of Waterloo Act one year later on 3 March 1959. Still, in Hagey's mind, the general parameters seemed clear; trust and goodwill, however, would soon be in short supply.

Some of these problems lay properly at the feet of Hagey himself. For example, in an attempt to limit the status of St. Jerome's College within the proposed university, he suggested to Smyth that in drafting the legislation, "It seems to me that we might not use the word 'federated' but simply use 'affiliated' for any college associated with us. This follows Western's pattern." And he noted, "I think that if Waterloo is not a federated college, St. Jerome's would have no objection to being an affiliated college."

Waterloo College Associate Faculties published a series of "personal reports" to explain the development of their university idea. The Industrial Conference was "very probably...a milestone in the history of higher education."
UWA

Hagey clearly intended to provide Waterloo College with a favoured position over St. Jerome's, for as he explained to Smyth,

> I am assuming that a special arrangement would be drawn up between Waterloo College and Waterloo College Associate Faculties ... This agreement would be to the effect that, in the establishment of a university, Waterloo College, or any corporate body succeeding it, would become the Arts Faculty of the University ... [Waterloo College] conducts the Arts courses for the university and the heads of its Arts departments would be the heads or chairmen of the Arts departments for the University ... [and] this agreement continues and is incorporated in the University Bill.

Hagey persisted in seeking to acquire separate university status for Waterloo College even after discovering that his previous information regarding Western's reliance on the Huron College charter to grant degrees in divinity was incorrect. He confided to Smyth that "I am hopeful that we may use this question as a means through which Waterloo College may procure a degree-granting charter."

In Smyth's draft bill for Waterloo College, Hagey suggested changing the corporate name from "Waterloo College" to "Luther College — If the name under which its Board is incorporated were 'Luther College,'" he said, "the Arts Faculty operated by Luther College could commonly be known as 'University College.'" Hagey's persistence in these matters was undoubtedly an indication of his desire to retain the Lutheran identity of his college and still have it remain the Arts Faculty of the university. In light of the subsequent criticisms of him from within his church, these proposals to Smyth are ironic and the criticisms of Hagey were fundamentally unfair.

By the time the discussion of the proposed university reached the Lutheran Synod in June 1958, Edward Hall's critique of President Hagey and the applied science program of the Associate Faculties had been the subject of considerable debate within the Lutheran community. Hagey's intentions and his concern for the Lutheran college had been called into question and a special committee of Lutheran pastors had begun meeting with Edward Hall and other senior administrators at Western.

In the midst of these tribulations, on 29 May Hagey wrote to Albert Lotz, the chairman of the Board of Governors of the Evangelical Seminary of Canada, to dissuade him and his board from separating Waterloo College from the Associate Faculties.[8] The previous meeting of the Board of Governors of Waterloo College

Taken in 1958 by E.M. Brookes, the superintendent of buildings and grounds, these photos are some of the earliest images of the new campus. President Hagey's plans for a university charter were set in the midst of a campus that was totally undeveloped. In later years, Hagey would concede that if they had known all that was involved in establishing a university they might never have had the courage to go ahead.
UWA/E.M. Brookes

had approved a motion to the effect that Waterloo College should seek a degree-granting charter as soon as possible, on the understanding that "in doing so the affiliation with Western would be continued." From Hagey's point of view, the pernicious influence of Edward Hall was evident, as was the threat that this action posed to the future of the Associate Faculties and the creation of a University of Waterloo.

Hagey was alarmed. This action could endanger the whole university project. He made no attempt to hide his concerns from Lotz with whom he had developed a good personal relationship:

> I feel a personal obligation in helping to fulfil the objective of the establishment of the Associate Faculties. This objective was made clear to the Board and to Synod — namely, that of bringing to Waterloo a university in which the church college relationship would be similar to the church colleges in the federation of the University of Toronto. Deterioration of relationships with Western is regrettable. This, however, does not justify a deviation from the planned programme at Waterloo. Dr. Hall's opposition to the co-operative course was understood previous to the acceptance of the affiliation of the Associate Faculties. It was not understood at that time that he would endeavour to use the power of the University to prevent the continuing development of the co-operative course. Our actions which have annoyed Dr. Hall can hardly be accepted as justification for him to endeavour

to prevent the development of the engineering course as it is established.

Any move to separate Waterloo College and the Associate Faculties could easily be interpreted as an effort to make the continuing development of the co-operative course more difficult.

Ironically, Hagey was then given the responsibility of enacting the Synod's June recommendation "to the effect that both the College and the Seminary should be incorporated with degree-granting authority."

The purpose of revising the University Act was ostensibly to give the seminary the power to grant divinity degrees, although there was much more to it than that. In 1958 St. Michael's College at the University of Toronto had revised its Act of Incorporation and changed its name to the University of St. Michael's College. Hagey was elated on learning this. With this precedent in hand, perhaps Waterloo College could legally acquire a status equal to the Associate Faculties in the new university. It would no longer be the Associate Faculties alone that would be achieving university status. If the procedure used by St. Michael's were to be applied at Waterloo, his concerns would be over. He immediately wrote to Smyth suggesting revisions to the draft legislation creating the University of Waterloo. The name of the seminary would be amended to Waterloo Lutheran University and it could then be a separate denominational university, "federated" with the University of Waterloo.[9]

The draft agreement in 1958 reflected the changes that had come about as a result of the crises with Edward Hall and the University of Western Ontario. The decision to seek university status for the Waterloo Lutheran Seminary, however, also directly affected the status to be accorded to St. Jerome's College within the proposed university. The St. Jerome's agreement with the Associate Faculties, Hagey explained to Smyth, "will be in a similar form"[10] to that of Waterloo College. Hagey's desire to elevate the status of Waterloo College to a position of equality with that of the University of Waterloo had profoundly changed the shape of the university-to-be and in this process had elevated St. Jerome's College to university status, something that Bishop Ryan had long wanted, but which had always eluded him.

By November 1958 the general outline was clear.[11] The Evangelical Lutheran Seminary, the corporate body operating Waterloo College, would seek degree-granting powers under the name of the Waterloo Lutheran University. Waterloo College, which it operated, would change its name to Waterloo University College and would "federate" with the University of Waterloo. Similarly, St. Jerome's College would become the University of St. Jerome's College, with identical rights and prerogatives, and it, too, would federate with the university.

In this draft document, Waterloo University College sought the right to appoint the university department chairmen for the courses taught in the college as well as the prior right to give instruction in the arts subjects that are part of the university's professional courses. The university was to agree not to duplicate instruction in arts courses offered by its federated colleges without an elaborate protocol to protect the colleges. Duplication of courses would only occur if mutually agreed to by the Boards of Governors of the federated colleges in addition to the University Senate and its Board of Governors.

As a final safeguard, Hagey asked Smyth to add the restriction that the agreements between Waterloo University College and the proposed University of Waterloo "shall be interpreted in light of the affiliation agreements between W.C. and W.C.A.F. dated June 21, 1956." With this in hand, Hagey thought that he could rest easy, although his legal counsel doubted that, in law, the affiliation agreement of 1956 could actually take precedence over the new agreement. As time would tell, the affiliation agreements of 1956 would come to haunt Gerry Hagey, but in 1960 he would be president of the University of Waterloo and many other circumstances would have changed.

There is something almost tragic in Hagey's attempts to balance so many conflicting interests, while also attempting to serve as president of both the Associate Faculties and Waterloo College. Criticisms of his efforts came from all directions and often in a manner to which he could never reply.

It is ironic that one of the most cogent criticisms of Hagey's plans for the development of the University of Waterloo came not from his traditional critics, but from the Executive Committee of the Associate Faculties. At its meeting of 6 November 1958 the Executive Committee for the first time saw the proposed charter of their university. Reminiscent of a previous challenge to Hagey from his Academic Advisory Committee, they asked, "through him" to convey their concerns "to the Board of Governors of the Associate Faculties."[12] Their main point of difference was their suggestion that, contrary to Hagey's proposal, at some time in the future it was quite likely that a non-denominational Faculty of Arts would be established by the university. They also took exception to Waterloo College's use of the name Waterloo University College which they said in Canadian usage "normally refers to the university's non-denominational Faculty of Arts." The committee was frank and even confrontational. In their opinion, "Waterloo College will not be the University College of the University of Waterloo, but rather will be a Lutheran College of Arts federated with the University."

The Executive Committee conceded that perhaps in the beginning Waterloo College would provide the arts instruction, and to function properly, department chairmen are required, but "the University, however, should have ultimate control over its Department Chairmen in anticipation of a non-denominational Arts faculty." Similarly, they thought that a future university could not be restricted to having all of the arts subjects in its professional program taught by another institution. "The University," they argued, "is responsible for the subjects taught to its students and therefore must have control over these subjects."

Battle lines were quickly drawn. The reactions were derived from very different conceptions of the university and of the role of its colleges. In this respect, the committee was adamantly opposed to the desire to bind the future university to the original 1956 federation agreement, which was for a very different situation and a very different kind of university. Instead of accepting the entire agreement, as Hagey had wanted, the committee suggested that "if there are clauses in the previous agreement which are relevant to the new situation, they should be stated explicitly in the new agreement." Their memorandum to the Board of Governors of the Associate Faculties was a fundamental challenge to Hagey's and the Lutheran Synod's vision of the place of Waterloo College in the future University of Waterloo.

As the university developed it was inevitable that debates arose about the curriculum, about how students would learn, and who would be responsible for teaching them.
KWR

President Hagey tried to explain to them that their letter to the board was based on a "misunderstanding," although, he said, "I appreciate the misunderstandings being brought to my attention."[13] Once again Hagey was on the defensive, and much was left unsaid as he attempted to explain the various clauses in the draft of the University Act. "The name 'Waterloo University College,'" he explained, "was primarily selected because it identifies the college as having university status in its own right. This was considered to be a protective measure for the College should it at any time desire to operate independently of another university." He admitted that this name did "present the possibility of the College becoming known as 'University College,'" but he said, "in this case [it] could represent the building housing the oldest Arts faculty on the campus." While it could be interpreted in this way, this was certainly not what Hagey had earlier intended when he suggested the name to J.H. Smyth.

Hagey sought to sidestep the issue of Waterloo College assuming the position of the Arts Faculty, suggesting first that department heads were appointed by governing boards, not by the university Senate, and, "therefore, [it] becomes logical for the University arts faculty department chairmen to be appointed by the governing board of Waterloo College." He denied that a non-denominational Arts Faculty would necessarily be established, and "Consequently, it seems illogical to legislate for the future until the future development is known."

In the end, Hagey resorted to quoting the 1956 Affiliation Agreement made between Waterloo College and the Associate Faculties, to the effect that "the Arts subjects are to be offered by Waterloo College instructors until such time as Waterloo College wishes to release subjects for instruction, either by the Associate Faculties or the future university." Waterloo College was not only in a preferred position, but that preferred position was central to Hagey's conception of the University of Waterloo.

Shortly after sending his reply to the Executive Committee of the Associate Faculties, with a profound sense of pride and achievement, Hagey rose in the Senate at the University of Western Ontario on 12 December 1958 to announce the plans by which the Associate Faculties would petition the Ontario Legislature in its next session to establish the University of Waterloo. He had clearly won in his struggle with Edward Hall and the University of Western Ontario.

So simple it seemed in theory. So complicated it would become in practice. Hagey had fought off the criticisms of Edward Hall and held fast to his belief in Waterloo's innovative co-operative engineering program. He had brought St. Jerome's College into the university, and the university was in Waterloo, based on the primacy of Waterloo College, not one in Kitchener in which he would have been an outsider.

CHAPTER NINE

The University of Waterloo

The new year of 1959 had begun with a tremendous sense of optimism for the University of Waterloo. The opening of the first building on the new campus in December 1958 had gone splendidly and the campus plans for the future were impressive. A $15 million expansion program had recently been approved, and in less than six years nineteen buildings were scheduled to be on a campus that was still only a dream, albeit one that was rapidly acquiring a reality in concrete, brick, and glass. The excitement was palpable; one could sense it everywhere.

Capital funding from the province had placed Waterloo on a par with Ontario's major universities, an accomplishment of singular triumph for Hagey and his colleagues who, only months earlier, had been threatened with stern disapproval from these same universities. A major fund-raising campaign with a goal of $2 million had recently been launched by some of Canada's leading industrialists and they were confident that it would succeed. Student enrolment had grown beyond every forecast and the acceptance of the co-operative program in applied science by industries in Ontario and beyond had surpassed everyone's most optimistic predictions. Now that Ira Needles's tenure at B.F. Goodrich was coming to a close — he had retired as president but would remain as chairman of the board until 1960 — he was spending more of his time in contact with his colleagues in government and industry, encouraging the development of the University of Waterloo.

Premier Leslie Frost officially opened the Associate Faculties' first building on 3 December 1958.
KWR

On 12 February 1959 John Wintermeyer moved the first reading in the Legislative Assembly of the bill to create the University of Waterloo. Second reading was on 20 February and on 3 March with unanimous approval, the act creating the University of Waterloo was passed into law. On Wintermeyer's motion two other universities, separate from but clearly integral to the University of Waterloo, were also incorporated that day. The acts establishing the University of St. Jerome's College and Waterloo Lutheran University had also been given third reading. It was understood that the two denominational universities had been accorded this status in anticipation of their intention to suspend their degree-granting rights, except in theology, and enter into federation agreements with the University of Waterloo where they would be "founding colleges." So much was this so that the proposed terms of their federation were appended as schedules A and B to the University of Waterloo Act.

The very idea of establishing a new university, however, soon gave rise to conflicting passions and aspirations. The name Waterloo Lutheran University signified a goal previously suggested by Edward Hall, the president of the University of Western Ontario. Hall's critique of Hagey and the Associate Faculties led the way to the breakdown of relations between Waterloo College and the Associate Faculties even before the university had begun to take root. Furthermore, Hall's personal criticisms of Hagey and his rejection of the academic respectability of the co-operative applied sciences program had resulted in a precipitous haste on the part of both institutions to acquire university status prematurely. Hall's interventions had instilled a fundamental distrust between Waterloo College and the Associate Faculties when he suggested that the

college should reject federation and seek independent status. His open criticism of Hagey and his advocacy of an independent status for Waterloo College encouraged some Lutheran faculty members from Waterloo College to go into the rural Lutheran congregations seeking justification for their desire to create an independent Lutheran university. Western's president had provided an element of legitimacy to their point of view when many of these same individuals spoke out against federation.

There had always been a vocal minority of Lutheran faculty members who distrusted any federation proposal, regardless of its terms. They preferred an independent Lutheran university. This group of Lutheran faculty members, G.F. Durst, A.B. Little, J.F. Little, Herman Overgaard, and R. C. Teigen had made this clear in a letter published in the *Canadian Lutheran* in May 1959. The proposed federation, they predicted, "might well lead to the Lutheran Church losing control of its college just as the Baptist Church lost control of McMaster University." It would be preferable, they suggested, to continue the relationship with the University of Western Ontario, or for Waterloo University College to become an independent university and to exercise its own degree granting powers:

> It is imperative that our Church retain complete control of Waterloo College because it is the only senior liberal arts college with university status in Canada operated by the Lutheran Church. This fact is doubly important in view of the anticipated merging of several Lutheran bodies in Canada.

Their primary concern was the future of the Lutheran Church. Although their article was written before the terms of federation had been discussed, indeed before the federation committee had even begun to meet, there would be little that anyone could do over the next months to answer so emotional an issue.

A major turning point in the relations between the two institutions occurred in April 1959 when the college decided to separate its administration from that of the University of Waterloo and to appoint its own president.[1] With this decision, the tightly interwoven structure established in the 1956 Articles of Affiliation began to unravel. The unique, symbiotic relationship between Waterloo College and the University of Waterloo so painstakingly set in place at the Evangelical Lutheran Synod had been breached. Gerry Hagey, for one, quickly realized that this was the first break with the terms of the 1956 affiliation agreement which "had presented the possibility of a continuance of the dual operation after University status is achieved."

With separate administrations, Hagey admitted for the first time that there may also be separate interests represented by the two institutions. Some of these may have been personal, but others most certainly were not. So much of what Hagey had done was based on the premise that Waterloo College and the University of Waterloo were one and the same and the separation of their administrations had come as an unwanted and emotional issue for him. Many of the contentious issues in the federation debate stemmed from Hagey's original conception of the role of Waterloo College in the university. Now he would leave his college behind and assume the presidency of the University of Waterloo.

The need for a separate administration was perhaps inevitable, but the full ramifications of it were not clearly understood. With

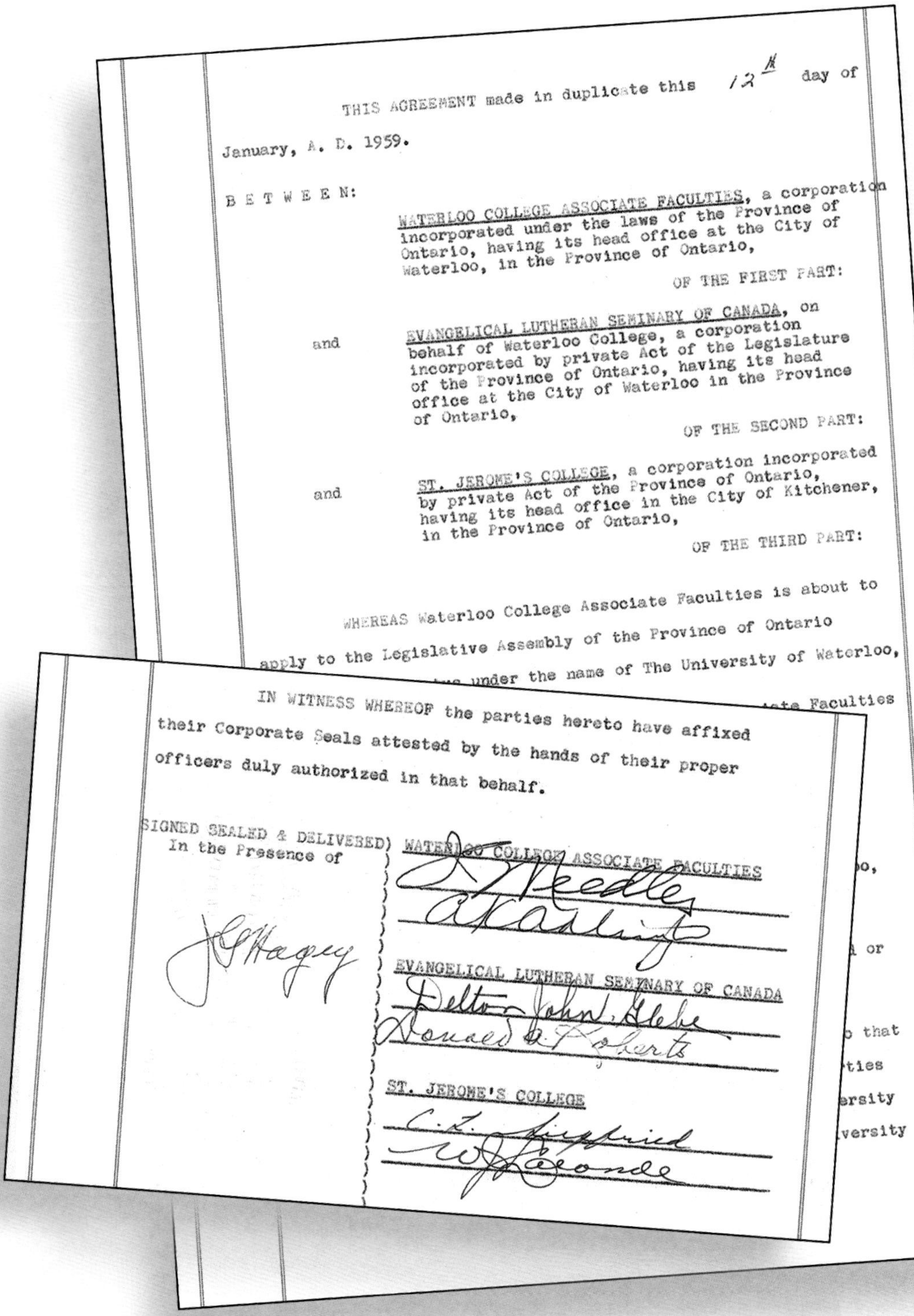

THIS AGREEMENT made in duplicate this 12th day of
January, A. D. 1959.

BETWEEN:

WATERLOO COLLEGE ASSOCIATE FACULTIES, a corporation
incorporated under the laws of the Province of
Ontario, having its head office at the City of
Waterloo, in the Province of Ontario,

OF THE FIRST PART:

and

EVANGELICAL LUTHERAN SEMINARY OF CANADA, on
behalf of Waterloo College, a corporation
incorporated by private Act of the Legislature
of the Province of Ontario, having its head
office at the City of Waterloo in the Province
of Ontario,

OF THE SECOND PART:

and

ST. JEROME'S COLLEGE, a corporation incorporated
by private Act of the Province of Ontario,
having its head office in the City of Kitchener,
in the Province of Ontario,

OF THE THIRD PART:

WHEREAS Waterloo College Associate Faculties is about to
apply to the Legislative Assembly of the Province of Ontario
—————— under the name of The University of Waterloo,

IN WITNESS WHEREOF the parties hereto have affixed
their Corporate Seals attested by the hands of their proper
officers duly authorized in that behalf.

SIGNED SEALED & DELIVERED)   WATERLOO COLLEGE ASSOCIATE FACULTIES
    In the Presence of

 J. G. Hagey

                               EVANGELICAL LUTHERAN SEMINARY OF CANADA

                               ST. JEROME'S COLLEGE

this bifurcated division, could Waterloo College expect that its dean would still serve as the dean of arts for the university? So long as President Hagey had also remained as president of Waterloo College the joint administrative arrangements of 1956 had perhaps seemed reasonable. Now they were not. The unseemly haste by which Hagey's presidency at Waterloo College had ended also left a bitter aftertaste. This was all the more so when the new president recruited to replace him, Dr. Herbert M. Axford, had been suggested by those faculty members in the college who had been the most outspoken in their criticism of Hagey and the Associate Faculties.[2]

The anti-Hagey faction had a natural sympathizer in Herbert Axford, who was dubious about federation and inclined to go in his own direction — wherever it would lead. The timing of Axford's appointment, the well-known hostility of his supporters towards Hagey and the Associate Faculties, and Axford's own lack of administrative experience seemed to be a disaster waiting to happen. Those who predicted it were not far wrong.

In April 1959, as president of the University of Waterloo, Hagey prepared his first report for the university's Board of Governors. The relationship between the university and Waterloo University College loomed large in his mind as he explained to the board that the terms of federation appended to the University Act were "only general terms" and that a federation committee would be established to "consider and recommend for Board approval the specific terms for federation." Now that the two institutions were separate, "it is important that the University maintain a centralized control over the academic affairs of the total university."[3]

The acting dean of science of the University of Waterloo, Bruce Kelley, was one of the first to show signs of frustration about the attitude of Waterloo College. He complained to Hagey in May of 1959 that "the Deans of Engineering and Science and all members of their faculties are perturbed by certain items which appear in the most recent Calendar of the Faculty of Arts, issued by Waterloo University College." It had described itself as the Faculty of Arts "when it was only the Faculty of Arts of Waterloo University College — not that of the University of Waterloo."[4]

Kelley also disliked the misleading references to the Associate Faculties becoming "in the future" the Faculties of Engineering and Science, "when it was known ... that the Associate Faculties had already become the University of Waterloo and not just two other faculties, apparently in a subservient position to the Faculty of Arts."

This complaint revealed more than a sense of unease. Kelley explained that the use of the name "Waterloo University" rather than the "University of Waterloo" was misleading, creating the

As dean of Waterloo College since Hagey had been president, Lloyd Schaus had been part of the major decisions that had shaped Waterloo College and the Associate Faculties. By 1959, however, he had begun to worry about the best interests of his college and possibly his own career. An ordained Lutheran minister and lecturer in Religious Knowledge, Schaus was a strong advocate of the primary position of Waterloo College as the Arts Faculty of the future university.
WLU

impression that Waterloo University College had a position beyond that to which it was entitled. He was quite emphatic about this last point. "We cannot help but feel that again there is a deliberate misrepresentation to give the impression that Waterloo University College occupies a position which, in fact, it does not so do ... We feel we must go on record to assert that we are aware of the advantage being taken of our known desire to achieve the best possible University." And, Kelley concluded, "we somehow dislike being 'put upon'."

As dean of Waterloo University College, the Reverend Lloyd Schaus was nothing if not tenacious. His primary interest was to ensure the position of his college within the university and his sense of this differed from many in the former Associate Faculties. Schaus considered Waterloo University College to be the arts college of the University of Waterloo, and as such, it would "serve the Liberal arts requirements of all other courses at the University." He had always seen Waterloo College and the Associate Faculties as equal partners and the terms of Schedule A appended to the University of Waterloo Act seemed to affirm a central position for Waterloo College.[5]

St. Jerome's College was also a federated college in legal and juridical terms, but in the metamorphosis of the Associate Faculties into the University of Waterloo Dean Schaus did not regard St. Jerome's as having equality with Waterloo College. The agreement of 12 January 1959, between the Evangelical Lutheran Seminary and Waterloo College Associate Faculties, appended to the University Act, had affirmed the "prior rights" of Waterloo College. Schaus's point of view was a natural outgrowth of the historical precedents as agreed to by President Hagey and Ira Needles when they had signed the schedules as part of the University of Waterloo legislation.

The singular role of Waterloo College as the Arts Faculty of the University of Waterloo, however, was not as clearly defined as Schaus would have liked.[6] Waterloo University College did have "the right to appoint the chairmen for all courses taught in the College," and unless mutually agreed, "these would also be the chairmen for the University." With regard to its position as the Faculty of Arts, the meaning was ambiguous. Waterloo College merely retained the prior right to give the instruction in the arts, humanities, and social sciences for courses which were part of the university's professional courses. For its part, the university had agreed not to duplicate instruction in arts, humanities, and social sciences, unless the Boards of Governors of both of the federated colleges agreed to such duplication, or if the colleges were unable to meet the university's requirements. These two clauses were to become the centre of a new debate.

ANALOGUE COMPUTER
SOLUTION
OF
EARTH SATELLITE
ORBITS

Hagey's original desire to see Waterloo College as central to the University of Waterloo had contributed to the complications he now faced. Negotiated under entirely different circumstances, these terms had stipulated that "it is to be clearly understood that the Board of Waterloo College shall at all times in the future have an equal voice ... in the establishment of policies and programmes that affect the overall development of higher educational facilities at Waterloo."

In 1956 Hagey had gone even further in assuaging the Synod's concerns about becoming part of a larger university, suggesting that any advantages resulting from provincial and other sources of revenue "shall not be used to the detriment of Waterloo College or of the position of the Lutheran Church ... [and] wherever practical, ... shall be used to improve [the] academic standards and instructional facilities in Waterloo College as well as those under the control of the Associate Faculties." In light of these "understandings," it is not surprising that Waterloo University College developed a strong sense of its unique position within the new university. It would also be hard to imagine any two clauses that would be more limiting for the future University of Waterloo.

The leaders of Waterloo University College did not see themselves merely as a federated college within the University of

Physics professor Ian Dagg with an early analog computer that would soon re-shape Waterloo's curriculum in science, engineering and mathematics.
KWR

Waterloo. It was a point of view grounded in their history, in their sense of the college's importance within the Lutheran community. Anything that would alter this status within the University of Waterloo was completely unacceptable.

Not everyone at Waterloo College shared this view. One who did not was Ralph Stanton, chairman of the Department of Mathematics, who had arrived at Waterloo College from the University of Toronto in the confident expectation of being part of a new university beyond Waterloo College. By October 1959 Stanton had presented President Hagey with detailed plans for the foundation of a "University Faculty of Arts," arguing that "in view of the increasingly unsatisfactory service provided [by Waterloo College] in the Arts Electives," it would be prudent "to prepare a rough estimate of the requirements for an Arts Programme":

> The need for a University Arts Faculty is so great, and our uniqueness among Canadian Universities in possessing no non-denomination Arts Faculty is so striking, that I am sure that all of us in the Chemistry, Physics and Engineering Buildings, would be willing to squeeze up temporarily so as to provide both teaching space and office quarters for University people in the Humanities and Social Sciences.[7]

As a mathematician, Stanton had calculated the revenue paid by the university to Waterloo College for instruction for courses in the humanities and the social sciences and the likely enrolment of other students who would choose the University of Waterloo. "Provided we can have our Arts Faculty ready by December [1959]," Stanton

Provincial funding, the sine qua non of university expansion in Ontario, resulted in the creation of Ontario's University Affairs Advisory Committee which visited the University of Waterloo in July 1961. (Left to right) Senator T. D'Arcy Leonard, R.W. Mitchell, Chief Justice Dana Porter, Education Minister John Robarts, and Floyd S. Chalmers.
KWR

suggested, "there should be no difficulty in obtaining a minimum of 80 students for First Year Arts."

> This would in no way injure Waterloo College, since we would expect to draw students who prefer a non-denominational institution, and who are desirous of the high standards which we would demand ... Naturally, with the present delicate situation, this memorandum cannot be discussed even informally with more than a handful of people and the only copies are held by yourself, Mr. Adlington, Dr. Batke, Dr. Cowan, Dr. Wright and myself.

The rapid expansion of the engineering program resulted in a new urgency for a decision about the possibility of Waterloo College being able to meet the university's needs. In November 1959, a planning meeting attended by Bruce Kelley, A.P. Gordon, the university's new registrar, and the ubiquitous Ralph Stanton, predicted that by the fall of 1960 some 280 students would be "wishing to take new electives. By January 1 the number will have increased to 369." The university was committed to offering a range of courses from Year I to Year IV and, "it would be highly irregular for another institution, Waterloo University College, to be entirely responsible for so major a university program."

By mid-November of 1959 Stanton had also addressed his concerns directly to Bruce Kelley, whom he regarded not only as dean of science, but also as a de facto if not de jure dean of arts.[9] In the meantime, the protracted negotiations with Waterloo University College over the federation agreement had led Hagey to explain to a joint Science and Engineering Council meeting on 11 November that "it was the hope of the Board [of Governors] that the University would not be forced to create a Faculty of Arts solely because of a failure to federate on the part of Waterloo College." Stanton agreed that this was "a very reasonable point of view ... shared by most people." Still, he argued, "whereas all persons are desirous of seeing a proper federation built up, it would be a valuable *complement* to federation if the University were to create its own Faculty of Arts at the same time."

> [This] would put us on the Toronto model, and would have great virtue for our future development ... Such a move would actually tend to allay certain fears on the part of the Lutheran Church if it were suitably presented, since if there were a University Faculty of Arts, which were non-denominational, then there would be no need nor danger of any persons pressing for the secularization of the Lutheran-related College.

The reality of university status had imposed its own imperatives on Waterloo's university community. Circumstances had altered previous arrangements, and Stanton's own department, Mathematics, already transferred to the University of Waterloo, he said, would be served best by being within a non-denominational Faculty of Arts:

> There is also the additional point that Waterloo College is both unwilling, and probably unable financially, to provide an Arts group of stature and strength which the University needs. Their faculty is appropriate for an affiliated college within a larger university, but is not even adequate to properly give the Arts elective programmes which we are giving at the present time ... A University Faculty of Arts would allow us to build up a strong group which could complement the work of the Federated Colleges ... The function of the University Faculty of Arts is not to compete with the Federated Colleges but to complete the work which the Federated Colleges do up to a certain extent.

Stanton's views had some merit, but they created even more uneasiness on a campus that was already badly divided. President Hagey had become alarmed at the spate of rumours surrounding the future relationship between Waterloo College and the university. As an indication of his pent-up frustration he issued a directive urging that, "At this stage in the discussion of federation agreements, it would appear to be desirable for statements of opinion to be recorded. This will prevent the possibility of them being misunderstood, misinterpreted, [or] misquoted." If Hagey's frustration was beginning to show, it was for good reason.

The official induction of Herbert Axford as president of Waterloo University College on 4 November 1959 had been a moment of respite from the ongoing debate and the spate of misleading rumours about the federation agreements between the two Waterloo institutions. Arriving from Washington for the ceremony, Reverend Gould Wickey registered his "surprise that the Articles of Federation had not been signed," as he had assumed that the troubles of the past were behind. As in the past, however, Wickey was once again besieged by those wishing to tell their side of the story.

This time Wickey decided to take direct action.[10] After meeting privately with Dr. Hagey on 4 November 1959 he suggested a "luncheon conference" with Hagey and Axford, at which time a frank discussion took place on "what may be called the problem points." "It appeared that on some of these there was agreement on the basis of certain affirmations of Dr. Hagey," Wickey recalled, but "on others there was evidence of some uncertainty and lack of assurance."

Before leaving Waterloo, Wickey was given a copy of the "Memorandum re: Federation Agreements" which Hagey was presenting to the Federation Committee on 10 November and which he assured Wickey "would cover most of the problems discussed." Wickey had also received from Pastor Baetz the Waterloo College Planning and Development's nine-point document "on the basis of which Federation might be effected."

Wickey noted that "during the past two years [since 1957] there has developed an unusual amount of personality tension and distrust. If these could be eliminated," he suggested, "it seems to me most of the problems could be solved. I am convinced it is the duty of all parties concerned to make a serious effort to dispel all mistrust. If this cannot be done, then it would be wholly undesirable for the Federation [of Waterloo University College with the University of Waterloo] to take place."

There was little in Wickey's memorandum that had not been said before. He noted with a degree of consternation, however, that "during the past year or two, something has happened to effect a situation in which the College will not be the University College and ... St. Jerome's will also be a federated college rather than an

The installation of Herbert M. Axford as president of Waterloo College was a happy moment and a respite from the tension in the relationship between Waterloo's two post-secondary institutions. President Axford is at the left; next to him is the Rev. Dr. Gould Wickey, executive secretary of the Board of Higher Education of the United Lutheran Church of America, with Rev. Albert Jacobi, president of the Evangelical Lutheran Synod of Canada, and Rev. Lloyd Schaus, dean of Waterloo College.
KWR

This slightly later photo shows a very happy Gerald Hagey in the board room of the University of Waterloo, flanked by senior administrators and the deans of science, arts, engineering and graduate studies at the University of Waterloo.
UWA/Roy Purkis

affiliated college. I have not been able to ascertain why the change of attitude or why the new situation."

What had also changed was the sense of achievement by the Lutheran community in Ontario. "Waterloo Lutheran University possesses a prestige and a standing in the academic community never before possessed," he stated proudly, and "it has degree-granting power in its own right." Furthermore, "the Synod is more awakened to the importance of Christian higher education than ever before, and is minded to support it in the largest degree possible."

These last two sentences reveal as much about the dispute as all of the clauses and sub-clauses in the articles of federation. Waterloo Lutheran University could become an independent university. Wickey now recommended "that all parties concerned seriously endeavour in a Christian manner to dispel all tension and distrust." Despite Wickey's directive, some Lutheran faculty members and some church leaders foresaw an independent Lutheran University on the horizon. It was a goal that many had sought. Now it was attainable. Fortune had played into their hands in a most surprising way.

The University of Waterloo's proposals for federation had moved in an entirely different direction from those of Waterloo Lutheran University or its constituent, Waterloo University College. Their proposal given to Gould Wickey was based on the principle of Waterloo University College becoming a "federated college having a relationship to the University [of Waterloo] similar to the relationship of the colleges in other universities having a federation or affiliation program." A general policy statement from the Board of Governors over the signature of Ira Needles was sent to both Waterloo University College and the University of St. Jerome's College on 29 November 1959.[11] It clearly set out the university's position in the changed circumstances since 1956 and its desire to honour its previous commitments to Waterloo College, explaining that:

> When the Associate Faculties was originally incorporated, it was expected that the assistance of a government-supported college would only be needed in Science, Business, and other specialized fields of study. Thus, the original incorporation document legislated against the Associate Faculties offering Liberal Arts courses ...
>
> As a result of Waterloo's Co-operative Engineering Program, the expansion of higher education at Waterloo was so rapid that university status became essential at a much earlier date than anticipated ...
>
> University status carries with it an obligation to offer a universal education [consistent with the powers in the University of Waterloo Act, 1959].

Needles and the members of his Board of Governors recognized that the agreements with Waterloo Lutheran University and the University of St. Jerome's College, which were appended to the University of Waterloo Act, gave the two church-related colleges "privileges that would apply when they became federated with the University."[12] The specifics were clear:

> These [privileges] included an agreement with the federated colleges to the effect that the University would not duplicate instruction in Arts, Humanities, and Social Sciences offered by Waterloo University College ...
>
> [The University of Waterloo] is prepared to sign federation agreements with Waterloo University College and The University of St. Jerome's College on the basis of the University of Waterloo Act and its appended schedules A and B — recognizing the present status of the Church Colleges' development in Liberal Arts Courses as well as their desire for further development and protecting them against the unnecessary or uneconomical duplication of instruction that would react to their detriment.

In return, the university asked that the colleges respect the obligation of "a non-denominational and publicly supported University to serve the educational needs of the community and the province by continuing the academic growth of the University in co-operation with its ... colleges." The university would be responsible for co-ordinating the academic programs of its faculties and schools and those of its departments along with the federated and affiliated colleges. Similarly, it would provide general administrative direction, through university-appointed deans, for all university faculties including arts, science, and engineering and through university-appointed directors for its extension and athletic programs.

Anticipating that this was a particularly sensitive area, Needles quickly assured the colleges that "This does not prevent federated or church-related colleges appointing their own college Deans or developing their academic programs in accordance with the University Act." This memorandum, Needles explained, contains "a principle which, in our opinion, is basic to federation — that is, that the relationship to the University would be similar to the colleges in other universities having a federation or affiliation program."

The Boards of Governors of both St. Jerome's and Waterloo University College accepted the general principles in the university's memorandum. Waterloo College, however, wanted a separate addendum that modified the university's proposal. They asked that Schedule A be interpreted to mean "that Waterloo University College is to continue to be the Major Arts College of the University to the extent that Waterloo University College is able to provide the courses of instruction required." Here at least was the basis for negotiation that seemed to satisfy the needs of both institutions.

It is doubtful whether either Gerry Hagey or Ira Needles — or for that matter the Board of Governors of Waterloo University College — fully understood the commitment of a minority of faculty members to create, at any cost, an independent Lutheran University. Even had they understood, they sincerely believed that an independent denominational university could not survive. The list of denominational colleges that had failed was a long and distinguished one. More important was their wish to make Waterloo a university in which the denominational colleges could flourish and thereby enrich the university.

On 5 January 1960, as the Board of Governors of Waterloo Lutheran University met to consider their college's future, Ira Needles sought to reassure them of the desire of the university to make federation a success. The announcement the previous day that Dana Porter, now the chief justice of the Supreme Court of Ontario, had agreed to become chancellor of the university was helpful to those who wanted a symbol of the acceptance of Waterloo as a provincial university. The well-known friendship and profes-

sional relationship between Dana Porter and Leslie Frost, "who had encouraged Porter to accept the appointment also signified the province's approval of the new university and its colleges."[13]

Needles thought that it was perhaps also of interest that three other religious denominations—the Anglicans, the Mennonites, and the United Church — in addition to Waterloo University College and St. Jerome's College, had indicated an interest in building residences to accommodate the students of their denominations who would be attending the University of Waterloo. The preliminary campus planning, Needles explained, "indicates the probability of the two hundred acre site being adequate for church college residences in addition to the University's requirements." St. Jerome's College, having already agreed to the terms of federation, had asked to purchase a ten-acre site in order to construct buildings for teaching, administration, and students' residences.[14]

Needles hoped that there would be a similar willingness on the part of Waterloo University College to join the university. In this regard, Needles continued,

> The University Board, its administrators and faculty recognize and appreciate the extent to which Waterloo University College has developed its Faculty of Arts. We are hopeful that at all times the actions of the University will prove to be to the benefit of its federated colleges ... The University Board is aware of the many needs that a University is expected to provide for Arts students in addition to those now available at Waterloo University College or the University ... The university realizes that funds not available to the federated colleges will need to be allocated for such purposes ... [and] we appreciate the concern and fears that your Board is facing in contemplating the final stage of the federation program undertaken in 1956. These are similar to the concerns and fears of other church-related Boards recorded in the histories of the development of higher education in this province over a period of many years.

Ira Needles was sympathetic to the concerns of the Lutheran board members. He knew many of them personally and respected and admired their leadership in the community.

He reminded his colleagues on the Waterloo Lutheran board that with the exception of three members, "all of the original members of the Associate Faculties Board are continuing to serve the University," and that "the men who were appointed to the Charter Committee approximately two years ago ... are now continuing to serve as members of our Federation Committee." These were the same community leaders who had brought forward the idea of a university to the Evangelical Lutheran Synod in 1956 and who remained committed to the best interests of the community. The federation proposals were not those of Ira Needles or Gerry Hagey alone. They were brought to the table by some of the leading business and professional leaders in Kitchener and Waterloo. They were as free of denominational or religious bias as any group would ever be. As Needles put it, they were "the more active members of our Board [and they] have a good appreciation of the problems that are involved in federation."

Much had occurred since the modest university plans were laid before the Evangelical Lutheran Synod in 1956, Needles admitted:

> We are aware that in a progressive development such as that taking place here, there must of necessity, be changes in the

THIS IS
WATERLOO

Published bi-monthly by the Alumni Association of Waterloo University College in the interest of the Association and the College

| VOLUME 4 | ★ DECEMBER, 1959 ★ | NUMBER 1 |

THIS IS WATERLOO ! !
BY WAY OF INTRODUCTION

This issue of the bulletin has been designed to serve a special purpose, but before we begin, we are anxious that you know how it came about.

Inquiries from Alumni members, questions from expansion fund contributors and expressions of confusion from the student body led several members of the executive to become concerned about the apparent breakdown in federation proceedings between Waterloo University College (formerly Waterloo College) and the University of Waterloo (formerly the Associate Faculties). We had presumed, as had the public at large, that federation of the two institutions was imminent following the acts of incorporation for both institutions last spring. Initial inquiries of officials resulted only in added confusion and therefore your bulletin staff constituted three of its members as a committee of inquiry who, with Alumni executive sanction, interviewed officers of administration, faculty members and the board chairmen of both institutions.

Interviews were based on a series of questions concerning: rumours of broken agreements; the possible development of two universities side by side; the financial support available to both institutions; the status of a mathematics graduate school operating since the opening of this autumn semester and changes in the intended role of Waterloo University College within the University of Waterloo and its federated colleges.

As the interviews progressed (from 10:15 A.M. to 5:30 P.M. on Wednesday, Nov. 11) several other issues became apparent and information was sought concerning these as well. This data will be presented as the main text of this bulletin, but first we have some general facts which we feel will serve to clarify these details. Also, we wish to express our appreciation to those interviewed. Busy people sacrificed much time from a day filled with commitments and administrative details to accomodate our committee with complete and forthright answers to all questions.

FEDERATION PLANNED! — FEDERATION HALTED!

When the Associate Faculties were formed, agreements upon whose basis the College would federate with the proposed University of Waterloo were formulated — the assumption at that time being, that federation was pre-supposed. Reports to the press and those carried in this bulletin implied the above assumption. This was premature, as it appears now, since the negotiations for federation have met with some complications.

One of the complications stems from an interpretation of the word "university". The College interprets the word in reference to the corporate body and therefore if the college is to play a dominant role in the development of the University (according to the original agreements) the College must have a strong voice in representative organs such as the senate and planning committee.

The University, on the other hand, uses the word to denote the total academic community and claims that the 'dominant role' should be one of influence and moral suasion thereby negating the need for "legislating themselves (the College) into a position of dominance".

This difference of interpretation manifests itself in the confusion surrounding the arts faculty clause in the original agreements.

Further complications arise from the fact that St. Jerome's College now insists on a federation agreement with the University rather than the affiliation agreement as originally planned. Although the difference is insignificant, representation in the senate is affected and both colleges (Waterloo and St. Jerome's) would share equal status. Again the University claims that the College is underestimating its potential for influence while the College fears a loss of identity and reputation through absorption.

With this backdrop for a setting, here then is the situation as it presently exists on the two campuses on Dearborn St.

OFFICERS CLARIFIED

To avoid further confusion, we are publishing the following list of officers for both institutions.

Waterloo Lutheran University
President and Chairman of the Board —
Rev. A. J. Baetz (not a full-time position)
Business Administrator — Dr. H. M. Axford

Waterloo Lutheran Seminary
President — Dr. Ray Houser
Dean — Dr. Ulrich Leupold

Waterloo University College
President — Dr. H. M. Axford
Dean — Dr. Lloyd H. Schaus

University of Waterloo
Chairman of the Board — Ira G. Needles
(not a full-time position)

President — Dr. J. G. Hagey
Dean of Science — Prof. Bruce Kelley
Dean of Engineering — Dr. D. T. Wright

RELATIONSHIPS CHANGED

The following charts will demonstrate graphically the changes of relationship which have resulted from the acts of incorporation.

PRIOR TO SEPT., 1959

Evangelical Lutheran Seminary
Associate Faculties — Waterloo College (affiliated with U.W.O.)

AFTER SEPT., 1959

University of Waterloo

| Faculty of Science | Faculty of Engineering |

Waterloo Lutheran University

| Waterloo University College (affiliated with U.W.O. until June, 1960) | Waterloo Lutheran Seminary |

The University of Waterloo now has the power to grant its own degrees as has Waterloo University College. As long as the College remains in affiliation with another degree-granting institution, this power must remain dormant. The seminary, presently, holds this power and will continue to exercise it.

relations between the colleges and the University. As such changes take place, they should, to the best of everyone's ability, be structured to serve the best interests of all parties. It was with this desire that our Board members worked with the colleges in the development of the University Act.

Needles also reminded them that this was not the first change since 1956 that required the mutual consent of the two boards and that "Some of the agreements made during this intervening period have changed materially the original conception of the way in which the two corporations would work together. We have continually recognized the need for close co-operation, and we believe that it is only through mutual trust and respect that a federation program will work to the benefit of all parties."

Needles's case was based on reason, trust, and goodwill. The proposed federation on the model of the University of Toronto, he believed, would best protect the interests of the Lutheran Church and was essentially the concept, as he understood it, in the original affiliation agreement:

> It is a position similar to that of the Arts colleges at Toronto that the University is now offering the Arts Colleges here. We believe such a relationship to be in the best interest of the churches and permits their maintenance of colleges with a Christian character and personality in accord with their denominational preferences.

All of this may have seemed reasonable. Certainly it was for St. Jerome's. Waterloo University College, however, sought a different role for itself in the new university and in the end Needles finally addressed this difference as he explained the system of colleges proposed by the university:

> We believe that any agreement of federation which would place any one church college in a position of administrative control over other federated or affiliated colleges — or prevent the over-all development of a faculty within the university — would be a continuous source of irritation and would not be in the best interests of either the University or of its federated and affiliated colleges.

After months of doubt and debate, the relationship between Waterloo University College and the University of Waterloo was in the open. The academic rights and privileges of the college would be protected, its academic programs secure, its denominational development unhindered, and the size and prominence of its arts departments would give it a leadership position in the university, but it would not have exclusive control of the Arts Faculty of the University of Waterloo. Countless details remained to be debated, but the parameters had at last been set down.

On the same day in January 1960 that Ira Needles had sent his detailed statement, the Board of Governors of Waterloo Lutheran University met to consider their response. Their reply was affirmative, although guarded and reserved, but still hopeful that the university idea would work. "After full consideration of all the factors affecting federation," they agreed, on behalf of Waterloo University College, "to enter into federation with the University of Waterloo as of 1 July 1960, on the basis of agreements reached to date and such other terms as may be mutually agreed upon."[15] Discussions would continue, but the decision in favour of federation was made. The community and the students at Waterloo University College could be assured that the university idea would go forward.

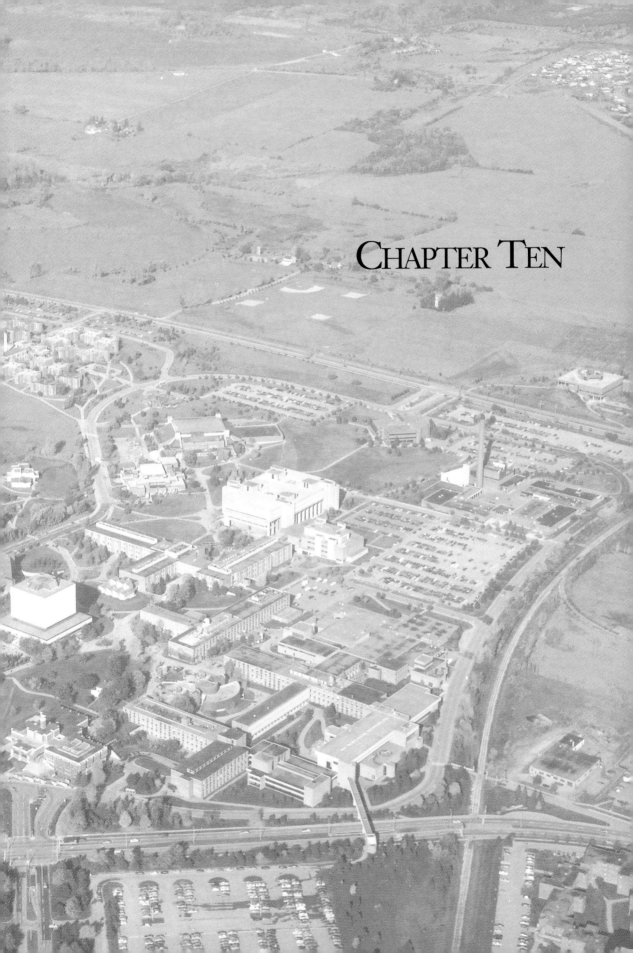

CHAPTER TEN

The Battle of Waterloo:
An End and a Beginning

As the decade of the 1960s began, plans for the University of
Waterloo seemed to be moving forward. On 5 January the
Kitchener-Waterloo Record announced that an agreement had been
reached by which St. Jerome's College and Waterloo College
would become federated with the University of Waterloo. "After
July 1, [1960] arts students enrolling at the Colleges will receive
their degrees from the new university."

In February Reverend Lloyd Schaus, dean of the now-named
Waterloo University College, and Dr. Herbert M. Axford, its newly
appointed president, explained to the students that "next year's
graduates will receive their degrees from the University of Waterloo."[1]
But it was not to be.

On 26 March 1960 a committee of six Lutheran faculty members of Waterloo University College, Reverends George Durst, Robert Langen, A.B. Little, J.F. Little, L.H.Schaus, and R.Teigen, circulated a letter to members of the Evangelical Lutheran Synod, petitioning for clerical support for a special meeting of the Synod to discuss the federation question. At first, the president of the Synod refused, stating that the reasons for the special meeting were not clearly defined. A second letter was sent on 30 March. This time the president of the Synod, Dr. Albert Jacobi, had no choice. The purpose of their request was clear: they wished the members of the Synod to rescind the 5 January federation agreement. A special meeting was called for 12 May.[2]

The reaction of the University of Waterloo was immediate. On 6 April the Board of Governors empowered its administration to establish an arts program and to hire its own faculty.[3] The following day Waterloo University College was notified that the University of Waterloo intended to create a non-denominational Faculty of Arts. Responding to the concerns of some students who were asking questions about the status of their future university degrees, Dean Schaus publicly revealed his own agenda, including his opposition to federation with the University of Waterloo and his disapproval of the policies of President Hagey. According to Dean Schaus, "federation would not take place."

At the same meeting, Dr. Hagey announced that the university intended to offer a full arts program of its own. Students would not forfeit their degrees. In fact, both announcements were somewhat premature. Waterloo College was not in a position to offer a complete arts program; nor was the university able to offer an arts program on its own and the question of federation was still very much alive. From the students' point of view, this crisis was very real and a profound sense of anxiety and worry engulfed the campus.

At the very moment when the student assembly was in progress, the Executive Committee of the Waterloo College Board of Governors was also meeting, rejecting their dean's directive, and reaffirming "the January 5th decision to federate with the University." The Executive Committee thus asserted its authority, temporarily taking the initiative away from Axford and Schaus.

President H.M. Axford of Waterloo College along with President Hagey and representatives of the Anglican, Mennonite, Roman Catholic, and United Church discuss the location of their college sites on the campus of the University of Waterloo on 5 January 1960.
KWR

Students from Waterloo College took a break from the political debate surrounding the "university question" to meet with Liberal leader Lester Pearson to discuss politics at another level as the students planned a protest march against apartheid in South Africa on 5 April 1960.
KWR

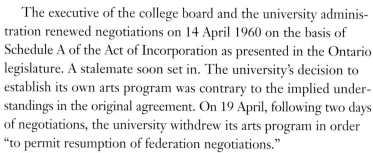

The executive of the college board and the university administration renewed negotiations on 14 April 1960 on the basis of Schedule A of the Act of Incorporation as presented in the Ontario legislature. A stalemate soon set in. The university's decision to establish its own arts program was contrary to the implied understandings in the original agreement. On 19 April, following two days of negotiations, the university withdrew its arts program in order "to permit resumption of federation negotiations."

The next day college and university board members established a steering committee "to work out the details of a basis for federation suitable to both institutions." Agreement seemed to have been reached. On 22 April Reverend Alvin Baetz, president of the Waterloo University College Board of Governors, told students at the college, that "the University had withdrawn its arts program; that the Senate would be asked to re-establish the curriculum of the College as a basis for the University's arts curriculum and that all courses and credits earned at the College would be accredited by the University [as if federated]."

"Great progress had been made toward federation," said Pastor Baetz, and "more progress was foreseen." On 27 April the university Senate re-established the college arts curriculum in confirmation of negotiations proceeding. On 6 May the Board of Governors of Waterloo University College ratified the actions of its executive, agreeing to federate with the University of Waterloo. Federation was back on track. Waterloo University College would again be part of the University of Waterloo. Compromises would have to be made, but the ultimate goal was once again attainable.

Within the hallowed halls of Waterloo College ferment of another kind had left many faculty members upset and uncertain of their future in the Arts Faculty of this new university. In December, when the idea of an independent Lutheran university had arisen, a majority of faculty members and staff had voted in favour of an amendment to the Waterloo Lutheran University Act to include a majority of non-Lutherans on the board. The governance of Waterloo University College would then be given over to a non-denominational Board of Governors. Not only would this permit the college to receive "substantial government grants," but it would also allow it — as a non-denominational institution — to be the central Arts Faculty for the university. Signed by twenty-one members of the Faculty Association, the brief was to be sent to the Board of Governors of Waterloo University College for its meeting on 16 December 1959.[4]

As Dean of Science, Acting Dean of Arts and Chairman of the Academic Advisory Committee, Bruce Kelley played a powerful role in developing the university. During the autumn of 1959 and the early days of 1960 a committee met privately in his home to prepare a shadow arts curriculum in the likelihood that Waterloo College would not federate with the university. With Dean Kelley's untimely death on 9 May 1960 the university lost a man known for wise counsel and sound advice.
WLU

In a first draft of a personal letter to Stewart Reid, the executive secretary of the Canadian Association of University Teachers, James Stone, the president of the College's Faculty Association, had been candid about the internal divisions within Waterloo College. The faculty, he said, is split on the issue of federation with the University of Waterloo: "Twenty-one members of the faculty association are in favour of federation or of independence with the same academic guarantees as federation will offer, and approximately eight are for independence with no guarantees except religious affiliation." "The minority group," he continued, "composed mainly of Lutheran ministers and others who have vested interests, have for months now been very vocal in proselytizing, to the extent that we of the other persuasion feared that the Board of Governors of the College would assume that the minority reflected the opinions of the majority." Life in Waterloo College had begun to resemble a battle zone and a majority of the faculty members were trapped between the Lutheran interests and those of the university.[5]

The decision of the Board of Governors on 5 January 1960 to federate with the University of Waterloo intensified the debate about the Lutheran identity of Waterloo University College. On

President Hagey, meeting on 16 September 1959 with Father Siegfried of St. Jerome's College and President Axford of Waterloo College, plan a curriculum that was never to be.
KWR

Protest Church Move

E. G. SCHAFER
Belair

D. A. ROBERTS
Belair

FRANK C. HODDLE

MERVYN LAHN
Record Photo

4 Governors Quit Over Synod Veto

BULLETIN

A fifth member of the Waterloo College board of governors, Robert Bornhold of Milton, has tendered his resignation to the Evangelical Lutheran Synod of Canada.

By GEORGE TODD

Four members of the Waterloo College board of governors have resigned and 24 faculty members have lodged a protest as reaction continues against a decision not to federate the college with the University of Waterloo.

The decision not to federate was made by the Evangelical Lutheran Synod of Canada after an all-day meeting in Kitchener.

tors of Twin City Lutheran churches.

Commenting on their decision to resign the four board members said they had little other choice after the synod reversed a policy passed by the board.

"Since the synod is not prepared to follow the recommendations of the board of governors it is clear the board no longer commands the confidence of the synod," Mr. Schafer told The Record.

"It is in the best interests of the college that the board should share the thinking of the synod, otherwise the board holds an untenable position."

Synod." Dr. Little was strenuously opposed to the "pernicious campaign of theological liberals to accommodate the Christian faith to current secular trends or thought," and as one scholar has written, Dr. Little had built a system of theology, "designed to protect 'Fortress Lutheranism' against every deviation, however small." [14]

Little insisted "that absolute doctrinal purity was necessary to resist what he felt to be the unionist danger of pan-Protestantism. Otherwise Lutherans would be 'among the increasing number of organizations that pervert the Word of God and desecrate the Holy Sacraments.'" [15] It was the Reverend Dr. J. F. Little, son of the Reverend Dr. C. H. Little, who stood before the Lutheran Synod, on 12 May 1960, to plead the role of Lutheran orthodoxy in the face of a proposed federation with the secular, modernistic University of Waterloo. For many members of the Synod it would have been difficult to disentangle the emotional plea in his arguments for independence from the theological propositions of his father.

Reverend Norman Berner of Kitchener, assistant to the president of the Synod, offered two main reasons for the Synod's decision: "First, he said the University of Waterloo is refusing to give Waterloo College the position of 'the' arts faculty of the university ... Secondly, it was contended it would cost the college more financially in federation than it would to remain an independent school ... It was [also] felt [that] the college would become secularized in federation under the university's terms." [16]

President Hagey announced that "the University of Waterloo was shocked, and regrets that the Evangelical Lutheran Synod of Canada has decided to oppose the decision of the Lutheran College board of governors which favoured federation of the college with the university." [17] Both sides were leaving much unsaid, but the hurt and the bitter feelings of betrayal and distrust would linger for years to come.

In the aftermath of the Synod's decision, twenty-four of the thirty-five full-time faculty members at Waterloo College lodged a formal complaint against the Synod. Seven faculty members resigned in protest, as did the entire executive of the Alumni Association. The Board of Governors at Waterloo College also felt rebuked; a majority of its members, all of them laymen, and board chairman, Pastor A.J. Baetz, resigned in protest and former board members publicly spoke out against the Synod's decision.

Perhaps most remarkable were the sentiments expressed by Albert Jacobi, president of the Synod, as he offered his resignation to the Synod at its regular meeting on 8 June. His comments expressed his sadness at the events that had led to the extraordinary meeting of the Synod in May:

I have been unable, however hard I have tried, to convince myself that the campaign which prefaced the special convocation of Synod can be accepted as in keeping with good Christian ethics. I cannot refrain from the judgement that the lobbying and politics that induced enough pastors to sign a petition for a special meeting of the Synod was not in the spirit of Christian procedure that should be evidenced in the Church.[18]

Waterloo College was not a college like the others and its destiny had been profoundly shaped by its own history. Within the City of Waterloo two new universities had been created on that 12th day of May, 1960, separated by a short distance and a long history.

The synodical decision that Waterloo University College would pursue a course of independence marked the end of the college's relationship with the University of Waterloo and with the University of Western Ontario. It also marked a new beginning. The University of Waterloo was free to pursue its own destiny unhindered and unshackled by past restraints. Preparations were begun immediately to sever ties with Waterloo College. Library resources and laboratory equipment would have to be divided. Staff would have to choose new employers. Some faculty would stay at the college; others would be invited to join the new University of Waterloo; still others would resign in protest hoping to find academic appointments at other universities. Relationships were strained, friendships lost. Fear and foreboding consumed some, while others revelled in their new freedom.

Some students nearing graduation transferred immediately to Western; some remained at Waterloo College; others accepted President Hagey's invitation to earn their degrees in Arts as well as Science from the University of Waterloo. These were exciting days that no one was likely ever to forget.

A shadow arts curriculum had been designed under the aegis of Bruce Kelley who in January had been named acting dean of arts in addition to his post as dean of science. With Dean Kelley's untimely death only four months later, work on the implementation of an Arts curriculum was delayed until Professor Keith Thomas, newly appointed as acting dean of arts, hurriedly arrived from Acadia University in Wolfville, Nova Scotia.

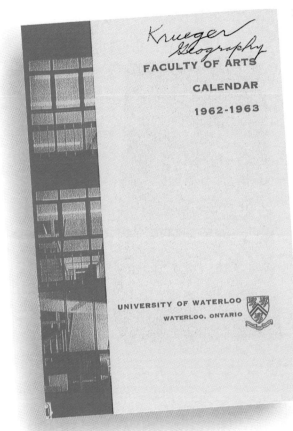

Little more than a month after the synodical rejection of federation, on Saturday, 18 June 1960, the University of Waterloo held its first convocation and the installation of its chancellor, the Honourable Dana Harris Porter, Chief Justice of Ontario and former minister of education and treasurer of Ontario. When Chancellor Porter addressed convocation he spoke of the tentative request to him for support for the "Waterloo Plan" in 1956 made by Ira Needles and President Hagey, recalling that he was "much impressed with the whole concept of the plan of combining alternate academic studies and the application of them by actual employment in industry." This, he said, was "a novel project in this country." "Today," he continued, "three years later, the building programme is well advanced, a staff of distinguished men of learning has been assembled, more than 600 students are enrolled, 250 industries have undertaken to assist in training on the job [and] in addition to the provision made for the sciences, the University has now established an Arts faculty which will open this Autumn. This is indeed a great achievement in so short a time. I am proud to have had some part to play in that inception." Dana Porter's part was of greater consequence than his words suggest. Without his personal intervention in 1957 there would not have been a University of Waterloo.

As Chancellor Porter mounted the dais to begin the conferment of degrees he must have felt more than a little pride in seeing this university come into its own. Dana Porter would have been pleased, too, to see that the first degrees were graduate degrees — a master of arts and seven masters of science in applied mathematics. For Dana Porter, as for the faculty at Waterloo, a commitment to research and the advancement of knowledge was a sine qua non of what universities were about. He would, I think, also have enjoyed the remarks of the honorary graduand, Dr. James Talman, the historian and chief librarian from the University of Western Ontario who received an honorary LLD. Dr. Talman spoke to the graduating class about the ingenuity, diligence, inventiveness, and remarkable industrial growth of Waterloo County — characteristics, he suggested, which were evident in the creation of the University of Waterloo. "We can only conclude that they will be just as successful in developing the intellectual resources of the future," he continued. "With the evidence before us, the conclusion is inescapable. The University of Waterloo can look forward to a brilliant and successful future." With that, the chaplain offered the Prayer of Benediction and the chancellor dismissed Convocation. The University of Waterloo's graduates emerged into a bright, sunny June afternoon ready to face the future with the assurance that their university would fulfil its destiny.

An Afterword

With Convocation completed, the university settled in for its first full term. New faculty members and their families began to arrive to prepare to meet the onslaught of students in September. One of those newly arrived in Waterloo was Paul Cornell, a Toronto Ph.D. and a former vice-dean at Acadia University in Wolfville, Nova Scotia. Paul Cornell and his family had come to Waterloo that summer to establish themselves in the community and to begin life in Ontario. At the University of Waterloo he was appointed professor and chairman of history and he also served as acting chairman of political science, economics and geography. One of his tasks was to recruit other senior professors to fill out the roster in the Faculty of Arts. One of those to whom he wrote was K.A. MacKirdy, a fellow historian teaching at the University of Washington, who was anxious to return to Canada. Cornell's letter, printed below, is a remarkable set piece describing the university and the city as they appeared to him in February 1961.

Dear Ken,

I have just received your letter of 28 January, and am happy that you are giving us a second and third thought. I think it will be best if I go through your letter, item by item first, and then see what generalisations follow at the end.

The (twin cities) are over-grown Ontario towns, still clustered about a seven mile King St. that runs throughout the two towns. Mostly brick. You can see the boundaries, in concentric circles where the post WWI, and post WWII expansion began, about the earlier nucleus. Generally they have planned to have residential areas proximate to industries-so you come on factories and plants pretty generally throughout the two cities. In the more newly built fringes they hive industry [off] in areas, and have blocks and blocks of new bungalows and split levels. (I am saying this frankly). There are a few older houses sprinkled about. We have bought an old brick farm house, at the western city limits, now surrounded by new split levels etc: but we have fields behind, and a golf course across the way. A number of the faculty have bought farm houses in the country, up to 10-14 miles away. There are possibilities of getting older "conventional" houses in the built up, heavily treed areas of town. About 90% of the houses are owner occupied, and there are not many houses for rent, though given some months it is possible to find a rental proposition. The Pol Sci man that came in from Saskatchewan last summer has a big sound 3 bedroom, 7 room house on an old street at $125 a month. Housing is not nearly as expensive as Toronto, and for buying, there is lots of choice. There is the inevitable problem that the new (undesirable to us) houses can "be financed" much more reasonably than the older houses. With hunting and waiting, I would guess that you could get something reasonably desirable in an older house for about $13,000. A temporary less desirable something could be had, I think, for approx $10,000. [The] Campus is very new and just a building. Two buildings up in the last three years, one more $3 1/2 million building is under construction for next fall. Campus is on the N.W. just beyond the Waterloo built up area. Beyond it a new super posh residential area is just beginning to be developed. Back S.E. into Waterloo there is a large area of post WWII housing some very cheap, some medium and some dear. About 25 minutes walk would take you into older Waterloo. The university has no scheme that I know of to help with housing — there is no endowment here for anything, we live on government grant and aid from industry and fees.

Education: quite good, at the H.S. level particularly. A colleague from Acadia, in Psychology, was hired by the navy to evaluate their whole program for choosing and training H.S. recruits. One byproduct of his research was that two Canadian areas seemed to stand out for the calibre of their schooling— the Kitchener-Waterloo area, and some area in B.C.. Ontario Dept. of Ed. is currently doing a great reappraisal of H.S. education with some good insight, and in a direction away from "progressive" and back to disciplined learning. Ontario never did go overboard for the "new look" in Education. I think the local collegiates come close if they don't equal the big Toronto Schools (eg. Humberside, etc.). Primary schools are sprinkled all across the cities, and usually available within 8 or so blocks of wherever you are. I think the answer on education is good.

Shopping: a great many super-markets on the fringes and within reach of most areas. Hardware, shops etc usually on King St. and competing, therefore not too bad for price. Generally our prices are Toronto prices on all appliances and consumer goods. We don't get sale prices as low as those advertised in Toronto papers. Probably Marg. [Mrs. MacKirdy] would want to do semi annual shopping for her own costumes, in Toronto. (By contrast with N.S. [Nova Scotia] we are thrilled). There are no "extra" taxes.

Hospital etc: Kitchener-Waterloo Hospital is not very large, but has a very good feeling of kindness and homeliness. We have been involved as X-Ray cases — out patients. There is the Ontario Hosp. Insurance scheme which is province wide and paid in premiums of about $4+ per month per family. There is no medical school, but there are a good assortment of specialists. We have found a physician as G.P. for our family, an excellent young chap, good with kids, just a year or two out of Med School. Young, serious, exacting, but very good personality. His boyhood chum is also newly set up as Dentist. With the Highway 401 open to our southern outskirts we are about 1 1/2 hours away from U of T, or medical arts building, etc; so in case of need we are not too much further away than, say Richmond Hill, or Weston.

Recreation — You are right — no lake. We have picnicked on the Grand River and at Doon etc. It is quite rich farm land with quite a lot of good scenery, etc. on the Grand River Valley. We also found last summer quite tolerable at home. Elevation is about 1 000 feet, with a breeze a lot of the time. All our [university] buildings are air conditioned. The kids swam happily in the Waterloo Pool. Waterloo park isn't as corny as the name suggests — it is large and heavily treed. The twin cities have about a dozen parks in various stages of development — (some with swans). Stratford, as you say, is 20-25 minutes away. Established families have cottages on small lakes to the north, others go to the Owen Sound — Collingwood area, away north on Georgian Bay, or over to the shore of Huron. There isn't any obvious answer to water (but is Toronto's waterfront not polluted?) We have the usual winter assortment of film societies, little theatre, symphony, fine arts concerts, Art Gallery, etc. Certainly, the University should do a lot in the next decade to give these a lift. We are affiliated with the Doon School of Fine Arts and hope to join in on the academic side of Stratford Shakespeare business by being strong in Shakespeare and seeking some sort of affiliation and service — There is a firm staunch, active Presbyterian church in Waterloo.

University Arts: I came here because on examination the promise of building a real, proper Humanities School looked good, and the sound of the people on the ground rang true. I still think the same way. The battles that we have fought have been between Arts men, this year, mainly on the lines of drawing up a curriculum. In the working out of our needs for office and teaching space we arrived at 634 as the minimum Arts enrolment in 1965. We're building, as the preliminary thinking goes at the moment, for approx 1 000 in Arts.

I don't sense the feeling that this is to be a pale copy of M.I.T., although there will have to be constant vigilance. In the budget, there is a tendency to need a computer, but to haggle about the salaries of say (yourself) a key Arts appointment. But this is a natural enough problem. There are 59 Arts students at the moment, while the university registration is 1000+. There is the inevitable banter about "unpractical" arts men, etc. But the whole faculty is young. Very few people are 40, and all the key administrators are 40ish or younger. They are quite open to experiment and co-operation on pilot schedules to bridge Arts-Sci-Eng gulfs.

The Board of Governors dream of a "proper" university. The board is weighted in a group of a fast vanishing type: the individual millionaire who has built his industry personally and continues to run it personally and not as a corporation. There are 4 or 5 of these.

Personalities:

President — J.G. Hagey — non academic, into Waterloo College from public relations chief of Dominion Rubber [B.F. Goodrich]. Quite astute but not confident in his own judgement in academic decisions. Has the effect of passing academic policy decisions down to Deans, Heads and meetings of the general faculty. Wants the total university to go — 55ish.

Comptroller — Al Adlington — from Dominion Electrohome. Very tidy mind: quite fair within the realms of what is financially possible — 40's.

Superintendent of Buildings and Grounds — Mike Brookes — northcountry Englishman loves archaeology, drama, etc — as well as an engineer, 40ish.

Dean of Engineering — Doug Wright, formerly of Queen's, dynamic, good administrator, reads broadly, friend of Arts, 38ish.

Dean of Science — W.A.E. MacBryde ("Pete"), Chemistry, from Toronto, has the makings of a good friend: interests & view broad. 40ish.

A/ Dean of Arts (till July) — permanent Dean not designated & Head of English, Keith Thomas, 34, PhD English from Toronto, many scholarships, came with me from Acadia where he had been Head of English for 4 years.

Head of Math, (Chairman of Faculty of Grad studies): Ralph Stanton, bachelor, 40ish, Western Grad, Toronto PhD, also does Portuguese which he taught at Toronto. Heads largest, very strong and effective department. Opinionated, an "old hand" ie. has been at Waterloo College, and through the shifts that have created this university. Individualist, likes to play king maker.

Head of German & Russian — Wilhelm Dyck: born in Russia of German stock, out of Russia during the war, learned English in the States, taught at various places, Oberlin; another "old hand" in that he was at Waterloo College and came across to the university ahead of all the arts people. Hopes for great things. A good humanist — A.B. (Bethel), MA (Missouri), PhD (Michigan) 40ish.

Me

The above four have been the quadrumvirate in Arts, with rank of Prof and

Head. We divide most issues Stanton, Dyck vs Thomas, Cornell. We are eager to break the tie.

Other Arts people: 12 or 13 Math people, including Ken Fryer, formerly at Queens (or RMC)

Jim McKegney BA (Western), MA (Oregon), PhD (Washington): French and Spanish — formerly Sec, Royal Society of Canada, etc. 58ish.

Dorothea Walter MA (Queens) 50ish — M.D.'s widow, from Quebec city, quite a mature person — continuing next year in French.

Terry Qualter BA (New Zealand), PhD (London) — literary approach to Pol Sci — specialty in "propaganda" 30ish.

Carl Miller MA (Western), PhD (Clark) — 2nd yr of teaching — specialty money & banking, from Civil Service Ottawa. 30ish ...

There are others, but this gives the idea. There was a great scurrying around in late spring and into the summer gathering a cadre to teach a 1st year of arts and "get off the ground." From here we must try to build in the face of a seller's market. We will be as good as the faculty we can assemble. (Haven't mentioned St. Jerome's faculty. They are of fairly good calibre. The Order is Congregation of the Resurrection. I haven't found any duffers among them. They have an excellent Superior, who has played an impeccable hand in ensuring that everything runs smoothly. They will build and be on the campus by 1962.) Renison College is still an embryo — an Anglican residence plus a faculty of about 4 humanists is planned. This year Renison supplies [Jim] Horne (nearly "PhD" Philosophy) and Alan Barker (M.A. Geog) to teach these 1st year courses for us. Both are clerics. [The principal, Wyn Rees, is an historian.]

ARTS — General

As to the "new league" idea — and fitting. This is one of the few cases where we can still make many of our own rules and establish our own traditions. It seems to be in the cards that humanist fields will be favoured 1st. Some of the flavour of Western Ontario, and Waterloo College lingers, for many of the people have local connections. But the dilution will be progressive. I'll want the best advice of yourself and [Wyn] Rees, to hew an optimum path in finding new faculty, and helping to give a new flavour to the new creation.

We are embarking right away, on a selective group of Honour Courses. Our curriculum is agreed to by the Dept of Education, we are able to carve out areas where we feel we should carve, without the restraining hand of a parent University. (This is rather a soul searching business; Mathematics can, and is offering graduate work, but History will have to wait till our resources are riper — but when we think we can do grad work, we can go ahead, the administrative machinery is taking shape already.

If our 58 freshmen are a true sample, then our students will be quite challenging. I've had more lift this year, than any year at Acadia generated by student enthusiasm.

I'll send the mimeographed sheets of what is to be our 1st Arts calendar. We finally agreed to these items in a meeting last night. It is the product of *many hours of open debate and committee work. It contains compromises, but these are compromises between opposing ideas within our faculty. The debate continues — everyone is involved in the debate. As we settle down, it appears that very great initiative is left to the Departments in detailing the curriculum of their own "Majors" and "Honours" students. (I would guess that we would have about 6 or 7 honour students next year (ie 2nd year).*

I've just been leafing though paper trying without success to get the proposed library budget. As I remember, History gets $8 000 next year, out of an Arts budget of $35 000. Another $15 000 for history comes from the budget for the Teachers' Summer School. The librarian is a her, a history graduate of Toronto, and very much on the side of Arts. I was counting on your experience, ideas and know how to help with this whole library problem. The exact policy for administering the library and its acquisitions is in debate. Mrs. Lewis is an effective debater (age 40ish), but of course the thing will have to be regularized. The next building, by the way, may be a library built large, with arts camping in, until the stack etc; area crowds us out.

SALARY

1960-61 (ie with engineers)	7 1/2 mo. teaching load	9 mo. teaching load
Prof.	9 915	11 898
Assoc Prof.	8 120	9 744
Asst Prof.	6 330	7 596
Lecturer	4 765	5 718

This scale is an Ontario average without Toronto calculated in. My choice of 9 000 was a round figure beyond which I didn't have a hope of getting an O.K. from the President. Before making the offer I was instructed to try elsewhere. I made the other inquiry quite mechanically and half-heartedly — found the man engaged at U of London from Christmas on. I didn't make any effort to see whether his engagement runs beyond summer. I do believe that $ 9 000 is the most I could extract in the circs. The earlier offer corresponded to three offers made to three people in fields other than History. For people very roughly the same teaching experience. We are new enough to have no firm doctrine on increments. A going rule of thumb is $206 a year.

Occasionally something can be done about moving expenses, but it may be difficult this year, for the budget is very tight.

I must stop in a minute to get this in the mail.

In general, there is a spirit of a going concern, young, eager. For myself, I'd like to assemble a department of specialists, who are congenial, but who will see areas of our work as their own. As we build toward specialization, and we must, there will be debate, but we must end by going strong in one or two or three areas, so that we may build library resources. I've been holding off this sort of decision making until we can talk it out together. There will be battles ahead, and we must present a united front where facing the opposition. I think we are compatible, and can be frank. I want you to be here.

I've not had time to look this over. I hope it isn't too bad a picture ... I've tried hard to give you the whole view.

Yours Sincerely,

Paul

A Postscript

In recent years a spate of university histories has appeared. Often in two volumes, they chronicle the development of Canadian universities from Newfoundland to Vancouver Island, from Memorial, St. Francis Xavier and Mount Allison to Queen's, Dalhousie and McGill. These histories are much more than lists of buildings and of the achievements of administrators, students and their professors. They also reveal that universities reflect and respond to the values of the society of which they are a part. In this respect, the University of Waterloo is no exception. While other universities have long histories and traditions that have shaped them, Waterloo is a university of the post World War II world. What is remarkable in its history is the degree to which the values and aspirations of post-war Canada shaped this new university and its students.

Universities are unique institutions. Despite their size and complexity they are also very personal institutions and we respond to them in very personal ways. The story of the founding of the University of Waterloo is replete with a variety of emotions — fear, uncertainty, pride, determination, anger and defiance to name only some, and these have all been very much a part of its history.

When I was first approached and asked to consider undertaking a series of oral history interviews about the founding of the University of Waterloo, little did I realize the adventure on which I was embarking. The idea was both timely and challenging and the project seemed possible. Enough time had passed since the intense emotional division over the separation of Waterloo College (now Wilfrid Laurier University) and its offspring, the Waterloo College Associate Faculties (now the University of Waterloo), that one could hope to achieve a degree of objectivity from the pain and tensions of those difficult years.

As I was trying to explain this new university's history, my daughter Janet, then age eleven, innocently asked, "Does every city have two universities?" Her question was not without merit. Coming of age in Waterloo it was entirely reasonable for her to assume that every city would have two universities. (If one includes St. Jerome's College, which in 1959 was incorporated as a separate university along with UW, for a moment in time Waterloo had three universities.) Clearly this was a story worth the telling.

In 1990, while attending the Learned Societies at the University of Victoria, I conducted the first oral history interviews for the UW history project. I met with Howard Petch, Waterloo's former president pro-tem and vice-president academic, then president of the University of Victoria and with Elaine Reaman who had had a long career in the Dana Porter Library and whose father had been active in UW's early years. In Vancouver I spoke to Bruce Gellatly, whose career had begun at Waterloo College and who had become vice-president finance at UW and then vice-president of the University of British Columbia. The early history of Waterloo had begun to take shape.

When in 1992 I was invited to give UW's Thirteenth Annual Arts Lecture, entitled "Dreaming In Technicolor," I sought to describe the hopes of Gerald Hagey, UW's founding president. For the first time, I learned of the concerted opposition to the plans for developing the University of Waterloo. Strident objections to The "Waterloo Plan" of co-operative education, the alternating work-study program, by the deans of engineering at two Ontario Universities had been sent to the minister of education in Toronto, while the president of the University of Western Ontario, with which Waterloo College Associate Faculties was affiliated, urged the removal of Gerald Hagey as president. By now I was completely captivated by the unfolding Waterloo history.

Under the creative eye of the first superintendent of buildings and grounds, E.M. Brookes, following the innovative designs of the internationally acclaimed landscape architect, Hideo Sasaki, by 1958 two hundred acres of raw, scruffy farmland had begun to be transformed into a picturesque campus as students from across Ontario and Canada's provinces came to study here. The lack of esteem with which Waterloo was still held by other Ontario universities, however, had given the university "a license to be radical" in its campus design as well as in new areas of research and new ways of teaching and learning. This was often said by Douglas Wright who arrived in Waterloo in 1958 as chairman of civil engineering and at the age of 32 was soon to be the youngest dean of engineering in Canada. Wright's experience was not unique. W.A.E. "Pete" McBride, the soon-to-be-appointed dean of science, had a similar response. So did many others.

UW's first students had heard the criticisms of their university, but they were undeterred. They had often come from careers in the workforce and they were determined to make Waterloo succeed and a strong sense of comraderie soon developed between students and professors alike. The commitment to academic excellence combined with exuberant student pranks became part of the definition of university life as Waterloo's co-operative education program began on this new and undeveloped campus. Disdain for the co-operative Applied Studies program was replaced with respect and acclaim as Waterloo soon became the largest undergraduate engineering school in Ontario with a strong reputation in graduate research. A remarkable series of educational initiatives followed. Many of these are unfortunately beyond the bounds of this study, although in the photographs we have tried to re-create the look and something of the Waterloo ethos in these early years.

This book has been about the often complex founding of this very unconventional university. From the earliest days in 1956, Gerald Hagey and the board of governors of the then Waterloo College Associate Faculties were committed to creating a university that would be relevant for the lives of Canadians in a rapidly-changing world. Their credo was a curriculum that combined the best in science, technology and the humanities, setting a course that looked to the future rather than one based on past university precedents.

"Major changes in established universities are difficult," the early board members had suggested. "Many of the major changes that have been made in higher education programmes during the last century have developed through new colleges rather than through previously established universities. Consequently, Waterloo, in organizing a new university, is challenged to develop courses in line with our country's present and future needs." Waterloo was never thought of as a regional university; it was to be a Canadian university. This would be evident in Waterloo's curriculum, in the design of its campus, in the research and publications of its faculty and staff, and in the excellence of its students and graduates.

The British historian, E.H. Carr, once advised readers to study the historian before they studied the facts of history. This advice may be particularly apposite. I first came upon the UW campus as a young high school student. There were two buildings then: Chemistry and Chemical Engineering as one, and Physics and Mathematics the other. My first year as a student in 1961 was spent not in Waterloo, but at the Kingsdale Campus of St. Jerome's College in Kitchener. By my second year, St. Jerome's had moved its arts program to the UW campus, and the Arts Building (now Modern Languages), with its leaking diamond shaped skylights ever-filled with murky water and the overpowering odour of silicone sealant, the new building and the new campus was almost ready for us. When I graduated with an Honours Degree in history in 1965 the university library was still shelved on part of the top floor of the Physics and Mathematics building; the library had two microfilm readers, but essays were still reproduced on Gestetner machines rather than by Xerox photocopiers. UW, however, had acquired its first computer. The future was at hand. What I remember most is that Waterloo was an intensely exciting university, but not without its flaws. That sense of excitement and fascination with the university has remained with me ever since. I hope that I have been able to convey some sense this excitement while remaining true to the university's history.

What's In A Name? A Note About Waterloo Nomenclature

The similarity of the names Waterloo College, Waterloo University, Waterloo University College, Waterloo College Associate Faculties, the Associate Faculties of Waterloo College, the Evangelical Lutheran Seminary of Canada and Waterloo Lutheran University has led to considerable confusion. Contemporaries often used many of these names interchangeably and most often without regard to legal or jurisdictional distinctions. From the beginning of the post-war era, the expansion of Waterloo College was the primary issue facing the Board of Governors of the Evangelical Lutheran Seminary of Canada. Meetings about the future of Waterloo College were held in the Waterloo College board room and agendas referred to the Waterloo College Board of Governors and its committees. Board members met regularly and conducted college business referring to themselves as members of the Board of Governors of Waterloo College. And so they were. In legal terms, however, they actually served as members of the Board of Governors of the Evangelical Lutheran Seminary, for the college existed only under the authority of the seminary, a distinction that was frequently blurred in this era of university and college expansion.

President Hagey's career as President of Waterloo College illustrates some of the reasons for this confusion. As an alumnus of Waterloo College he had been elected "Vice-President of the Board of Waterloo College and Seminary." Subsequently, he was appointed President of Waterloo College and Administrator of the Seminary. His predecessor as President of Waterloo College, Helmut Lehmann, had also been President of the Evangelical Lutheran Seminary of Canada and he retained his position as President of the Evangelical Lutheran Seminary when Hagey became President of Waterloo College, for the first time separating the presidency of the college from that of the seminary. To complicate matters still further, the chair of the board of governors had the legal title of President of the Board, so that in some documents there appear to be three presidents. As President of Waterloo College, Gerald Hagey became president of two institutions, Waterloo College and Waterloo College Associate Faculties, and he reported to two different boards of governors. In the drive toward university status, Waterloo College Associate Faculties ultimately emerged as the University of Waterloo. Before doing so, the Associate Faculties were affiliated through Waterloo College with the University of Western Ontario. Waterloo College's own affiliation with Western, however, was through the Evangelical Lutheran Seminary of Canada. Few understood all of this, especially when Waterloo College, not the seminary, was represented on the senate at Western.

In 1959 when the University of Waterloo emerged from the cocoon of the Waterloo College Associate Faculties, Waterloo Lutheran University took its place alongside. In legislative terms, Waterloo Lutheran University was the "body corporate" previously known as the Evangelical Lutheran Seminary of Canada and its board of governors continued as the board of the university. In 1960 it was not unusual to read of the Board of Governors of Waterloo College, sometimes referred to as the Board of Waterloo University College, but most often the names were used interchangeably.

The University of Waterloo tried to eliminate some of the misunderstanding over the names of the two institutions by publishing a declaration in 1960 stating that, "Waterloo University College was NOT federated with the University of Waterloo." The President of Waterloo Lutheran University, who was actually the President of Waterloo University College, and several faculty members from Waterloo University College, wrote passionate letters to the Premier of Ontario justifying the retention by Waterloo College of its historic name and suggesting that the University of Waterloo change its name. In response, the University of Waterloo petitioned the province to grant it the exclusive use of the name, "Waterloo University." (AO RG 32-1, file 151). This matter was not finally resolved until 1973 when, in return for provincial funding, the Board of Governors of the Evangelical Lutheran Seminary of Canada surrendered control of Waterloo Lutheran University and the university acquired the name of Wilfrid Laurier, one of Canada's most famous prime ministers. Ever the astute politician, Sir Wilfrid, one suspects, would have understood. Not for nothing had Laurier been prime minister of Canada for fifteen years.

In order to simplify matters, I have followed the conventions of the day, using the nomenclature as it was employed by contemporaries rather than attempting to define the names according to legal or jurisdictional distinctions. Inevitably some misunderstandings may result from this decision, and I hereby apologize. The detailed chronology below serves as a helpful guide through this maze.

Chronology of the Development of the University of Waterloo

Prepared by Ross Fair and Kenneth McLaughlin

Associate Faculty= WCAF

Board of Governors= B of G

St. Jerome's College= SJC

University of Waterloo= UW

University of Western Ontario= UWO

Waterloo University College= WUC

Waterloo College= WC

1925

February 18

➤ WC federation with UWO begins

1927

➤ first graduating class of WC

1928

➤ Hagey graduates from WC

➤ hired by B.F. Goodrich (but does not stay)

➤ Hagey begins advertising career with Brigdens then with Merchants Printing

1935

➤ Hagey rehired by Ira Needles at B.F Goodrich as national public relations and advertising manager

1943

➤ SJC begins fund-raising drive toward university status

1947

➤ WC announces an expansion and fund-raising drive

February 20

➤ SJC B of G approves the purchase of the Centreville [Kingsdale] property

1949

➤ Hagey elected alumni representative to WC B of G

➤ SJC announces its expansion plans

➤ anticipates that construction can begin in 1950 of the two buildings, one residence and one administration and teaching

1951

➤Hagey elected vice-president of B of G

1953

➤ WC erects a dining hall and kitchen and an administration and teaching building

March 25

➤ *KW Record* announces that SJC will offer courses in science and business administration at the new Kingsdale campus of SJC as soon as conditions warrant

April 29

➤ Hagey offered WC presidency at special B of G meeting

June 24

➤ Hagey accepts presidency

June 25

➤ Rev. Lloyd Schaus appointed dean of WC

➤ Lehmann's letter of resignation as president of WC effective July 15. He remains president and dean of seminary

July 26

➤ Hagey assumes duties of president of WC

September 7

➤ Premier Frost opens Kingsdale campus of SJC

October

➤ WC sends flowers to SJC with congratulations

November 23

➤ Lehmann's letter of resignation as president and dean of seminary dated Nov. 4 read to the B of G

1954

June 8

➤ meeting of Executive of B of G

➤ purpose to make recommendations to fill Lehmann's position

➤ four clergymen from the US suggested

1955

April 28

➤Hagey presents a special report to the B of G outlining his plans for the WCAF

May 30

➤ WC B of G meeting to consider establishing a non-denominational college

➤ recommends matter to Synod

June

➤ Synod approves plan, 101-21

October/November

➤ letters sent to selected community leaders regarding a proposed "science college" to be "associated" with WC

December 16

➤ first meeting of the B of G members
➤ agree to establish a "science college"

1956

January 19

➤ letter from Hagey to Hon. W.J. Dunlop, min of ed, showing interest in provincial government plans to establish schools offering technical training
➤ Hagey points out that KW is a logical location

April 4

➤ WCAF is established as a legal entity

April 19

➤ Siegfried records his view concerning federation with any new university in a letter to MLA C.P. McTague

April 25

➤ WCAF's first resolution: that if a university charter obtained will entertain petition from SJC for association

May 22

➤ letter from Hagey to Needles
➤ informs him that WCAF move for university charter unlike experience of Assumption and McMaster. WCAF, not the sponsoring college, will seek the university charter

June 11

➤ first discussion of the "Waterloo Plan" at a meeting of the committee for curriculum studies

June 12

➤ letter from Hagey to J.G. Althouse, co-ordinator of higher education
➤ mention of "considerable amount of controversial discussion." Notes SJC interest in the WCAF. SJC's plans to seek university charter
➤ support from UWO for charter

June 19

➤ First presentation of "Waterloo Plan" at B of G meeting of WCAF

August 26

➤ Ira Needles' talk to the Rotary Club: "Wanted 150 000 Engineers and Technicians: The Waterloo Plan"

September 26

➤ letter of Hagey to President Edward Hall
➤ outlines why he thinks the establishment of co-op should not discourage UWO's recognition of affiliation of WCAF

October 2

➤ Hagey notified that UWO's B of G formally approved affiliation of WCAF

October 3

➤ Hall's letter to Hagey approves students in preliminary year and pre-engineering co-op not being registered with the UWO

December 18

➤ WCAF B of G meeting
➤ still discussion of a tech school with students going to other universities for degrees

December 19

➤ cautionary letter from Bishop Ryan to Siegfried warning that it would be a mistake to negotiate federation by himself with Hagey

1957

February 15

➤ letter from Siegfried to WCAF B of G requesting clarification of SJC position in the proposed university
➤ full support of the 25 Apr 1956 resolution of the WCAF to make the facilities available to SJC if and when university degree granting abilities are reached

February 22

➤ Joint B of G meeting of WC and WCAF approves that the first section of the applied science course be offered beginning, 2 July 1957

February 27

➤ WC B of G meeting
➤ many members do not support the third year in technical training
➤ fear that the technical aspect may overshadow the engineering emphasis

March 5

➤ Hagey reports to WC B of G on his discussion with Dept of Education concerning the possible removal of the third year technical certificate course

May 31

➤ WCAF B of G meeting
➤ approval to purchase Annex I and II from Ratz Lumber

July 2

➤ first classes of the WCAF begin. 74 students registered

October 15

➤ meeting with the new architects Shore and Moffat, recommended site on WC campus for new Science building

October 29

➤ Academic Advisory Committee sends Memo #1 requesting a reconsideration of the WC campus site for university expansion

October 30

➤ Hagey's reply. Opposed.
➤ Move would be politically difficult and nearly impossible

November 5

➤ Academic Advisory Committee replies to Hagey
➤ points out that there is no suggestion of WC campus being abandoned
➤ request to present matter to B of G at next meeting

November 12
> presentation of Memo #1 at B of G meeting

November 14
> Memo #2 from Academic Advisory Committee to Hagey
> request for a general secretary for the WCAF. First step toward a separate administrative structure

November 29
> letter from Hagey stating engineering curriculum has now been approved by UWO but there is a need to discuss it with UWO

December 3
> meeting of the Management Committee of the B of G of WCAF
> letter from Major Holdings offering a tract of 150 acres, open to Dec. 31
> limit of December 31 too close, but if limit could be extended, study of the matter would begin
> B of G meeting also recognized the need to appoint a dean of engineering

1958
January 9
> Report of the president
> suggestion of relocation of WC
> presentation of WCAF moral obligation to WC

January 14
> Joint B of G Committee meeting of WCAF and WC
> approval of WC B of G for WCAF to purchase new campus

January 25
> Address by Rev. Lotz, president of the Lutheran Seminary to faculty
> unanimous approval of land purchase
> WC will automatically become the arts faculty of the new university and WC faculty members will automatically become the arts faculty

January 25
> press release from Hagey about purchase of new campus site
> press release from Ira Needles that at the appropriate time the WCAF will apply for a university charter. Notes that other colleges may join the University on its new campus site

February 11
> memo notes that by October 1959 the already crowded new building will no longer be adequate

March
> the arts faculty of WC submits a detailed memo to the B of G of WC outlining the academic prerequisites of university status and the needs of the arts faculty to develop to meet these levels

March 20
> Brief to WCAF B of G from Hagey concerning his views on the reasons for obtaining a university charter and his views on the structure of its administration

> notes that the university is not to set up an arts faculty to compete with that of WC
> announcement of resignation of George Dufault from co-ordination department and that this department will receive closer attention by Hagey

March 27
> memo to Academic Advisory Committee from Hagey
> states requirements and qualifications for faculty

April 28
> recommendation that WC establish an arts faculty no later than Oct. 1962

May 28
> Hagey's presentation to the B of G of WCAF regarding the intentions of President Hall at UWO

June 13
> E.M. Brookes hired as superintendent of buildings and grounds

A Day to Remember
for Education and Industry

June 23
> purchase of 1 1/2 acre Hergott property and 0.7 acres from Bauer Ltd draws the two campuses ever closer together

August 12
> C.L. Emery resigns

August 29
> Hagey issues statement of the church colleges' position in the new university and the structure of the university's administration

September 13
> move of Annex I and II to new campus begun

September 22
> meeting of Charter Committee
> both WC and SJC table subjects for consideration concerning the charter

September 29
> move of Annex I and II complete

December 3
> Premier Leslie Frost officially opens the Chemistry and Chemical Engineering building
> first building on the new campus of what would become the U of W

December 11
> SJC B of G meeting
> all members approve the terms of federation, but felt Siegfried should try to have the wording changed concerning WC "prior" right to teach the students who attend the university proper. The word "prior" was a problem, but if it could not be changed the issue should be dropped

1959
January
> Siegfried reported that letters would be filed that SJC will have prior rights over its own students in the denominational subjects, regardless of the economic arrangements
> the SJC B of G voted in favour of purchasing 55 acres of land north of the WC campus, separated by Columbia Street. This would never be acted on

January 12
- agreement reached between the WCAF and SJC to be included in the University Act
- inaugural meeting of the Engineering Faculty Council
- inaugural meeting of the Science Faculty Council

February 13
- letters sent to mayors of Kitchener and Waterloo inviting them to become members of the B of G

February 20
- letter from Hagey to the deans noting the rapid pace of development of the engineering curriculum
- points out new process of changing curriculum in order that problems be avoided

February 28
- Hagey appointed by B of G of WCAF to the office of the president of the U of W

March 5
- Royal assent given to U of W Act, Waterloo Lutheran University Act and University of SJC Act

April 16
- Hagey resigns as president of WC

April 20
- Report of the Executive Committee
- Alan Gordon to be appointed to position of registrar of UW

April 25
- B of G meeting
- noted administration would have to be moved from WC buildings for the fall term

May 14
- personal letter from Hagey to Dr. Willison concerning his resignation
- suggests he did not expect this development to occur so quickly
- Engineering Faculty Council decide that the degree granted in engineering should be a BSc

May 26
- UW Senate agrees to establish the Senate Advisory Committee
- includes all members of Senate and principals and faculty reps of SJC and WC who would be members of Senate upon federation

June 2
- reported that SJC B of G did not purchase the 55 acres of land. An agreement with the university allows it to build on the university campus

June 18
- WC B of G meeting
- affiliation between WCAF to be terminated as of June 30, 1959 Federation agreement with the UW to be reached as soon as possible

July 20
- Herbert Axford named new president of WUC

July 24
- Federation negotiations put on hold until Dr. Axford arrives in September

August 12
- A.P. Gordon named registrar

September 1
- Senate Advisory Committee for one year or until Federation, which ever comes first

October 8
- Memo from Stanton to Hagey concerning his views of the university's ability to develop its own arts faculty with little cost

November 3
- Kelley, Stanton and Gordon meet to discuss a university arts faculty

November 5
- Axford installed as president of WC

November 12
- Memo from Kelley to Stanton includes mention that the likely home for math will be the arts faculty and Hagey's hope that an arts faculty does not develop only as the result of a breakdown of federation, but rather as a complement to federation

November 21
- letter from Axford to UW B of G requesting terms on which land could be secured for WC

November 25
- request from WC B of G to acquire 20 acres of land on UW campus

November 26
- UW issues policy statement to WC and SJC

November 27
- petition sent to Hagey from Stanton includes signatures of math department members supporting the placement of math in the arts faculty of the university, but not in arts of any federated college

November 30
- Science Faculty Council passes motion to introduce to Senate the plan to offer summer session in 1960 of general science for teachers who wish to upgrade their skills

December 2
- SJC B of G unanimously endorses UW policy statement re: federation

December 8
- letter to Axford from UW B of G stating land given only once a federation agreement reached

December 11
- WC presents its "10 points" for federation

December 12
- colours picked for UW

December 17
- UW imposed deadline to WUC for federation of Jan. 1, 1960 extended to Jan. 15

1960

January
- J.F. Little's "Our College at the Crossroads" published in the *Canada Lutheran*

January 5
- WC B of G meeting considers policy statement
- approves a motion to federate as of July 1
- leaves details to be worked out by administration
- Hagey issues memo to the B of G of UW concerning the possible need and costs of developing an arts faculty at Waterloo

January 7
- Dana Porter appointed chancellor of UW

January 8
- *KW Record* announces WC and SJC will federate on July 1, 1960

January 15
- Douglas Wright appointed dean of engineering
- Bruce Kelley appointed dean of science and acting dean of arts
- B of G meeting of WC
- no decision made on policy statement

January 19
- Joint Executive Committee meeting with members from all three institutions to discuss federation

February 3
- Bruce Kelley announces that W.A.E. McBryde will be the new chairman of the chemistry department

February 8
- Memo from Executive Committee recommends land grants of 5 acres to each of the federated colleges; additional lands may be purchased

February 10
- Physics and mathematics building officially opens

February 11
- Report of the president
- stating a good deal remains to be done to complete federation

February 15
- Arts Faculty Council meeting
- reading of the B of G resolution concerning the math department's location in the arts faculty

February 19
- Memo from Hagey concerning arts curriculum and the printing of calendars

February 21
- Al Gordon receives letter from Keith Thomas inquiring about Waterloo's plans to establish a faculty of arts

February 23
- Joint Executive meeting
- WUC presents memo concerning academic place of a church-related college, admission procedures, relationship among deans of arts, minimum admission standards
- UW presents memo of Feb. 19

March 4
- Kelley informs Thomas (at Acadia) of federation problems and cannot answer when or if a university faculty of arts will be established

March 14
- Kelley informs Al Gordon of his information that WUC plans to offer summer school courses for this summer and has not gained Senate approval

March 15
- Gordon informs Axford that no university credit can be offered for courses not approved by Senate

March 22
- letter to Axford from Hagey
- pressure for WC to agree as Hagey sees negotiations as delaying the university from addressing other important matters

March 26
- Lutheran Faculty Committee of the college circulates a letter requesting Synod members to petition for a special meeting of Synod to discuss federation.
- Dr. Jacobi discovers a technical fault in the letter which would prevent him from calling such a meeting

March 29
- Policy statement considered by WC B of G
- no absolute decision

March 30
- A second, amended letter regarding opposition to federation is circulated by the Lutheran Faculty Committee

April 1
- Memo from Hagey
- University has committed itself to the development of an arts faculty

April 6
- UW Board gives authorization for UW to start arts program as it feels federation will not occur in time for a program to be established for the fall term

April 7
- WC is notified of this intention

April 8
- Upon request of the student government, Dean Schaus informs the students that federation under the present terms would not take place. Hagey informs them of the new university arts program
- College B of G meets to reaffirm the 5 Jan. decision to federate
- the B of G assumes negotiation responsibilities from the administration
- letter from Bruce Kelley to Keith Thomas informing him of the breakdown in federation negotiations and the situation in which Thomas would begin to develop an arts program

April 11
- Memo from Hagey
- University proceeding with the development of arts and courses will begin fall 1960
- university will offer transfer for those students expecting a degree from UW if federation does not occur before fall 1960

April 14
- Negotiations are resumed between the College B of G and the university but are stalemated because of the UW's decision to develop its own arts program

April 18
- memo from UW B of G to WC B of G regretting the delay in the federation decision
- offers suspension of arts program to show good faith

April 20
- College and university B of G reps establish a steering committee to work out the details of a basis for federation which would be suitable to both universities

April 21
- meeting of Executive Committee of UW and WLU
- statement of suspension of developing a university arts program

April 22
- College Board President Baetz announces to the student body that the university had withdrawn its arts program and that the Senate would be requested to re-establish the curriculum of the college as a basis for the university's arts program and that college credits would be accredited by the university (as if federated); also noted was progress of negotiations

April 25
- Kelley writes Thomas "The turmoil continues unabated." Impossible to offer him a position under present conditions
- hopes to be able to make a firm commitment next year

April 27
- The university Senate acts as Baetz had suggested it would and re-establishes the college's arts program

May 5
- Overgaard makes a "Circuit Rider" speech to the Lutheran congregation in Zurich

May 6
- WUC B of G ratifies the actions of its executive with regards to federation

May 9
- Bruce Kelley dies while attending university meetings. He will be sadly missed

May 12
- Special session of Synod votes against federation

May 13
- the College Alumni Executive passes two motions
- the first deplores the actions of Synod in overruling the B of G and the second authorizes a mail poll to determine the students' enrolment plans for the coming year

May 16
- WC alumni censures Synod
- 4 WC B of G resign and twenty-four faculty members lodge a protest

May 17
- drop in enrolment at WC predicted
- Dean Schaus issues academic freedom statement

May 21
- Keith Thomas appointed UW's acting dean of arts

May 24
- College B of G president resigns

May 27
- Seven College faculty members resign in protest against the Synod's decision

May 31
- UW announces the re-establishment and start of its own arts program in the fall term of 1960
- College alumni president, vice president, and four members resign from the executive

June 2
- Adlington sends a memo to Axford concerning library arrangements; the university will establish its own library and take with it equipment from WC library that was purchased by the university

June 3
- Wright issues a memo concerning switching co-op to a three-semester system from a quarter system

June 6
- Hagey sends a letter to Renison and SJC expressing his hope that federation for July 1 can be announced at Convocation as well as final details of the affiliation agreement that the B of G is to approve on June 17

June 8
- Thomas issues his report as acting dean of arts noting the appointments made to the faculty and the present state of the program

June 30
- end of WC affiliation with UWO

July
- SJC and Renison join UW

July 8
- letter from Axford to Hagey asking UW to share facilities with WC without federation

July 11
- letter from Hagey to Axford informs Axford that the two universities are separate

July 15
- Thomas issues his draft proposal for the arts curriculum

August 2
- Arts Faculty Council meeting notice that arts curriculum established by Bruce Kelley is still in existence
- problem of two Senate-approved curriculums for arts

August 9
- Arts Faculty Council need to request province to delay approval of the complete curriculum until Dec. 1, 1960

September
- UW places ad in *KW Record* declaring that UW has no affiliation with Waterloo Lutheran University

November 9
- At the Engineering Faculty Council meeting, Dean Wright recommends studying the removal of the pre-engineering year in the near future. (comes effective following 1963-64 session)

1970
- Gerald Hagey receives an honorary LL.D. from Waterloo Lutheran University

1973
- Waterloo Lutheran University becomes Wilfrid Laurier University, surrendering Lutheran control to become a provincially funded university

1975
- Gerald Hagey receives an honorary LL.D. from the UWO

A Note About Sources

Of the many scholarly monographs, articles and dissertations written about universities and their histories, several may be of interest. Oscar L. Arnal's *Toward An Indigenous Lutheran Ministry In Canada* (Waterloo, 1988) subtitled, *The Seventy-Five Year Pilgrimage of Waterloo Lutheran Seminary*, provides an overview of the seminary's development, with some references to Waterloo College. C.M. Johnson's two volume history of McMaster University (Toronto, 1976 and 1981) is a detailed scholarly account of McMaster's development from a small Baptist-affiliated college to a provincially-funded university. Although Volume 2 ends in 1957 coincident with the beginning of the Waterloo College Associate Faculties, the development of McMaster's Hamilton College is described in some detail. *Cold Iron and Lady Godiva, Engineering Education at Toronto, 1920-1972*, edited by Robin Harris and Ian Montague (Toronto, 1973) outlines major trends in the education of engineering students from a variety of points-of-view and offers a contrast to the Waterloo experience. P.B. Waite's two volume history of Dalhousie University published by McGill-Queen's University Press (1994 and 1997) is a marvellous example of the historian's craft. His 1987 *Lord of Point Grey, Larry MacKenzie of U.B.C.* (Vancouver, 1987) will elicit a resonance for those reading about Gerald Hagey's tasks and torments at Waterloo. Claude Bissell's *Halfway up Parnassus, A Personal Account of The University of Toronto 1932-1971* (Toronto, 1974) suggests that all university histories are fraught with elements of personal anguish and exultation. Paul Axelrod's detailed analysis of the relationship between politics and economics in the development of the universities of Ontario between 1945 and 1980, *Scholars and Dollars* (Toronto 1982) is mandatory reading for anyone wishing to understand the prevailing social, economic and political trends influencing universities in Ontario. Similarly, Roger Graham's 1990 study, *Old Man Ontario: Leslie M. Frost* explains much about Ontario's politics and politicians during Waterloo's formative years. One of my personal favourites is *Student Days, An Illustrated History of Student Life at McMaster University from the 1890's to the 1980's,* (Hamilton, 1986) by C.M. Johnson and J.C. Weaver. Students are too often overlooked in university histories. *Mea Culpa*. A most impressive study relating to Ontario's universities is A.B. McKillop's *Matters of Mind, The University in Ontario 1791-1951* (Toronto, 1994). Although McKillop's monumental study ends just as the period of the post-war expansion of universities begins, it is necessary reading for anyone wishing to understand the "life of the mind" in the university tradition of this province. These studies are only a partial listing and they are supplemented by numerous government reports, projections of student involvement, economic forecasts and the musings of various royal and lesser commissions. There is a plethora of graduate student research papers and dissertations, newspaper articles and special reports. Fascination with universities, their societal purpose and their historical identities, is an enduring feature of the Canadian landscape.

The major sources for *Waterloo: The Unconventional Founding of an Unconventional University* are the numerous reports, correspondence and memoranda, documents and personal letters, in the Archives of the University of Waterloo, St. Jerome's College, Wilfrid Laurier University, the University of Western Ontario and the Archives of Ontario. In addition, the University of Waterloo Archives (UWA) houses a series of oral history interviews. These are identified by the date, the subject of the interview and the name of the interviewer. Those interviews conducted under the terms of UW's Oral History Project are identified with the abbreviation OHP.

Several individuals have provided extensive personal archives to me. These ultimately will be deposited in the University of Waterloo Archives, but pending an accession number I have indicated them as Personal Archives. It is the intention of the University History Project to create a CD-ROM version of this text and that of the 27 May 1997 Founders Lecture, including all illustrations to be searchable by text and image. Pending its release, I have sought to provide these end notes and this note about sources as an indication of major references relating to the university's history.

Abbreviations are as follows:

University of Waterloo Archives: UWA
University of St. Jerome's College Archives: SJCA
Wilfrid Laurier University Archives: WLUA
University of Western Ontario - Regional History Collection: UWO-RHC
Archives of Ontario: AO

Notes

CHAPTER I

1.   Oscar L. Arnal, *Towards An Indigenous Lutheran Ministry in Canada* (Waterloo, 1988), 25.

2.   Kenneth McLaughlin, *Waterloo: An Illustrated History* (Burlington, 1990), 60,61.

3.   *Waterloo College Cord*, November 1949, 13, 14.

4.   WUA A80-41-07, Hagey to G. Brakeley, 8 February 1957.

5.   A.B. McKillop, *Matters of Mind: The University in Ontario, 1791-1951* (Toronto, 1994), 549.

6.   WLUA, Waterloo College Board of Governors, n.d., 1947.

7.   Arnal, *Indigenous Lutheran Ministry*,32, 33.

8.   WLUA, Waterloo College Board of Governors, 4 September 1947.

9.   Ibid.

10.   *Waterloo College Cord*, October 1948.

11.   WLUA, Waterloo College Board of Governors, 28 April 1955.

12.   Ibid., 6 March 1951.

13.   UWA B88-27-1-3 J.G. Hagey unpublished manuscript, n.p., n.d.

14.   Ibid.

15.   Ibid.

16.   Ibid.

17.   Ibid.

18.   Ibid.

19.   Charles M. Johnson, *McMaster University*, Vol 2: *The Early Years In Hamilton, 1930-1957*, (Toronto, 1981), 121, 123.

20.   Private Archive, J.G. Hagey to Academic Advisory Committee, 30 October 1957.

21.   Peter M. Meehan, "From College to University: The Basilian Fathers and Assumption", (M.A. thesis, University of Windsor, 1991), 40, 78.

22.   UWO/RHC Memorandum of G.E. Hall, 22 March 1955.

23.   UWA B88-27 Special Report, Board of Governors, Evangelical Lutheran Seminary, 25 April 1955.

24.   Minutes of the 93rd Annual Convention, Evangelical Lutheran Synod of Canada. (June, 1955) 99-113.

25.   UWA Oral History interview, J.G. Hagey, June 1985 (K. McCracken).

26.   Minutes of the 94th Annual Convention, Evangelical Lutheran Synod of Canada. (June, 1956) 57-58.

27.   WLUA, Special Report to Board of Governors.

28.   UWA A78-14-30-32, J.G. Hagey to Norman Schneider, 18 March 1957.

CHAPTER II

1.   UWA, *National Conference on Engineering, Scientific and Technical Manpower* (St. Andrews, New Brunswick, 1956) n.p. See also Paul Axelrod, *Scholars and Dollars, Politics, Economics and the Universities of Ontario. 1945-1980* (Toronto, 1982), 23ff.

2.   Axelrod, *Scholars and Dollars*, 24.

3.   UWA Miscellaneous, Ira G. Needles, "Wanted 150, 000 Engineers The Waterloo Plan" (Kitchener, 1956), 8.

4.   UWA A77-4-203, Hagey to G.E. Hall, 6 September 1956.

5.   National Conference, 1.

6.   Axelrod, *Scholars and Dollars*, 23.

7.   UWA A77-4-203, Hagey to G.E. Hall, 26 September 1956.

8.   Axelrod, *Scholars and Dollars*, 23.

9.   Ibid.

10.   UWA A77-4-278, The references to this and subsequent meetings with the minister of education are in this file.

11.   Ibid.

12.   UWA A77-4-79.

13.   Ibid.

14.   UWA A77-4-79, J.G. Hagey to W.J. Dunlop, 12 October 1955.

15.   UWA A82-1-01, Board of Governors, WCAF, 16 December 1955.

16.   UWA A81-1-01, 25 April 1956.

17.   UWA A77-4-79, J.G. Hagey to W.J. Dunlop, 6 January 1956, and UWA A77-4-79, C.A. Pollock to W.J. Dunlop, 19 January 1956.

18.   Axelrod, *Scholars and Dollars*, 85.

19.   Ibid.

20.   Axelrod, *Scholars and Dollars*, 86.

21.   UWA A82-01, J.G. Hagey to the Board of Governors, WCAF, 17 May 1956.

CHAPTER III

1. UWA A82-1-01, Board of Governors, WCAF, 19 June 1956.
2. Ibid.
3. UWA A82-1-02, 3 July 1957.
4. UWA A77-4-274, Henry H. Armsby to C.L. Emery, 3 July 1956.
5. UWA A77-4-255.
6. Ibid., L.A. Wright to Hagey, 16 July 1956.
7. UWA A77-4-79, Hagey to W.J. Dunlop, 4 September 1956.
8. Ibid.
9. Ibid.
10. Ibid.
11. Ibid.
12. UWA A77-4-203, Hagey to G.E. Hall, 26 September 1956.
13. UWA A77-4-275, S.H. Deeks to Hagey, 27 August 1956.
14. Axelrod, *Scholars and Dollars*, 24.
15. UWA A80-41-07, J.G. Hagey to G.A. Brakeley, 8 March 1957.
16. Ibid., Brakeley to I.G. Needles, 24 June 1957.
17. UWA A82-01-07, Hagey to Board or Governors, WCAF, 14 March 1957.
18. UWA A77-4-79, W.J. Dunlop to A.S. Mackie, 29 October 1956.
19. UWA A77-4-78, J.G. Hagey to Hon. Dana Porter, 1 March 1957.
20. UWA A77-4-276.
21. As cited in C. Dufault, unpublished manuscript, 22 December 1996, 16.
22. UWA A77-4-276, 4 March 1957.
23. Ibid.
24. UWA A82-1-07, President's Report to Board of Governors.

CHAPTER IV

1. UWA A82-1-02, 3 July 1957.
2. UWA A78-14-30-32.
3. Personal Archive, Faculty Advisory Committee, 29 July 1957.
4. Ibid.
5. Ibid., Academic Advisory Committee, Memorandum No. 1 to J.G. Hagey, 29 October 1957.
6. Ibid., J.G. Hagey to the Academic Advisory Committee, 30 October 1957.
7. Ibid.,Academic Advisory Committee to J.G. Hagey, 5 November 1957.
8. UWA A82-01-03, 9 January 1958.
9. Ibid.
10. Ibid.
11. Private Archive, Reverend A.J. Baetz to all pastors in the Synod, 22 January 1958.
12. Ibid., Address by the Reverend A.W. Lotz, president of the Board of the Evangelical Lutheran Seminary of Canada, 25 January 1958.

CHAPTER V

1. H.B. Neatby, "Visions and Revisions: The View from the President's Offices of Ontario Universities since the Second World War," presidential address, Canadian Historical Association *Historical Papers* (1988), 2.
2. UWO-RHC, Memorandum, G.E. Hall, 22 March 1955.
3. Ibid.
4. Ibid., G.E. Hall to Hagey, 29 August 1956.
5. UWA A77-0-203, Hagey to G.E. Hall, 6 September 1956.
6. UWO-RHC, G.E. Hall to Hagey, 3 October 1956.
7. Ibid.
8. UWA A77-4-79, Hagey to W.J. Dunlop, n.d.
9. J.G. Hagey Report to Management Committee, Board of Governors, WCAF, regarding the meeting of 27 March 1957 at UWO with Dr. Hall and Professor L.S. Lauchland.
10. UWO-RHC, Stiling to Hagey, 15 June 1957.
11. Ibid.
12. UWA A77-4-203, Hagey to F. Stiling, 18 October 1957, and UWO-RHC, Stiling to G.E. Hall, 11 December 1957.
13 UWO-RHC, Stiling to G.E. Hall, 28 February 1958.
14. Ibid.
15. Ibid., A.W. Lotz to G.E. Hall, 17 April 1958.
16. UWA A82-1-03, contains the reports of this series of meetings: 1) 28 April 1958   2) 30 April 1958 A Report Re: Meeting at Western 3) 28 May 1958 Report to the Board of Governors of Waterloo College Associate Faculties   4) UWA A77-4-203 5) UWA A82-1-03 n.d. May 1958 Draft report to the president of the board of governors of Waterloo College and the chairman of the board of governors of Waterloo College Associate Faculties.

CHAPTER VI

1. Axelrod, *Scholars and Dollars*, 71-73.
2. UWA A80-4-7ff, The Brakeley Report.
3. UWA, A.S. Barber papers, n.d.
4. UWA A80-4-7, 24 June 1957.
5. Ibid., Hagey to G.A. Brakeley, 8 March 1957.
6. Ibid.
7. Ibid.
8. Private Archive, Waterloo College Associate Faculties Academic Advisory Committee (Federation File), Memorandum to President Hagey signed by J.A. Cowan, 28 April 1958.
9. Ibid.
10. Ibid.
11. UWA A82-1-03, 28 May 1958, and n.d. May 1958, draft report.
12. UWO-RHC, D.J. Glebe to G.E. Hall, 4 August 1958.
13. Ibid., G.E. Hall to D.J. Glebe.
14. Ibid., Gould Wickey to G.E. Hall, 19 August 1958.
15. Ibid., G.E. Hall to Gould Wickey, 9 September 1958.
16. UWA A77-4-203, Report of Committee Meeting with Western, 12 September 1958.
17. Ibid., "A description of Waterloo's plans" presented to the Senate, UWO, 12 December 58.
18. UWA A77-84-200 Hagey to N. Willison, 14 May 1959.

CHAPTER VII

1. Private Archive, university press release, 25 January 1958.
2. UWA A82-1-3, 14 January 1958.
3. UWA A77-4-79, I.G. Needles to W.J. Dunlop, 6 November 1958.
4. UWA B88-27-1-3, J.G. Hagey unpublished manuscript. n.p., n.d.
5. *Kitchener-Waterloo Record*, 18 October 1972.
6. G.J. Stortz and J.A. Wahl, "Enthusiasm for the Truth" (unpublished manuscript St. Jerome's College) 6:3.
7. Ibid., 7.
8. Ibid., 9.
9. Ibid., 11.
10. Ibid., 13.
11. Ibid., 17.
12. SJCA, C.L. Siegfried to C.F. Canon, 17 March 1953.
13. Stortz and Wahl, "Enthusiasm for the Truth," 6:23.
14. Meehan, *Basilian Fathers*,46.
15. SJCA General File, Synod Minutes.
16. UWA A77-4-278, Faculty of Science Progress Report No. 1, 19 July 1955.
17. See above, Chapter III.
18. Meehan, *Basilian Fathers*, 61.
19. UWA A77-4-278, Report, 6 January 1956.
20. UWA A77-4-79, Hagey to W.J. Dunlop, 6 January 1956.
21. UWA A77-4-278 Report, 28 February 1956.
22. Ibid., 15 March 1956.
23. UWA A77-4-79, W.J. Dunlop to Hagey, 17 April 1956.
24. Ibid., Hagey to J.G. Althouse, 12 June 1956.
25. SJCA, C.L Siegfried to C.A. McTague, 19 April 1956.
26. Ibid.
27. Stortz and Wahl, "Enthusiasm for the Truth," 6:2.
28. SJCA, C.L.Siegfried to J.F.Ryan, 23 July 1956.
29. Ibid., J.G. Althouse to Siegfried, 26 July 1956.
30. UWA A77-4-79, Hagey to W.J. Dunlop, 4 September 1956.
31. SJCA, J.J. Wintermeyer to Siegfried, 6 November 1956.
32. Ibid., J.F. Ryan to Siegfried, 19 December 1956.
33. Ibid.
34. Ibid., Siegfried to Board of Governors WCAF, 15 February 1957.
35. Ibid., Siegfried to C.F. Cannon, 17 March 1957.
36. Ibid., 10 March 1959.
37. Ibid., Siegfried to W.J. Dunlop, 10 March 1959.
38. Ibid., Board of Governors minutes, 11 December 1958.

CHAPTER VIII

1.   The Petition for Affiliation and the Articles of Affiliation are available in the Archives of Wilfrid Laurier University (WLUA).

2.   Hagey's remarks are subsumed within the actual affiliation articles and the petition as well as in the synodical reports, loc. cit.

3.   Kenneth McLaughlin, *Waterloo* 106.

4.   UWA A82-1-03, Board of Governors WCAF, 14 January 1958.

5.   As cited in C. Dufault, 22 December 1996, 26.

6.   UWA A82-4-28, Hagey to J.H. Smyth. See also C.M. Johnson, *McMaster University*, Vol 2, 177ff.

7.   UWA A82-4-28 Hagey to J.H. Smyth, 20 March 1958. Hagey's ideas about a future Waterloo Lutheran University are outlined in detail in his correspondence with J.H. Smyth, the lawyer retained by the college and seminary to draft the legislation for the future university.

8.   Private Archive, Hagey to Albert Lotz, 29 May 1958.

9.   UWA A82-4-28, Hagey to J.H. Smyth, 22 October 1958.

10.   Ibid. Hagey to J.H. Smyth, n.d., November 1958.

11.   Ibid. Smyth to Hagey, 28 October 1958.

12.   Private Archive, Executive Committee WCAF to Hagey, 6 November 1958.

13.   Ibid. Hagey to the Executive Committee WCAF, n.d., November 1958.

CHAPTER IX

1.   UWA A82-1-06, Hagey to UW Board of Governors, 25 April 1959.

2.   OHP, Reverend A.J. Baetz (K. McLaughlin and Shaun Browne), 8 November 1990.

3.   UWA A82-1-06, Hagey to UW Board of Governors, 25 April 1959.

4.   Private Archives, Bruce Kelley to Hagey, n.d., May 1959.

5.   UWA, "This is Waterloo" vol 4, no 1, December 1959; vol 4, no 2, February 1960.

6.   Ibid.

7.   UWA A78-24-8, R.G. Stanton to Hagey, 8 October 1959.

8.   Ibid., Committee Minutes, 3 November 1959.

9.   Ibid., R.G. Stanton to Bruce Kelley, 12 November 1959.

10.   Private Archive, Memorandum re Federation of Waterloo University College with the University of Waterloo, n.d.

11.   SJCA, I.G. Needles to C.L Siegfried, 29 November 1959.

12.   Ibid.

13.   UWA A77-4-208, Needles to A.J. Baetz, 5 January 60.

14.   UWA A81-7-25, C.L. Siegfried to Needles, 10 December 1959.

15.   UWA 77-4-208, A.J. Baetz to I.G. Needles, 15 January 1960.

CHAPTER X

1.   UWA, "This Is Waterloo," vol 4, no. 3, June 1960.

2.   This synopsis of synodical correspondence is from a private archive. These letters are in the public domain and printed in the Synod's Annual Report, loc. cit.

3.   This sequence of events is outlined in UWA "This Is Waterloo," June 1960.

4.   Private Archive, Waterloo University College, Faculty Association Brief, 14 December 1959.

5.   Ibid., James Stone to J. Stewart Reid, 16 December 1959.

6.   Ibid., "Notes on the Sandison Case," 25-27 January 1960.

7.   Ibid., "Document E, Report of the Sandison Case," 11 February 1960.

8.   OHP, Professor J.W. Dyck (Ross Fair), 9 December 1992.

9.   Private Archive, Report of the Committee on Academic Freedom and Tenure, 9 May 1960.

10.   Zurich *Citizens News* 5 May 1970, as cited in Ross Fair, "Dreaming in Technicolor: the Politics of Developing the University of Waterloo," n.d.:57.

11.   WLUA Special Session, *The Evangelical Lutheran Synod of Canada* (ELSC) (Kitchener, 1960)
      All quotations are from the official minutes of the Synod.

12.   Carl F. Klinck, *Giving Canada a Literary History*, (Ottawa: 1991), 4.

13.   Arnal, *Lutheran Ministry*,46.

14.   Ibid., 44

15.   Ibid., 46

16.   *Kitchener-Waterloo Record*, 13 May 1960.

17.   Ibid.

18.   Supplementary Report of the President, Minutes of the 98th Annual Convention of the Evangelical Lutheran Synod, June 1960.

CONCORDIA CUM VERITATE

TO ALL AND SUN[
WE, Malcolm Rognvald Innes of Edi[
Signet, Lord Lyon King of Arms, send G[

UNIVER

in the Province of Ontario, Canada, having by[
College Associate Faculties under The Corpor[
Province of Ontario the name of the Univer[
for and on behalf of the University of Waterl[
that We have Devised, and Do by These Prese[
Ensigns Armorial, as depicted upon the marg[
Public Register of All Arms and Bearings i[
three lions rampant Gules a chevrone[
Incorporation (VIDELICET:- a Salade Pr[
Wreath of the Liveries is set for Crest b[
and leaved all Proper, and in an Escrol[
demonstration of which Ensigns Armo[
Places of Honour, to be taken, numbered[
Noblesse of Scotland; IN TESTIMON[
Seal of Our Office is affixed hereto at E[
Our Sovereign Lady Elizabeth the Second[
and Northern Ireland, and of Her Other[
Defender of the Faith, and in the Year of[